Voices from This Long Brown Land

Palgrave Studies in Oral History

Series Editors: Linda Shopes and Bruce M. Stave

Sticking to the Union: An Oral History of the Life and Times of Julia Ruuttila, by Sandy Polishuk; foreword by Amy Kesselman (2003)

To Wear the Dust of War: From Bialystok to Shanghai to the Promised Land, an Oral History, by Samuel Iwry, edited by L. J. H. Kelley (2004)

Education as My Agenda: Gertrude Williams, Race, and the Baltimore Public Schools, by Jo Ann O. Robinson (2005)

Remembering: Oral History Performance, edited by Della Pollock (2005)

Postmemories of Terror: A New Generation Copes with the Legacy of the "Dirty War," by Susana Kaiser (2005)

Growing Up in The People's Republic: Conversations between Two Daughters of China's Revolution, by Ye Weili and Ma Xiadong (2005)

Life and Death in the Delta: African American Narratives of Violence, Resilience, and Social Change, by Kim Lacy Rogers (2006)

Creating Choice: A Community Responds to the Need for Abortion and Birth Control, 1961–1973, by David P. Cline (2006)

Voices from This Long Brown Land: Oral Recollections of Owens Valley Lives and Manzanar Pasts, by Jane Wehrey (2006)

Radicals, Rhetoric, and the War: The University of Nevada in the Wake of Kent State, by Brad Lucas (forthcoming)

Sisters in the Brotherhoods: Organizing for Equality, by Jane Latour (forthcoming)

For my mother

If one is inclined to wonder at first how so many dwellers came to be in the loneliest land that ever came out of God's hands, what they do there and why stay, one does not wonder so much after having lived there. None other than this long brown land lays such a hold on the affections.

Mary Austin, *The Land of Little Rain*, 1903

If I were now to visit another country, I would ask my local companion, before I saw any museum or library, any factory or fabled town, to walk me in the country of his or her youth, to tell me the names of things and how, traditionally, they have been fitted together in a community. I would ask for the stories, the voice of memory over the land.

Barry Lopez, "Mapping the Real Geography," 1996

Contents

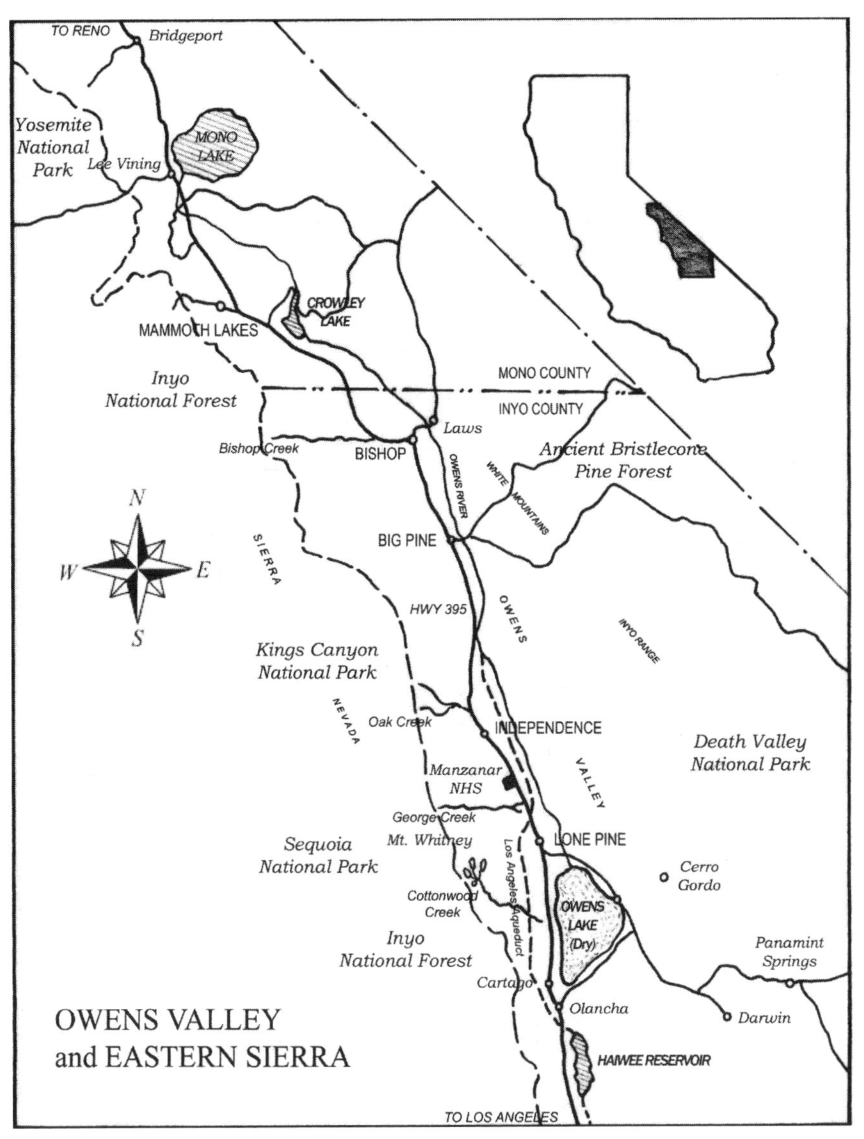

The Eastern Sierra region, including the Owens Valley. *Map by M. Wehrey/L. Gaillac*

Acknowledgments

William H. Michael, Director of the Eastern California Museum, 1986–2005, has been unwavering in his support for the project, generously granting permission for use of the fourteen interviews presented here. I thank him for that and his kindness in assisting me in numerous other ways.

For skills that often go unheralded, thank you to the interviewers, especially Richard Potashin, and the transcribers, especially Garnette Long. Both are masters of their respective crafts. To Palgrave Studies in Oral History Series Editors Linda Shopes and Bruce Stave, I extend my sincere appreciation for taking on the project and seeing it through, and for invaluable suggestions and encouragement. My warm gratitude to these friends and colleagues: Arthur H. Hansen, Professor of History Emeritus and Director of the Center for Oral and Public History at California State University Fullerton, who first offered me the extraordinary opportunities to practice the art and craft of oral history that led directly to this project; also at CSUF, Lawrence B. DeGraaf, Professor of History Emeritus, and American Studies Professor Michael Steiner.

Thank you to Alisa Lynch, Chief of Interpretation, Manzanar National Historic Site, and her staff; Ross Hopkins, first superintendent at Manzanar National Historic Site; Kathy Frazee, Center for Oral and Public History, CSUF; Anh-Thu Thi Pham and Michael DePrez, Los Angeles Department of Water and Power; Chris Langley, Beverly and Jim Rogers Museum of Lone Pine Film History; Sharon Dare, the *Inyo Register*; Archie Miyatake, Toyo Miyatake Studio; Loic Gaillac, Debra Gold Hansen, and others who provided assistance and encouragement. And especially, thank you to my family.

Lastly, I am grateful that the fourteen narrators consented, as far back as 1954, to the recording of their Owens Valley memories. They are the co-authors of this work. Over a decade or more, as I visited nearly all of them, they demonstrated the same enthusiasm for the project that is so evident in their life stories. I have valued their friendship and encouragement. I thank also these family members and friends who assisted and spoke with me about those they have known well: Dorothy and Turney Cornwell, Eleanor Taylor, Ron and Carol Taylor, Dan Gonzales, Karen Rockafellor, Dennis Eder, Paul Kashitani, Joanne Ikita, Roger Rystrand, and Jane Bright.

Introduction

The Owens Valley

The Owens Valley of eastern California is a bold and starkly beautiful land, a deep trough of high desert bounded on the west by the sheer granite flanks of the Sierra Nevada eastern escarpment and on the east by the dry, brown crests of the White-Inyo Range. The valley floor is narrow, 5 to 12 miles wide, with upward rises to the mountains on either side, and from the north slopes gently downward 90 miles to the far south end of Owens Lake. At a 3,700 foot average elevation, it is nearly 2 miles below the 14,000 foot peaks of the Sierra.

An environment of stunning contrast and extraordinary diversity, the valley lies at a rare geographic confluence, of the Great Basin, Mojave Desert, and Sierra Nevada. There, the geology, climate, plant systems, and wildlife habitats particular to each intermingle and overlap in close proximity. Snow-covered peaks are within sight of sand dunes, and desert scrub is minutes by car from alpine meadows. A passage of true seasons, unique in California's southern half, is marked by hot summers, cold, dry winters, and the colorful foliage of fall and wildflowers of spring. "A country of wonderful contrasts," John Muir called it in the nineteenth century.[1] Without dense forests, and unobscured by heavy vegetation, the shapes of the land are always visible; but perspectives change as light and shadow move across mountain crests and through desert canyons.[2] The sense of space is palpable, but the space itself is clearly bounded, and sheltering, too, as valleys are.

Markers of a complex geologic past, fault scarps, ragged lava flows, and weathered boulders stud and scar the desert floor. Formed by the uplifting of the Sierra Nevada, the Owens Valley is a deep basin of impervious granite filled now with thousands of feet of porous sediment; water stored there surfaces in springs and wetlands. Glaciers that sculpted and polished the Sierra walls deposited their rubble of rocks and boulders at canyon mouths, and glacial melting replenished the Ice Age lake that once covered much of the valley; Owens Lake, saline, with no outlet, and now dry, is its visible remnant. The shaping forces go on in modern time: an 1872 earthquake, said to be as powerful as the 1906 San Francisco cataclysm, fractured and lifted the valley floor near Lone Pine twenty-three feet.[3]

In this land of little rain, precipitation is scarce, but water can be abundant. Wet storms from the Pacific drop deep blankets of snow on the Sierra crests and western slopes, but leave barely six inches annually in the Owens Valley.[4] By spring, dozens of swift streams fill with clear snow water and tumble down the steep east face canyons into the valley below. Marked by lines of willow, birch, and aspen, they cross the desert scrub and join the Owens River, a narrow, meandering channel that rises in streams far to the north and ends in the sump of Owens Lake. From sixty miles north of that terminus, the river since 1913 has flowed into the Los Angeles Aqueduct.

The superlatives of the land draw the curious and the adventurous: A dozen Sierra peaks over 14,000 feet tower above this, America's "deepest valley." Mt. Whitney, at 14,496 feet the highest point in the contiguous United States, is little more than one hundred miles from Death Valley, where the barren sink at Badwater, at 283 feet below sea level, is the lowest place in North America. Active Sierra glaciers near Big Pine are the southernmost on the continent, and at 10,000 feet in the ancient Bristlecone Pine forest of the White Mountains, the oldest living thing on earth, the gnarled Methuselah tree, still clings to life after 4,700 years.

Politically part of California, the Owens Valley is so geographically isolated from it that only in recent decades have those living in the state's Central Valley, coastal foothills, and urban enclaves taken notice of the "undiscovered California."[5] With an area of nearly 28,000 square miles, the Sierra Nevada in places spreads 70 or more miles across. Once feared by settlers moving westward, it remains a formidable wilderness barrier, where deep canyons, vertical cliffs, ice, and summer lightning can trap the unprepared, and where no through roads connect east to west for more than 150 miles.

Euro-Americans came late to the land east of the Sierra, and settlement later still. Nearly three hundred years after Juan Cabrillo discovered *Alta California* by sea in 1542, the colonizing influence of Spanish missions, *presidios*, and *pueblos* that spread through much of the present state between 1769 and 1832 had not penetrated past the Sierra Nevada. The expedition of explorer Joseph Walker, pushing through the southern Sierra only in 1834, was the first recorded white presence to see the long valley to the east.

By then indigenous people had occupied the land for at least five thousand years. Those who met the white visitors called themselves *Numu*, or People, and the whites called them Paiute, for their cultural kinship with the Great Basin Northern Paiute people, of which they are the southernmost group. In bands of a dozen or more families, they lived in semipermanent camps of willow huts near streams and springs and followed a seasonal cycle of food-gathering actives that made use of the valley's varied resources: native grasses and plants, nuts from the pinyon forests of the Inyo and White mountains, and small game, fish, and insect larvae. Attributed to them was the earliest known manipulation of the valley's water environment, a simple but effective form of agriculture that used diverted stream water to flood meadowland plots of native plants. Augmenting their subsistence, they traded with the Yokuts, Miwok, and other groups on the Sierra western slopes, crossing the high passes on trails still in use today. Evidence suggests they traveled south as well and met Spanish speakers, from whom they may have borrowed words and phrases used in their language.[6]

Westward-moving wagon trains crossed through the valley in the years after 1845, but seldom lingered long in the arid desert landscape. In the same period, the reports of state-sponsored survey expeditions and military parties, sent to map new territories and open them for homesteading, were reaching prospective settlers. But there was little in them to spark interest in the Owens Valley: "Much inferior to that on the opposite side" [of the Sierra], a member of Walker's party had said of the Owens Valley land in 1834. State surveyor A.W. von Schmidt's 1855 assessment was less unequivocal: the valley was "Worthless to the White Man. Both in soil and climate." But the natives, he added, numbered about 1,000 and were "a fine-looking set of men." Edward Kern, traveling with a later Walker expedition, complained of the "strong, disagreeable, salty, nauseous taste" of Owens Lake; and Captain John Davidson, reporting on the Indians in 1859, noted that ". . . their character is that of an interesting, peaceful, industrious people, deserving the protection and watchful care of the government."[7]

"Heading to the top of the U.S.A." Mt. Whitney, elevation 14,496 feet, and the Sierra Nevada behind Lone Pine, ca. 1925. *Frasher's Photo. Author's Collection*

In the West, silver or gold often led the way for permanent settlement; and in 1860 as word of silver strikes in the Coso Mountains near Owens Lake spread, miners swarmed into the valley, and stockmen soon followed, driving their cattle from the drought-parched valleys of western California. As they found profitable markets for their beef at Owensville, San Carlos, Chrysopolis, and other rough camps, they built crude cabins and sent for families. Using the Preemption Act of 1841 or the newly-enacted Homestead Act of 1862, they claimed the prime watered lands that became the valley's first farms, ranches, and towns. One of the earliest to arrive, rancher John Shepherd homesteaded 160 acres near the stream that bears his name, land now encompassed by Manzanar National Historic Site.

The impact of white intrusion on the native people was immediate and devastating. Grazing cattle decimated grasslands and sullied streams, and miners and ranchers cut stands of pinyon pine for fuel and lumber, leaving the Paiutes without winter food stores. Desperate and facing starvation, the Indians stole cattle and raided white homesteads. As whites retaliated and loss of life mounted, the settler families abandoned farms and fled, and by early 1862, the Indians were again in control of the valley.

Sent to help, soldiers of the U.S. Second Cavalry, California Volunteers, raised the flag on July 4, 1862, over a crude outpost they named Camp Independence, their mission not the "watchful care" of the Indians envisioned by Captain Davidson, but a valley secure for white settlement by any means. Efforts at mediation brought a period of fragile peace, but after new Indian depredations and a white massacre of thirty Paiutes, soldiers turned to systematic starvation, destroying Indian food caches and shelters. In July 1863, they gathered nearly one thousand Indians—close to half the population—at Camp Independence and led them out, on a brutal march 200 miles across the desert, to a reservation in southern California. Most who survived the journey escaped the reservation, and many returned to the valley; the outbreaks persisted until 1865, when the army crushed the last of the three-year resistance that left an estimated sixty whites and 200 Indians dead.

For the next twelve years, the neat white buildings and uniformed soldiers at Fort Independence brought stability to the valley, and the post became an important market for the young farm economy. Settlement, ranching, and mining moved forward, small communities dotted the landscape, and in 1866 citizens chose Independence as the seat of the new Inyo County government.

For the Indians, the expanding white presence brought more destitution and new threats of removal. To survive and stay in the valley, they took jobs on road building projects and on the ranches that years earlier had displaced them. At his farm south of Independence, John Shepherd employed at least thirty Paiutes as farm hands, irrigators, and domestic helpers. Setting aside land on his property for their camp, he also gave them his surname, reportedly earning their trust and lifelong respect.

By the mid-1870s, a future in the valley looked promising; Homestead and Preemption claims had multiplied—most in the better-watered northern valley—and claims carried to patent outnumbered those cancelled, a sign that the exodus of early settlers had reversed. In 1880, the number of farms in the Owens Valley had tripled, to 222; average farm size was 200 acres, and improved, or irrigated, acreage stood at 26,261 acres, or 57 percent of land owned. Barley, corn, and wheat were the leading cereal crops, while alfalfa hay production increased after 1870. Large cattle herds, sheep raising, poultry, fruit, honey, and vegetables accounted for the remaining farm output.[8]

Extractive operations drove the Owens Valley economy in those years; the now-indispensable Indian labor enabled farmers to supply Nevada boomtown camps at Aurora and Candelaria and those east of the valley at Panamint and Darwin. Between 1870 and 1880, their strikes produced more than $75 million in gold, silver, zinc, and lead. Output at the legendary Bodie alone, in gold and silver, was an estimated $30 million in four years.[9]

But of all the region's mining legends, none matched the silver strike Mexican miner Pablo Flores found in 1865 high above Owens Lake. With total output valued at $17 million, Cerro Gordo, or "fat hill," was the richest silver mining district in California history. Owens Valley farmers and ranchers profited in the early years, supplying the rowdy camps with hay and beef, but the more lasting effect of Cerro Gordo in the valley was in the transportation monopoly held by freighter Remi Nadeau's Cerro Gordo Freighting Company. His twenty-mule team wagons hauled silver bullion across the desert to the harbor in Los Angeles for shipment to San Francisco. On the return trip to the valley, the huge wagons were loaded again, with food, spirits, hay, and equipment, all supplied by Los Angeles-area wholesalers and farmers. That unprecedented infusion of capital helped jump-start the transformation of Los Angeles from sleepy backwater town to booming metropolis, and transformed the future of the Owens Valley as well.

By 1880, with Cerro Gordo a virtual ghost town and other mines folding, the Owens Valley economy went into decline. The Carson and Colorado Railway, built in 1883 from Nevada down the eastern side of the valley to Keeler, had little business from the mines it was intended to serve; although the line opened up long-needed passenger and freight service, high shipping costs prevented all but cattlemen from profitably moving their products out. Costly mixed farming soon fell out of favor, and as farmers and former miners turned to stock raising and hay and grain production, the valley's economic base shifted from mining to agriculture for the first time.

As a new century began, Owens Valley residents seemed undeterred by the earlier downturn and gloomy economic assessments, when a San Francisco newspaper lamented that "owing to its isolated location, Inyo County has fallen far behind her sister counties in the marvelous development that has characterized California in the past ten years."[10] The years of uncertainty were giving way to optimism and faith in a new national Progressive agenda as gold strikes at Tonopah and Goldfield, in Nevada, poured money into the valley. An added stimulus to jobs and commerce, the Southern Sierras Power Company built new hydroelectric plants in the valley and exported electricity, most to the Nevada mining towns. Farmers in the north, meantime, still hopeful that a rail line south would materialize, had started work in 1878 on the McNally, Bishop Creek, and other large irrigation canals. By 1901, a network of seventeen ditches and small canals 200 miles long took water to dry farmland. That year, 141,059 acres of valley land were in agricultural use, of which 41,000 were under irrigation.[11]

In the southern areas, where the valley-wide trend in stock raising and larger farms was more pronounced, rancher John Shepherd had bought out neighboring ranchers during the downturn. By 1900, with more than 1,700 acres, he was among the largest and wealthiest landholders in the county.[12] His diversified approach to business—operating the toll road he had built, using Indian labor, to the Darwin mining district, selling horses to wealthy southern California ranchers, and his cattle, hay, and grain production—reflected a maturing valley economy and society at the turn of the century. The Shepherds' ornate Victorian ranch home, with eight children and a steady stream of visitors and travelers, was a lively center of social life for neighboring Independence and nearby George's Creek.

It was clear by 1900 that future irrigation projects in the valley would require substantial investments of capital. Huge flows of unused Owens River water were lost each year to evaporation in Owens Lake, and a storage project large enough to impound them was beyond the means of local cooperative companies. Without a reservoir, studies showed, little more than 30,000 acres could be successfully irrigated, severely limiting prospects for growth.[13] The Newlands Reclamation Act, passed in 1902, authorized federal assistance to rural areas in the West for large irrigation and water storage projects; within the year, officials of the new Reclamation Service had visited the Owens Valley and placed Long Valley, north of Bishop, on a list of potential reservoir sites.

Civic and business leaders in Los Angeles, meantime, had adopted growth as "a self-conscious plan."[14] The number of people in the city had doubled in the previous decade, to just over 102,000 in 1900, and would triple again by 1910—spurred on by aggressive land developers and promoters who proselytized that "God made Southern California—and made it on purpose."[15]

Missing from their schemes, though, was a long-term guarantee of water. Years of a low rainfall average and the limited supply from the Los Angeles River had depleted city reserves. Former Los Angeles mayor and Owens Valley landholder Fred Eaton had long eyed Owens River water for the city's use; there was a supply "adequate for any requirement Los Angeles may ever have," according to one study.[16] In 1904, he took Los Angeles water superintendent and engineer William Mulholland to the Owens Valley to assess the river, and Mulholland came away convinced he could build an aqueduct to carry its water to the city. What followed—Eaton's

Owens Valley Paiute camp of Mary Bell and Tom Bell, ca. 1915. *Andrew Forbes photo. County of Inyo, Eastern California Museum*

maneuvering for financial gain, his friendship with Reclamation engineer J.B. Lippincott and Lippincott's role in turning Reclamation studies on the Owens Valley over to Los Angeles, and the reputed dealings of wealthy southern California land investor groups—forms the core of a controversy that for over a century has been augmented by layers of conjecture, myth, and ill-will.[17]

It is certain that Mulholland drew up plans for the aqueduct, and Eaton quietly took options in his own name on more than $1million in land and water rights needed for the project—including the Long Valley reservoir site and land along nearly 60 miles of the Owens River—and later turned them over to the City. The *Los Angeles Times* broke the aqueduct story in July, 1905, amid jubilation in the city and outrage, disbelief, and a profound sense of betrayal in the Owens Valley—a "water theft," the Bishop *Inyo Register* called the plans.[18]

The following year, Mulholland, accompanied by Los Angeles officials, met with President Theodore Roosevelt in Washington, D.C. to secure backing for the aqueduct. Unmoved by pleas from Owens Valley citizens, Roosevelt threw his support behind the project. Citing "the greatest good for the greatest number" in utilizing Owens River water for municipal use, he authorized approval of a bill granting public land right-of-way for the aqueduct, withdrew support for the Reclamation project, and in 1908, by executive order authorized extending the Sierra Forest Reserve into largely treeless portions of the Owens Valley, warding off both speculation and further development.

With $23 million approved by Los Angeles residents, construction on the aqueduct began in 1908. A formidable design and logistics challenge, the project required the transport of tons of materiel and equipment into the desert and the housing and feeding of thousands of men and livestock. To supply construction in the Owens Valley, Southern Pacific built a standard-gauge extension from Mojave that connected to the 1883 narrow-gauge line, giving the valley a long-needed rail link to southern California. Completed in 1913 and hailed as a stellar engineering achievement of its time, the aqueduct still delivers water to Los Angeles by gravity flow alone through 233 miles of lined and unlined canals, tunnels, and pipes across rugged desert and mountain terrain.

In the first decade after the aqueduct opened, with only "surplus" —or water not used in the valley—sent south, agriculture remained viable and expanded modestly, mainly north of the aqueduct intake, near Bishop. Larger farm properties were subdivided and land sales were brisk, thanks to heavy promotion by developers and boosters who touted Inyo County as the "Switzerland of America."[19]

Los Angeles Aqueduct, 1913. Officials look on as the first Owens River water flows south from the intake near Independence. *Courtesy of Los Angeles Department of Water and Power*

Soon after the aqueduct plans were made public in 1905, John Shepherd had sold his 1,300 or more acres of land and water rights to southern California business interests headed by engineer and developer George Chaffey. Chaffey's experimental irrigated colonies east of Los Angeles were by then models for successful citrus-producing communities, and in 1910, the Chaffeys began subdivision of a new venture in the Owens Valley they called Manzanar, after the Spanish *manzana*, or "apple." Operating as the Owens Valley Improvement Company (OVI), they installed an innovative concrete pipe irrigation system, the first for the valley, to bring water from two adjacent creeks. The 10, 20, and 40-acre parcels offered for sale came with a guarantee of water, proportionate shares in a mutual water company, and the services of a *zanjero*, or water distributor. Agents advertised the "Manzanar Irrigated Farms" throughout the state and attracted buyers from southern California, the Midwest, and Europe. In the next two years, the company graded roads, planted 22,000 apple, pear, and peach trees, and built a school, community hall, and store in the town situated at the center of the subdivision.

Despite heavy promotion as the future hub of a major fruit-growing industry in the Owens Valley, Manzanar did not develop as expected. In ten years, the OVI had subdivided less than half the acreage it held, and half of that remained unsold. Reportedly, the company was entangled in litigation with Los Angeles over rights to the stream water that supplied the project. In 1920, 203 people lived in the area, including nine Indians and the fifty children who attended the two-room school. In good years, fruit harvests at Manzanar were huge and of exceptional quality, but unpredictable frosts, wind damage, and high shipping costs kept profit margins low.[20]

In 1920, slightly over half a million people were living in Los Angeles. Growth had far outstripped projections, and California was engulfed in a new cycle of drought. City agents returned to the Owens Valley to buy up stream and groundwater rights on agricultural land and gain control of the irrigation canals. Drought and depressed farm prices nationwide had left many valley farmers receptive to City offers; they sold outright as others joined together to force higher selling prices on Los Angeles. Some refused to sell altogether. Accusations of the City's "checkerboard" buying tactics and scenes of property owners angrily denouncing friends and neighbors left a lasting legacy of bitterness in the communities and toward Los Angeles.

With Los Angeles in control of 97 percent of the valley's farm and ranch land by 1927, and business in precipitous decline, town property values plummeted. Business owners demanded compensation, tensions mounted, and opposition to the City turned violent; explosions damaged the aqueduct system eleven times in 1927. On November 16, 1924, protestors from Bishop had seized the Alabama Spillway floodgates near Lone Pine, turning the aqueduct flow out into the desert. Over the next four days, a crowd of several hundred people at the site attracted the attention of

Manzanar town center, ca. 1912. The Owens Valley Improvement Company offered farm parcels and town lots for sale in the Manzanar Irrigated Farms subdivision. The town hall, at left, later doubled as a fruit packing plant. *County of Inyo, Eastern California Museum*

state and local officials, celebrities, and a sympathetic national press. Western movie star Tom Mix, filming on location nearby, reportedly brought a mariachi band to the festivities.

Despite the publicity, the resistors ultimately extracted from the City little more than a promise to pursue negotiations. In 1927, the opposition abruptly collapsed when the Inyo County Bank failed and its owners, resistance leaders Wilfred and Mark Watterson, were convicted of embezzlement. With the life savings of many Owens Valley residents wiped out—much of it in deposits from recent sales of their lands to the City—the economy spiraled further downward.

At Manzanar, the Chaffey interests were among the first to sell; with the majority shares of the Manzanar Water Company in Los Angeles ownership by late 1924, other property owners sold also in the following months. There and elsewhere in the valley, many who sold land and water rights opted to stay in their homes as renters and continue farming under lease—usually, without a guarantee of water. A City-employed farm superintendent managed operations on the former Chaffey-owned orchards for the next nine years, Los Angeles contracted packing operations to a southern California firm, and intermittent record fruit harvests were shipped out under a Los Angeles label. In 1934, as urban growth required more Owens Valley water in southern California, the City discontinued irrigation to Manzanar, and after the last family moved out in 1935, razed or burned some buildings and moved others to neighboring towns.

The valley languished in the early 1930s. As farmers left the valley and town commerce declined, Los Angeles bought up town properties as compensation. By 1933, the City owned nearly all valley farmland and 85 percent of town lots, and 80 ranches on thousands of acres of leased land had replaced more than 200 farms. With the large farm population, Bishop was the most severely affected; a third of its residents moved away and school enrollment declined 60 percent.[21] Hard hit, too, were the Indians, again destitute as their livelihoods all but disappeared with the sale of farms and ranches. Federal and local officials vetoed new plans suggested by the City to move the Indians from the valley; together with the local tribes, the agencies implemented instead the Owens Valley Land Exchange of 1937 that created new reservations at Bishop, Big Pine, and Lone Pine.

Throughout the troubled decade, 1924–1934, a small but steady flow of fishermen, hunters, and campers helped keep the valley's fragile economy afloat: 509 automobiles reportedly passed through Bishop in July, 1924. Extractive operations remained a viable, if intermittent, presence as well; tungsten mining near Bishop and soda ash recovery from dry Owens Lake south of Lone Pine employed local workers. In Independence, dozens of residents worked out of the City of Los Angeles headquarters office; many had only recently sold property to the City.

In 1937, valley business and civic leaders, led by Lone Pine priest Father John Crowley and Ralph Merritt—later to be the Project Director at Manzanar War Relocation Center—formed the Inyo–Mono Associates, their goal the revitalization of the Eastern Sierra towns and economy through tourism and recreation. Enlisted as a partner, Los Angeles opened lands to public recreation and began selling the nearly 88 percent of town properties it owned back to residents. In 1941, Los Angeles also opened the reservoir behind the new Long Valley Dam, part of the Mono Basin Project that added 105 miles to the aqueduct system and brought water from streams feeding Mono Lake through an eleven-mile tunnel under the volcanic Mono Craters. The reservoir, a popular fishing mecca that attracted 80,000 anglers its first year, was named to honor Father Crowley, killed the year before in a road accident.

In the 1930s, as the valley slowly pulled out of depression, a more diversified southern Inyo economy of mining, ranching, soda ash production, and movie making also proved more resilient.[22] Since 1920, when Hollywood filmmakers first went to the Owens Valley to make *The Roundup*, with Fatty Arbuckle, large studio crews and their stars had been a near-constant presence in Lone Pine. Often encamped for weeks at a time in local hotels, they filmed more than one hundred movies during that decade, nearly all Westerns, in the rugged Alabama Hills behind the town. Most memorable for local residents was the 1938 production of *Gunga Din* that lasted ten weeks, used 1,500 extras and hundreds of horses, and brought Cary Grant and a small contingent of elephants to the Owens Valley.

Amid the fear and hysteria that followed U.S. entry into World War II, a far more divisive presence was brought to the Owens Valley in the early months of 1942. The removal of nearly 120,000 persons of Japanese ancestry from the West Coast into ten "war relocation centers" in remote areas of the country began in March; in February, federal officials had selected the abandoned town site and orchard subdivision at Manzanar as the location of the first. Owens Valley residents reacted sharply to this new *fait accompli* thrust on them by federal authority. Ordered by the Army to relinquish control of more than 6,000 acres of Owens Valley land for the center, the City of Los Angeles, too, argued vehemently against locating the project in the valley, citing the security of the aqueduct—located less than a mile from the proposed camp.

"Wartime necessity" prevailed, and construction began March 16, 1942. Five days later, the first busloads of "camp" residents arrived to a bleak, windswept landscape of bulldozed land and partially built barracks. By December, when the population peaked, Manzanar War Relocation Center was the largest city between Los Angeles and Reno, with 10,121 people confined behind barbed wire in a square mile enclave of thirty-six residential blocks, each with fourteen barracks, a mess hall, latrines, and wash houses. Two-thirds were American citizens, and nearly a quarter were school-age children, including those in the Children's Village orphanage.

In the first months, primitive living conditions exacerbated pre-evacuation tensions among rival political and cultural factions. Most internees, however, willingly took on the task of getting a community up and running. Overseen by Caucasian

Farm workers with Mt. Williamson in background. Manzanar War Relocation Center, 1944. *Ansel Adams photograph, Library of Congress LC302141*

administrators, the internees manned agricultural, water, sewage, and building projects, and staffed schools, a hospital, beauty shop, camouflage net and garment factories, co-op, newspaper, police and fire departments. The War Relocation Authority employed a non-Japanese staff of two hundred, including many Owens Valley residents, most housed adjacent to the internee area. When mounting tensions in the camp erupted in a riot on December 6, 1942, that left two internees dead, the worst fears of many Owens Valley residents were confirmed, and both camp and community remained on edge for weeks.

Determined to prevail over the humiliation of confinement, the internees planned projects to beautify the bleak camp environment: elaborate ornamental and flower gardens, expanses of victory gardens, lawns, ponds, and parks within a few months had softened the drabness of the camp. In 1944, an internee construction crew built the high school auditorium/gymnasium that today houses the Manzanar National Historic Site Interpretive Center.

Over nearly four years of Manzanar operations, as local hostility evolved to a largely indifferent acceptance, town residents responded to invitations to attend open houses, musical programs, and sports events. A fall fair hosted by the internees featured music, dancing, food, and garden tours, and drew hundreds from the neighboring towns.

Implementation of a relocation program early in 1943 permitted internees to request "indefinite leave" from the camp. Required first, of all persons seventeen and older, was an ambiguous and divisive "loyalty" questionnaire: negative answers to two key questions branded their respondents as disloyal; they and their families—more than 2,200 in all—were sent to Tule Lake Segregation Center. Affirmative responses cleared the way for those with proof of jobs, sponsorship, or college admission to resettle east of the exclusion area: California, and western Oregon, Washington, and Arizona.

As residents moved out, the camp population declined steadily until the weeks before Manzanar closed on November 21, 1945, when fewer than 1,000 people remained. Project Director Ralph Merritt later reported that a tearful four-year-old was the last to leave the camp, the only home he had known. In the months following, more than 800 buildings were auctioned for lumber or removal to other locations, and the land returned to City management. Twenty-six former staff barracks temporarily housed Inyo County veterans and City employees, and the Independence Veterans of Foreign Wars used the auditorium/gymnasium as a social hall.

A relative quiescence settled over postwar Owens Valley. Helped by stabilized relations with Los Angeles, tourism flourished; expanded ski facilities at Mammoth Mountain, with an average 335 inches of snow annually, were attracting world-class skiers; throughout the Eastern Sierra, road, campground, and trail-building projects were under way, and dozens of new motels and coffee shops opened to serve the thousands visiting each year. Movie companies filled Lone Pine hotels, and scientists, researchers, and students of history, geology, and botany were discovering the region's remarkably intact evidence of natural and manmade environments.

More than thirty years after the economic collapse, the shift in business and employment seemed secure with the vitality of the sales and service sector and the nearly 20 percent of Inyo County's workforce employed in public agencies, most engaged with managing land and resources. By 1964, when the Wilderness Act placed over 100 miles of Sierra crest backcountry behind the Owens Valley into the John Muir Wilderness, Sequoia and Kings Canyon National Parks formed the western boundary of Inyo County; Death Valley National Monument lay to the east partially within the county, and mountain areas on either side were managed as Inyo National Forest. Agriculture, meanwhile, by then was concentrated in stock raising and alfalfa hay production on leased City-owned land. In 1960, 104 farms and ranches in the Owens Valley operated on more than 300,000 acres of valley land in grazing and farm use.[23]

In the same period, plans were underway in Los Angeles for a second aqueduct projected to increase water export capacity 50 percent. Placed into operation in 1970, the "second barrel," as it came to be known, flowed from the intake at Haiwee Reservoir 137 miles to Los Angeles, roughly parallel to the 1913 aqueduct. The City increased permanent groundwater pumping levels the following year, setting off a storm of protest from citizens and environmental groups. Alarmed at the potential adverse effects on plant and wild life of a rapid drawdown of groundwater, they pushed for action against the City.[24]

In 1972 Inyo County filed a lawsuit against the City, citing its failure to comply with the newly enacted California Environmental Quality Act (CEQA) in implementing the groundwater pumping program. A new era of protracted conflict over Owens Valley water moved into the courtroom, pitting the City against a host of local and national advocacy groups committed to monitoring the City's water export program and reversing the environmental damage they argued it was causing.

Years of litigation and negotiation produced the Long Term Water Agreement in 1991. A controversial and complex compromise, it called for joint county/city management of Owens Valley groundwater pumping by Los Angeles. A 1997 Memorandum of Understanding spelled out specific studies and mitigation projects required of the City and other parties, including vegetation analysis, sensitive habitat management, and turning water back into 62 miles of the Owens River below the aqueduct intake. Since then, the parties have returned to court repeatedly in new and acrimonious conflicts over implementation of the pacts, notably the river rewatering project and the levels set annually for groundwater extraction.

In the same period, air quality advocates were lobbying to have Los Angeles held accountable for decades of dust pollution from the dry Owens Lake. First noticeable when farmers in the nineteenth century used Owens River water for irrigation, the lake dropped gradually until aqueduct diversions starting in 1913 dried it completely. A 1998 Memorandum of Agreement between Los Angeles and the Great Basin Unified Air Pollution Control District imposed a 2006 deadline for the City to meet federal air quality standards.

In the decades after 1950, Manzanar lay in neglect. Desert reclaimed the camp landscape, and cattle grazed through gardens and orchards. Leased to Inyo County, the former high school auditorium for nearly forty years was a heavy equipment maintenance garage. As time passed, a stone cemetery monument, festooned with colorful origami cranes, coins, and toys, became a gathering place for returning former internees. "Soul consoling tower," the Japanese inscription said. Attendees at a pilgrimage in 1969 assembled there, as they have every year since, for a day of remembrance. Manzanar was listed on the National Register of Historic Places in 1976 and designated a National Historic Landmark in 1985. In 1992, decades of effort by Japanese American and other groups culminated in an Act of Congress that declared Manzanar a National Historic Site and placed it into the National Park system.

Since 1980, tourism and recreation, stock raising, geothermal development, and new extractive operations have shaped the economy and defined the social fabric of the valley. A reported three million people, many of them from Europe and Asia, traveled through the Owens Valley in 2003. Among the more unique events that swell the influx, Mule Days unfolds on Memorial Day weekend each year in Bishop, its roots in the century-long traditions of Sierra backcountry packing operations. In October, the popular Lone Pine Film Festival celebrates that town's movie-making heritage.

Federal, state, and local public agencies are joined in promoting the Eastern Sierra, but increasingly, their task is one of balancing that effort with upholding measures that protect fragile natural areas and wildlife from the effects of increased human activity. Bans on backcountry campfires, food storage requirements, quotas for popular trails into the Sierra wilderness, and hiker access only into once-open desert areas have dramatically transformed Eastern Sierra recreation in the decades since fishermen and campers first made the long trip across the desert into the mountains.

Slightly over 18,000 people lived in Inyo County in 2003, most in the Owens Valley. Of the county's more than 10,000 square miles, 92 percent is federally owned, and just under 4 percent, or about 400 square miles, is in City of Los Angeles ownership. Government remains the largest employer, followed by the retail and service industry. Unemployment is at or slightly below the California average; median household income lags behind both state and national levels.[25] With just 2 percent of land privately held, population growth has been slow in the past twenty years and may likely remain so.

The Owens Valley looking south, from above Manzanar, 2005. The National Historic Site Interpretive Center is at center; the camp layout is partially visible in the road grid and rows of foundations, used for the latrines and wash houses in each of the thirty-six residential blocks. *Author's Collection*

History, Memory, and Place: Remembering Manzanar

It is captivating, this saga of uneasy conflict and colorful players, and perplexing, too, in its myriad perspectives and multiple versions. No single, simple narrative of the past for this long land, history instead is gathered in and passed down, contested and refashioned in current perspective and prevailing myth. "Stories about ourselves," one author calls them, accounts of history's elusive truths that we tell and retell, leaving some of ourselves in them, as "inventors of [their] meanings."[26] More succinctly, writer Kathleen Norris suggests this about history in the West: that "one people's frontier is usually another's homeland."[27]

In the following pages, space has been set aside for fourteen people to tell their stories—and their histories—of the Owens Valley. They are the "ordinary" people of a place who go about their daily occupations, interacting with events, neighbors, news, and ideas. Though seldom given a voice in accounts of their communities' histories, they have nonetheless gathered extraordinarily wise and hard-won knowledge of those pasts, grounded in their deep engagements with the life around them. "Local companions," Barry Lopez has called them, "those people who can tell the names of things and how, traditionally, they have been fitted together in a community," who . . . "have a feel for the soil and history" of a place.[28]

Their vantage points of remembering are varied: an occupation or profession, a family, town or favored place in the Owens Valley; the particularity of ethnicity, gender, or race. All have lived there, or still do; some nearly all their lives, others little more than a few months. From the wealth of their combined age, experience, and perspective, these "local companions" relate nearly 125 years of Owens Valley history, and with remarkable insight and acuity, they convey—not surprisingly, but probably unwittingly—a uniquely interwoven, more inclusive account of its past than may have been told before.

Stories of the Owens Valley are many, but a few are so familiar as to be symbols of pasts deeply embedded in region and nation. The century-long presence of the City of Los Angeles as owner of land and exporter of water, and the political, social, and environmental issues attached to it, are, arguably, the most comprehensively documented. The World War II internment of persons of Japanese ancestry at Manzanar likewise has produced an expansive literature, a broad representation in the arts, and extensive media coverage. The remembering and recounting of both have generated their own parallel controversies, subjects for study and debate in their own right.

On these and other topics, the efforts of scholars and local authors, augmented by invaluable government studies, constitute a varied Owens Valley literature. Notable are these well-researched approaches to the water story: *Vision or Villainy*, by Abraham Hoffman; *The Water Seekers*, Remi Nadeau; *The Lost Frontier*, Robert Sauder, and *Western Times and Water Wars*, John Walton. From the hundreds of contributions to the internment history are: *Only What We Could Carry*, an edited collection from Lawson Inada; *Born Free and Equal*, with photographs and commentary of Ansel Adams; and *Camp and Community*, a study of local responses to Manzanar from the Center for Oral and Public History at California State University Fullerton. Fine guidebooks—especially *Deepest Valley*, edited by Jeff Putnam and Genny Smith—and local publications, articles, and websites chronicle the region's mining, railroad, movie, and mountaineering histories, among others.

John Walton's work notwithstanding, however, and recalling Bishop newspaperman W.A. Chalfant's sprawling 1922 saga, *The Story of Inyo*, accounts of the Owens Valley past, taken together, remain largely specialized, even narrowly realized. From that vantage point, a history can appear episodic or incomplete, as major episodes merit wider attention, and others and their historical actors, rendered separately, too, will be taken as detached from one another and the larger story they are part of. [29]

But the nearby past is neither fragmented in its parts nor detached from the far-off in history; as each gives access to the other, both are conveyed in more vivid hues of meaning and value. Stories of the Owens Valley soda ash industry cannot be told apart from those of the Mexicans who labored there, or the railroads, corporate businesses, world wars, and depression that impacted both. It is tempting, too, to ignore the messy conflicts and often unwelcome changes of the past; every community wants a history it can be proud of. But the "good old days" were not always so: at the colorful soda ash towns, the product itself was toxic. Embracing their more inclusive pasts, communities will discover the very uniqueness and character they endeavor to celebrate.

Recent studies confirm what most of us already know: we are more likely to be involved with the past by way of the "nearby" and the familiar—through stories heard from family and friends, perusing family photo albums, participating in community celebrations, visiting museums.[30] So we return to the fourteen "local companions," who perhaps will suggest a new kind of local history for the Owens Valley, one that alludes to distant events and people and doesn't back away from conflict and change. We can imagine their encounters with the past as ours too, as conversations that bring history "closer to home." Think of them for a moment, gathering in a coffee shop or meeting hall—as they often did—in one of the valley's small towns. We are there too, to listen, ask questions, and engage them in a dialogue about the past.

Used imaginatively, oral history helps this happen. It is a distinctively unique and effective tool of inquiry for anyone desiring to find out how, qualitatively rather than quantitatively, individual lives have affected and been affected by events of the past. It can capture the remembrances of historical actors famous and infamous, but is most effective in giving voice to ordinary people who would not otherwise be called on to document the past. At the heart of the process is a reliance, not on absolute historical accuracy or a literal recounting of events, but on human perspective—attitudes, biases, emotions—in recalling and conveying the past. The tape-recorded (and now, too, video-taped) interview, a record of a conversation, is more, in the subtleties it reveals: how people situate themselves in the past, for example, or weave events through personal experience—more significant, perhaps, than details of the events themselves. "Oral recollections tell us not just what people did, but what they wanted to do, what they believed they were doing, and what they now think they did," says historian Alessandro Portelli.[31]

That unique attribute of oral recollection may be as its flaw as well: the potential to mislead, confuse, and produce accounts of the past that are themselves flawed.[32] Interviews are not substitutes for the sources historians traditionally rely on—documents, records, letters, among others—nor are they free of biases. "There is no impartiality in oral history," says Portelli. "The partiality of the narrator . . . must be taken into account."[33] Oral history, in short, *must* be evaluated with a critical eye. But if not historical truth, oral narratives at the least can make us "uncomfortably aware" of its elusiveness, by lifting up for closer examination long-accepted versions of the past that trickle down through generations in a community.[34] From a number of the narrators come these mixed assessments, for example, of the 1920s Manzanar farm community: "thriving," encompassed "thousands of acres," some say, or conversely, its farmers "could never get ahead."[35]

People need to "place memories someplace," one historian has said."[36] "Life does not exist in a vacuum," says another; "everything takes place."[37] And so we call up memory most often by place. The benchmarks of our national past come to mind through the vivid images of where we first learned of them: the attack on Pearl Harbor, the assassination of John F. Kennedy, September 11, 2001. Closer to home, Nan Zischank locates her memories of escorting Manzanar internees out of camp within the tight confines of the large black government van she drove. Her perspectives seem sharper for the closeness of that space. Vic Taylor, too, locates his memories with clarity, but more so in the vast outdoor environment of the Owens Valley.

Places shape who we are: a profound axiom, though not, as one geographer commented, "a subject for rationale discourse." That intricately woven union of memory, identity, and locale resonates through the recollections of Vic, Nan and the other "local companions." Owen Cooper found it in the humble Jim's Place, as he made sodas and was absorbed into the community life of Independence. A "sense of place," some call it; others may confuse it with longings for the nostalgic and picturesque in a landscape. But by any name, we recognize the idea "that there is something intangible in certain places—a kind of quality that makes them worth defending."[38]

Of all the places of memory in the Owens Valley, Manzanar may most profoundly evoke that intense attachment to locale. Astonishingly diverse perspectives on the past and wide circles of experience intersect there, making of it a metaphorical meeting place for remembering in the valley, and in these recollections as well.[39] Among those memories, some are steeped in shattering life upheavals that occurred there, whereas others recount a simple brush with its past—a visit, a brief job. Both speak to the infinite meanings of place in human experience and suggest too, that Manzanar has been a place of immeasurable significance in some lives and in others, one peripheral to alternate locales where identity and sense of place were more sharply defined.

Places such as Manzanar defy simple description. As a geographic place, it lies about midpoint in the Owens Valley, but as a remembered place, it sits squarely at the center of the national debate on racism and guaranteed rights under the Constitution. History has taken place there often; a long sequence of human occupation attaches to the site and has transformed it repeatedly from "a land of the future to a [place] with a past."[40]

The "moral burden" of the American West is extraordinarily present in the empty landscape as well.[41] If the Owens Valley does not altogether "fit" the beloved frontier versions of the Western past, one need only examine the places the frontier usually became: where successive waves of people arrived and made use of land and resources to advance their economic and social interests, often displacing those who had gone before.[42] With little left to show for the hunters and gatherers, explorers, cattlemen and farm laborers, fruit packers, teachers, doctors, cooks, fishermen, photographers, and soldiers who have come and gone—and lacking a community of the present—Manzanar is now a landscape devoted to memory.

As a meeting ground of events in the Owens Valley past for more than one hundred years, Manzanar has been called a "microcosm" of local history. More accurate, perhaps, is the *suggestion* of broad impulses in the history of the American West common to both pasts that define each uniquely: a pervasive presence of federal policy and authority, the rise of corporate capitalism and its effect on rural areas, the growth of cities and concurrent decline of agriculture, and the West as a place of racial and ethnic diversity and strife.

The most recent of Manzanar's pasts, as a relocation center for Japanese Americans, demonstrates, too, how divergent perspectives on local and national histories can meet—and collide—in a place deeply infused with meanings important to both. The legislation that designated Manzanar a National Historic Site and was signed into law by President George H.W. Bush in March 1992, officially recognized the wartime relocation period of the site's history, 1942–1945, as the most nationally significant. Yet, asks historian David Glassberg, "when historians bound and mark certain places as 'historical' and distinguish them from ordinary places, which (and whose) version of community, place, and character will prevail? [Visitors] look for novelty in a landscape . . . whereas local residents look at the landscape as a web of memory sites and social interactions."[43]

As Manzanar was transformed in the decades since 1945 from neglected local landscape to national symbol of remembrance, residents in the Owens Valley remained ambivalent, and in some instances, outwardly hostile, to fully embracing a commemoration of the events—and the reconstruction of physical reminders of them—that took place there in World War II. At the same time, ideas proposed locally for tourist amenities at the site, such as a picnic area and campground, met with equally strong adverse reactions from Japanese Americans, many of whom regard the site in near-sacred terms.

Reflected in the local viewpoint is the conservatism of an older generation that includes revered combat veterans of World War II and other conflicts. There is, too, a residual awareness in local memory that the removal and relocation, now acknowledged as a grim episode in the national past, was carried out in close proximity to the small towns of this quiet valley, and without their citizens' consent. Over the long term, that closeness may have diminished local racist attitudes, but it was the nature of the confinement itself that provoked the strongest reactions. Most who remembered took exception to the now-iconic images of the camp's bleakness. They recalled the first weeks of dust and drab barracks, and how the people inside transformed it within months to a lush landscape of gardens and farms, proof they were well-off and content. Local residents questioned, too, the relative significance of four years of camp operations measured against the valley's long history, some calling the other, longer occupations of the site the "real" Manzanar.

The pasts of Manzanar loom large in Owens Valley memory. The irrigated environments present in each, for example, suggest a local historical perspective based in the symbolic meanings and historic uses of the valley's water. The demise of an agrarian way of life at the Manzanar orchard community in the 1920s—and throughout the Owens Valley—was a clear benchmark of local memory and history. More than eighty years later, it still belongs to the debate over the future of land and water in the valley. In the 1940s, moreover, the irrigated landscape at the relocation center earned internee gardeners and farmers the admiration and respect of Owens Valley residents, grateful to watch as Manzanar was returned, in their eyes, to its former days as a green and productive agricultural area.

My own web of memory at Manzanar began in childhood, when I accompanied my parents on excursions to pick apples in the old orchards, abandoned for the second time after the relocation center closed in 1945. Fed intermittently by years of good rain and a high water table, the trees still produced. A few buildings from the camp remained: white-painted staff barracks used by veterans, and the high school auditorium, now the National Historic Site Interpretive Center. On these outings, I heard stories about the two-room school my mother had attended at Manzanar, the general store my grandparents owned, and the ice cream stand, old-time dances, and acres of orchards. Not until many years later did I separate those images from others, of the "Jap Camp" also called Manzanar that the locals still talked about, where the orchards, gardens, and farming seemed nearly identical to the place of my mother's youth.

Memory in a community forms in layers of stories about a past held in common. These fourteen people speak here from the diversity of their remarkable experiences and the vividness of personal recollection, but among their memories, some have undergone testing, critiquing, and reshaping over decades, in conversation and debate with friends and neighbors, to become the collectively held "code of things it's all right to remember" in a community or a nation.[44] Acknowledging then, the pull of perspective, both personal and collective, in memory, history, and place in the Owens Valley, we can listen as these "local companions" recount their stories.

Presenting the Past: Editor's Notes

The fourteen people who speak here first did so in tape-recorded and transcribed interviews, now in the oral history archive of the Eastern California Museum (ECM) in Independence; they are used with the full permission of the Museum Director. A small local agency, the ECM has been a "keeper of the community past" in the Owens Valley for nearly eighty years.[45] Outstanding collections of Paiute and Panamint Shoshone basketry, historic photographs, and Manzanar artifacts have garnered it accolades throughout the region. In an archive of more than 1,000 audio tape hours in 500 interviews, remarkable oral recollections encompass nearly 125 years of Owens Valley and Eastern Sierra history. Notable among them are Nettie Fausel's memories of early Independence, the closest to the pioneer experience of Inyo County's first residents, and Stub Lydston's 1954 interview, the first completed under the aegis of the museum. Both are testaments to that particular urgency present in every oral history interviewing effort: to capture the memories of historical actors, young or old, while it is possible to do so.

Interviewing at the museum began informally fifty years ago and produced recollections sporadically until 1990, when a more focused effort generated most of the collection. Working from a loosely structured, broadly applicable set of questions developed by museum staff, interviewer Richard Potashin spoke with more than two hundred present and former Owens Valley residents, asking them to reflect on the region's people, events, and economic, social, and natural environments from their perspectives of gender, ethnicity, and occupation. I reviewed and catalogued the collection early in the 1990s and, in a later project, listened to dozens of tapes relating to the recently designated Manzanar National Historic Site. From both projects, I gained a broad familiarity with the contents of the archive and, as often happens in oral history, became immersed in its stories and drawn into the places and events of their narrators' lives.

These unexpected encounters with the Owens Valley past were the inception of this anthology. The remarkable stories I heard were passionate, amusing, surprising, sometimes tragic, and always informative. Conveying a knowledge of place available only to those who have lived and worked there, they could potentially broaden existing accounts of the local past and give new insights into the ways people in a community view their own history.

Because these interviews had spoken to me so compellingly, I could visualize bringing them out of boxes and file cabinets, into a public forum. Imagined as dialogues or conversations, they would engage readers with history, provoke curiosity, and enliven understanding of the Owens Valley past. I recalled when a group of students had met some years before with Nan Zischank, a narrator in this volume, and two other local residents; all three had worked at Manzanar during World War II. At the Eastern California Museum, as we gathered around them, listening and engaging in a dialogue, our questions led to conversations they carried on among themselves; pulling up memories, they seemed almost to forget we were there.

In the early thinking about the project, two criteria seemed obvious: first, the organizational metaphor would be the series of dialogues I had imagined; and, significantly, I would use only existing interviews in the ECM collection. This latter step is a departure from conventional starting points oral historians often use for such projects, in which they may generate a body of interviews from a specific research plan or problem of limited focus and incorporate them into a specialized study.

The ECM collection, however, is eclectic, even serendipitous, in its assortment of interviewing styles, question lists, transcription formats, and interview topics and settings. Embedded in each interview, nonetheless, is a consistency of intention, or collection philosophy—of why the interview was done in the first place—derived from its origins in this local agency's mission, administrative priorities, and operational constraints. Using interviews exclusively from this collection better preserves and illuminates the projects grounding in the local Owens Valley community.

As intersection of experience and perspective in the Owens Valley past, the place and historic occupations of Manzanar are here a loose focusing device for memory. The extensive references to Manzanar found throughout the entire archive reflect its significance in local memory; more extended Manzanar recollections were in a number of interviews already in transcript form, providing a logical and practical means of narrowing the choices. Each interview, then, recounts a firsthand life experience or contact with the place of Manzanar. It was not my intention, however, to compile a collection exclusively about Manzanar. Rather, I was looking to explore how references to it weave through Owens Valley life stories and memory. A decision to use an interview, therefore, took that into account and other considerations as well.

Progressively, however, interview selection became more intuitive than systematic. Representation, for example, typically requires a voice for gender, ethnicity, and occupation; in the Owens Valley, there would be towns, north or south valley, and events as well. Existing themes or topics would require locating interviews to "fit" them—the railroad and water history, among others. Or, more intriguingly, the so-called themes and categories could instead derive from the life experiences themselves. The stories of Mary Nomura, Truman Buff, and Connie Salas are steeped in their respective ethnic and cultural contexts, but are not markers here for ethnicity or race. In its many guises, ethnicity flows instead from all the interviews, according to the story told. Rather than address fixed areas of experience, it was more satisfying, finally, to hear Emily Roddy describe with captivating authenticity the railroad community at Owenyo and discover its sub-themes of multi-ethnic populations and racist attitudes.

Though decidedly an "intangible," it is that honesty of expression I heard in Emily's story and others, and the attitudes and perspectives it reveals, that best connects audiences to narrators and the pasts they recount. "The telling of the story is part of the story being told," oral historian Alessandro Portelli said. Here, a close reading of Nan Zischank's stories of driving Japanese Americans leaving Manzanar suggests that although her early life amid wealth and privilege is missing from her narrative, it is present nonetheless in its telling, adding a richness and texture to her account not found in details alone.

A careful reading will also reveal how a narrator organizes and conveys the complexity of his life experience—rarely around chronology or theme, but more often chaotically, and by association, with place, people, community, job, or family responsibility. Likewise, I asked how narrators articulate a "sense of place." Connie Salas recalls her modest childhood homes, where amenities mattered less than family closeness; Mary Nomura, too, links sense of place to the presence of family and friends.

At some point, most narrators will exaggerate, speak through others' experiences, pass on hearsay, nostalgically long for the past, or recount inaccurate details. This is part "of the story being told." But if these appear to be the primary means of conveying recollections, they call into question the validity of the experience being remembered and/or the condition of the memory itself. Still, there are exceptions: Stub Lydston's account is filled with nostalgic longings for the "good old days," but Stub, a story-teller, uses nostalgia as a narrative device. I did reject accounts seemingly informed by intended distortions of events or whose narrators appeared motivated by prejudice, personal feuds, or local politics.

Retaining the question and answer format would be essential to conveying dialogues as conversations and drawing others into them. Oral historians are often reluctant to keep dialogue formats intact for public presentations and will remove questions to achieve a more autobiographical style of narrative. Stylistic considerations aside, however, a more serious consequence of omitting questions is the loss of transparency in conveying the dynamics of the interviewing process. Narrators respond to specific questions asked of them by the interviewer—who is a full partner in creating the interview. That relationship, with its potential to subtly influence the perspectives, even the honesty, of the narrator—and with it the outcome of the interview—lies within the dialogue.

Exceptions to this format are the interviews of Nettie Fausel and Stub Lydston, whose roughly typed and carbon-copied transcripts did not include questions when I found them. With no tape recordings in the archives, and only brief notes from the interviewer, it is unclear to what extent questioning actually elicited these narratives.

Editing of oral history has been described as "meddling" with the form of a primary source. At its most basic, editing renders the chaos and clutter of the raw oral history transcript intelligible and usable. Michael Frisch takes that a step further: "aggressive editing," including "substantial manipulation [of the interview text]," he says, better protects the integrity of a transcript than its literal reproduction.[47] Beyond technique, however, editing embraces an aesthetic component more closely attuned to literature than history. Buried in each interview is a story, a narrative and its components of dialogue, plot development, and cast of characters. It is the editor's task to locate them. Editing, then, becomes a process of eliminating all that obscures and detracts from each interview's unique storytelling apparatus and the values and experiences that attach to it. This differs in both mindset and technique from extracting usable portions of a dialogue from the text, perhaps to reassemble a new interview version. Instead, peeling back layers of extraneous detail, trivia, and nostalgia illuminates the essence of a narrator's story, and how he or she articulates it.[48] That process produced substantial reductions in the original transcript lengths, of 60 percent or more, yet still allowed the unhurried conversational style of the dialogues to unfold.

To give coherence to the dialogue of the raw transcript, while remaining faithful to the structure of the narrators' presentations, I removed repetitive sections and phrases, combined others, and if it did not substantially alter the narrator's style or intent, compressed and combined statements. I did not alter the narrators' words, substitute, or add others, except where indicated by brackets, and then usually to improve the flow of dialogue or to clarify dates, places, or other references. Longer explanations and definitions are found in the notes. I did eliminate, shorten, or combine interviewer questions that were repetitive or extraneous. The interviews began with similar introductory questions; I eliminated those and gave instead the narrators' opening statements gleaned from their early responses.

Transferring the spoken word to the printed page is fraught with pitfalls. What seems acceptable in speech may appear ungrammatical, awkward, or simply embarrassing in print. I eliminated usages that would reflect unfavorably on the narrators, but have retained others representative of their natural modes of speaking, personalities, and backgrounds. To better capture those patterns in the editing process, I compared transcripts with tapes; my visits with the narrators were helpful as well.

Lastly, of the options for a coherent presentation, chronology in the Owens Valley past, age of narrator, thematic ties, or date of interview were most likely. A "loosely chronological" order did emerge, but out of the time period, locale, or set of events that seemed most compelling in each recollection: how, fundamentally, each narrator related his/her experience in the Owens Valley past. Capturing the interwoven quality of the memories, too, would enable their common and contrasting threads of experience to resonate through the entire work. The three brief recollections by young women who left their homes in Los Angeles and went to Manzanar are the first internee voices we hear; they are placed ahead of Mary Nomura's more comprehensive account of her music activities before, during, and after camp. But between them is the counterpoint of Nan Zischank's descriptions of the Sierra wilderness—a constant in the upheavals of wartime—her complex perspectives on the camp, and her role in taking its confined residents to their freedom—among them, most likely, the three women who have just spoken.

Word biases present unique editorial dilemmas: in this case, the pejorative "Jap," used by a number of the narrators. I have retained it without alteration or annotation as a clear indication of oral history's ability to transport us to a time when people of otherwise good character could use such epithets seemingly "in a descriptive, unmindful way."[49] The inherent subjectivity of the oral history process invites readers to form their own opinions about the actions and character of the narrators—all of whom were encouraged by their interviewers to reflect spontaneously and honestly on their pasts in the Owens Valley.

The terms used to describe the War Relocation Center at Manzanar carry political and cultural overtones as well. Known variously as a "concentration camp," "prison," or "internment camp," Manzanar was officially designated a "war relocation center" during World War II. The National Park Service uses that historic term in its exhibits and other materials, and I have chosen to use it here as well. Likewise, Manzanar's residents have been called "prisoners," "inmates," "evacuees," or "internees." Officially, they were "evacuees," but Japanese Americans will often use "internees." The Park Service uses both, and I have again followed its lead. Throughout the text, "City," "Los Angeles," "Department," and "DWP" are used interchangeably for the City of Los Angeles Department of Water and Power.

Established oral history procedure calls for the return of the unedited or partially edited transcript to the narrator for review. The ECM in some cases bypassed this step prior to making the transcripts available for research and public use. When possible, I returned my own edited versions to the narrators or their family members; in each case, they made only minor corrections or none at all. The tapes and transcriptions are available at the Eastern California Museum in Independence, California, for those who may wish to explore them more fully.

The Interviews

The telling of the story is part of the story being told

Alessandro Portelli

ONE

Nettie Roeper Fausel (1874–1968)

I raised some coyotes once

Introduction

In these witty and plainspoken recollections, Nettie Fausel reaches back in memory to her girlhood in the Owens Valley of the late nineteenth century. Nearly ninety-three when she talked with Eastern California Museum volunteers Bessie Poole and Jan Hillis in August 1967, she had lived in Independence most of her life and presided over the local post office for forty-two years. But of all her legacies, none has endured longer than the coyote she once kept as a pet. The hapless creature and its exploits amused the townsfolk, although some reportedly took a dim view of its presence in the community; it was a discomfiting reminder, perhaps, of those not-so-distant frontier beginnings in a desert wilderness that still lies just beyond the town's last street of shaded homes.

As the nineteenth century drew to a close across the West, the dusty *pueblos*, isolated mining camps, and frontier towns of Spanish colonizers and white pioneers were shedding the last vestiges of their rough-hewn origins, some to become one day the region's great urban centers of commerce and society. In the Owens Valley, years of depression and downturn seemed nearly over, and a welcome air of permanency settled over its small communities. Filled with optimism and civic confidence, their white settler citizens looked ahead to a new century; with it would come, they were certain, modernity, progress, and prosperity. It was a time, writer Mary Austin later said of the Owens Valley, when "life stood at the breathing pause between the old ways and the new."[1]

South of Independence, near Manzanar, Nettie pointed out the land her German immigrant grandparents had homesteaded in 1864. They and other white pioneers went to the Owens Valley as early as 1861, their reasons as incongruous as their origins in dozens of states and foreign countries.[2] A dream of prosperity brought most, but the promise of "social mobility in proportion to industry and probity" was as attractive.[3] Once there, and faced with isolation, Indian warfare, and a capricious climate, many left and moved on, joining thousands of other once-hopeful homesteaders whose abandoned sod huts, wood shacks, and log cabins still littered the western landscape decades later.

Those who stayed drew together in communities of mutual aid and shared struggle. Out of frontier exigencies, they fashioned civic order and community infrastructures; and by the late 1880s, their efforts were tangible in the thousands of acres under cultivation, miles of irrigation ditches, and the gracious homes, hotels, schools, emporiums, and churches in Bishop, Big Pine, Independence, and Lone Pine.

The formation of local government marked a milestone of progress in western communities and affirmed the optimism of their earliest settlers. When Inyo County was established in 1866, newly elected and appointed officials assumed the civic functions—in name at least—once performed by citizens. But lacking funds and promised federal assistance, the new agencies more often than not turned responsibility for essential services—fire protection, law enforcement, and schools among them—back over to volunteers.[4]

Despite the best efforts of government and citizens alike, the fledgling communities remained vulnerable to lawlessness, disease, and sudden disaster. The conflagration that swept through Independence on June 30, 1886, destroyed thirty-eight buildings and razed the main street. It clearly impressed an observant young Nettie Roeper, who recalled that without fire service or a town water system, hoses and buckets were no match for the wind-driven flames.

In predominantly Euro-American, Protestant communities like Independence, fraternal orders—Freemasons in particular—fostered leadership groups, and civic stability rested in the moral authority of the town's upstanding wives and mothers. A social order structured largely by ethnic origin relegated a nearly invisible cluster of Chinese laborers to the bottom, objects of the same nativistic derision suffered by "Orientals" elsewhere in the West; faring better were Paiute farm and ranch workers, essential to the valley's prosperity.[5]

Nettie recalls writer Mary Austin, an enigmatic figure who moved to Independence in 1900. From her "brown house under the willow tree," she wrote *The Land of Little Rain*, the elegant paean to the desert that earned her literary fame and entry into a coterie of western writers and artists that included Jack London, Lincoln Steffens, and John Muir.[6] Coping with a failed marriage and the heartbreak of a mentally impaired daughter, she found solace among the Mexican families of Lone Pine and inspiration in the folkways of the Owens Valley Paiute. But the guardians of correctness in Independence, troubled by Austin's outspokenness and

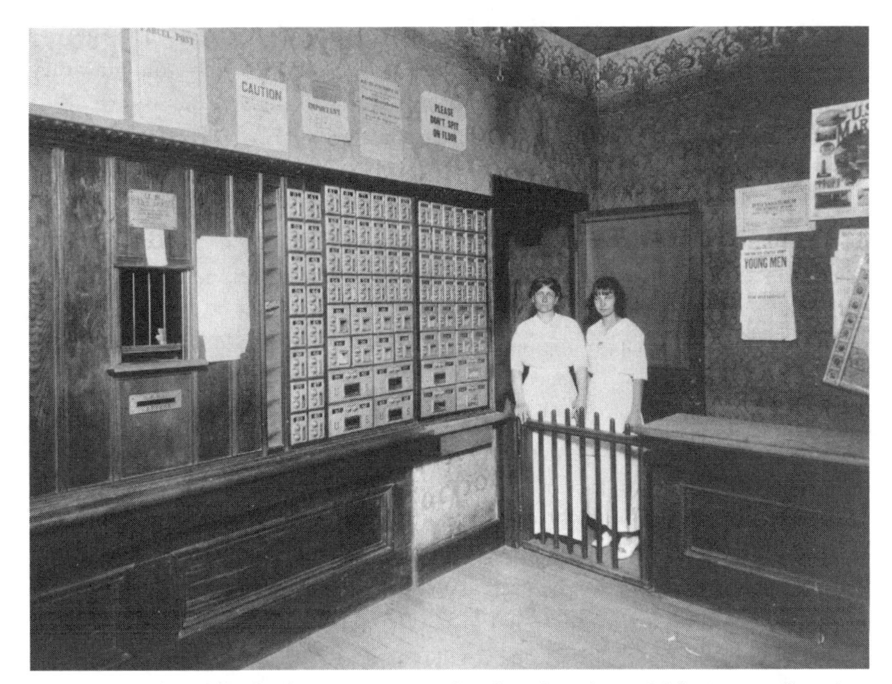

Nettie Fausel, left, with her daughter Norma, ca. 1916, in the Independence, California, post office, where Nettie was postmistress for forty-two years. *County of Inyo, Eastern California Museum*

early feminist zeal, frowned on these "unorthodox" associations: "A committee of ladies . . . used to call on me occasionally to ask what I meant by taking part in Indian dances," she wrote. "There was a suspicion that my interest in these things was touched by failure to apprehend the proper social distinctions."[7]

Nettie Fausel—Interview

My father and his father many years ago put down the artesian well by hand out there at the ranch just past Manzanar, and in '72 [1872] when they had the big earthquake it shut off almost all the flow. Now there is a small pond where the stock can drink. My father's name was Charles Julius Ferdinand Roeper. He was born in Germany and they came out here a long time ago when he was a boy. My husband was born in Germany, too. We had been married fifty-one years when he died in 1950. He came from Chicago to Los Angeles, then came up here to visit a man who had a mine in Mazourka Canyon and was persuaded to stay. But instead of going into mining he barbered for fifty-five years.

My mother came as a young person from Independence, Missouri. She was married when she was fifteen and she lived down there on the ranch. You know they got married early then. I didn't get married until I was a little past twenty-five.

My birthday was July 28, 1874. I had one brother and two sisters. I stayed down there on the ranch until I went to school in Lone Pine when I was eight years old. My father sold the ranch then and went up opposite the Fort [Independence] and had a lot of cattle. He had sort of a dairy, and I still remember sitting in back of the house where it made a big shade, and he did the churning of the butter and taught me. And when I was ten years old we came to town and I was ahead of the children here in school. My father had taught me on the ranch.

I've been here in Independence since 1884. My father had a business of his own—he had the market many years until he passed away. And he was postmaster. But he was too busy to be in the post office, and he just turned it over in my favor. It was a little different going into the post office than it is now. The Central Committee—Democratic or Republican—voted on you and put you in the office. You went four years and then the Central Committee wrote in and had you put back in office again. Then later, of course, I took the examinations. The last examination I took was in Bishop and it was all true–false. I went in as a Republican, but the Democrats treated me just as nicely. They didn't ask me any questions, they just put me in. Then after I was on Civil Service, of course, they had nothing to do with it. When we bought this place on the main street the post office was in front and then there was a partition and living quarters at the back where the postmistress ate and slept and cooked. I was postmistress forty-two years in this building and I've had my home [here] sixty-three years.

When I first came to town the Chinatown was right north of the courthouse and on the alley. This Chinese restaurant and laundry was there right in front of where [the] Walters used to live. Then later it was moved down where the old Robinson ranch is. That was where the red light district was. That was the only street going east and west. The Chinese laundry moved there, too. The old racetrack was south and west of Independence, south of Tin Can Clark's place. I've been there to the track many times. The judges' stand was the building that was moved into town and fixed up as the district attorney's office. Tin Can Clark's place was made out of tin cans.

Mary Austin's husband worked in the land office. [Her] house was part of the Parker Ranch [on Oak Creek] which burned down, except for the barn, which was made into a house, and then it was sold to the Austins.

We were going camping up there Seven Pines way, near Flower Lake, and she asked if she could camp by us, so we said sure. So she rode—we all had to ride horseback, you couldn't get up there with cars, you know. And she had blond hair, and very heavy, and she wore her hair all slicked back like a Chinaman with the braid hangin' down. And all the people there thought, "Well, they're bringin' the Chinese cook." When they got closer they realized it was Mrs. Austin. So she camped right by us and she's very interesting to be with. She knew everything and she did painting and she knew the names of all the flowers, but she made the most mournful sound at night that I've ever heard. Her tent was close to our tent, you see. I don't know what she was doing—I thought maybe she might be writing, I didn't know.

Mr. Austin [had been] superintendent of schools and my father was too, for a long time. That's how I was able to get my education. We had no high schools here, you see, and he went and talked to the teachers and made arrangements to get extra instruction for me. You didn't get your high school certificate like you get it now. You had to go to the courthouse and they'd give you your certificate after you took an examination.

My daughter was born in that house on the main street south of the Legion Hall. That's where I lived when I was first married. The *Inyo Independent* was issued in that building in the early days, and it was a two-story building. We didn't have sidewalks or anything, you know, and it was all dusty. In the early days there was wells all around this town. We had streams, but we depended on wells. There was one there at the Woods' store back of the jail, one back of where the cafe is, one back up here where the blacksmith shop was. The fire hydrant there at the back of Omie Mairs' parking lot was one of the original wells. The creek flowed right down in front of where Mamie Reynolds lived and ran through the brewery and through the courthouse yard and down by our school. I remember Judge Dehy making his Fourth of July speech in that place where the water ran through.

Sixty or seventy years ago or more the town burned down. We were just coming out of school and where Eckerts' oil station is was the livery stable and just south of that was a little shanty in there, and then there was a blacksmith shop. Some of the children evidently got in there smoking. And at about 4 o'clock there was a fire call, and we had no fire service and no water service, nothing, and the wind came up and blew the shingles clear to Kearsarge Station and the whole place burned. We went out of school and walked down to the Symmes Ranch and we stayed there till the evening and then they brought us home. I can still see the whole town—live coals. The only water in town was a brewery, and my father stood on top of that building with the hose running on top of him and put the fire out there, and it didn't go west. I think the Norman House [Hotel] was three or four stories and it went in the fire. It was rebuilt and then burned again. The Independence Hotel went too, but was rebuilt.

Everyone went to San Francisco in those days. We couldn't get out south, you know. We'd take the narrow gauge here and go through Reno. During the First World War, I went that way and, oh, it was so crowded and everybody pushing everybody to get on the train, you know, to be sure to get on. I lost my hat and I didn't dare to stoop to pick it up because I'd have been trampled. My sister, when I got there, said, "Where's your hat?" And I said, "It's in Reno." To go to Los Angeles, we had to go to Sacramento and down, way around the world to Los Angeles. Then when the City Department of Water and Power came in here they brought the railroad in, you see, and that's how we were able to get out south. They had sleeping berths at night. You could get on down here at Kearsarge Station, go to bed, wake up, and be in Los Angeles.

When I was a girl there wasn't too much trouble with the Indians. Mother came here when the Indians were still hostile—there were lots of Indians here then. [The women] all walked, only the men rode. They had those great big deep baskets with the strap over the head and they carried sacks of flour and everything on their backs in these baskets. They had a chief here and whenever they met that chief they all separated, and he walked through the center.

In a scuffle a man fell on the chief's stomach and killed him and this woman never quit till she got the one who killed him. She was the chief's wife! And how do you suppose she got him? He got brave and went to her place and she gave him parsnip tea. Wild parsnips grow along the streams. She made tea out of that and poisoned him. She never forgot. I knew her—she used to come to the post office. She lived down there on the Symmes Ranch, and it was quite a few years from the time of her husband's death until she got rid of the man who killed him.

The Hessions came here when Mabel and the others were little children. We lived next door to them, and they didn't know, they thought that they were killing a fox, and they were killing a coyote to eat and they ate the coyote. How we remember, we saw it all, you know, and we knew it was a coyote and not a fox.

I raised some coyotes once. There was two and somebody brought them from way up here in Mazourka Canyon. I raised them, and one I gave to a man in Lone Pine and it stayed just like a dog in the place where his business was. This one I had loved my daughter and she'd take Norma's arm all in her mouth—just like she was loving her. The first place she'd go when she'd come into the house was right in the center of my bed. When she was little there was a chicken, an old hen, and it had frozen feet and came to my yard, so I just took care of her, fed her and everything, and while the coyote was little the old hen would peck him. So one day the coyote came to my back door and, oh, she was so excited and her tail was wagging. I followed her and she took me out and showed me she'd killed the old hen.

Somebody finally killed *her*. She got out while I was on my vacation and Charlie Robinson came down and said he'd [found] my coyote and given her some milk that morning. So I said, "Well, all right, I'm awfully busy. I'll get her a little later." And during that time she wandered down on the Baxter Ranch and evidently got in the chicken house and John Baxter killed her and then came and asked me if I wanted the hide and I told him no. When I kept her in the yard I kept a chain on her and I had one of these old-fashioned irons that you used to use, you know, to iron clothes, that was tied on the end of the chain to keep her from jumping over. But evidently she dug out while I was gone. Maybe nobody gave her attention and she left.

In the early days, Mother told me, there was a family that lived down at Manzanar somewhere around there. The husband did something wrong—robbery, I don't know. And so he went up in the mountains and during the different times he would visit [his wife] the officers were watching for him, and when they got there, they thought they'd caught him. But you know women wore those dresses with great big hoop skirts. Where do you suppose she hid him? Under her hoop skirt. I guess they never did get him.

I knew the Shepherds and the Gunns down at Manzanar. I used to stay there when Dora Shepherd was living. Dora was Mrs. Gunn's sister [John Shepherd was their father]. Mrs. Gunn lived here in town later on right across from Pete Mairs on the north where all those cars are parked. I said the other night, "Wouldn't Mrs. Gunn be surprised if she'd wake up and see all those cars parked there where she used to live?"

TWO

W.C. "Stub" Lydston (1870–1957)

The valley is nothin' like it was in the old days

Introduction

By all accounts, Stub Lydston was a skilled storyteller. He wove these 1954 stories of the Owens Valley "good old days" from memories of his hunting rambles in the Sierra and ranching and fruit-growing days at Manzanar in the 1920s. Then eighty-four, he recounted them to Bessie Poole, a longtime friend and staff member at the Eastern California Museum in Independence.

Stub's yarns belong to a Western vernacular tradition that celebrates the ingenuity, bravery, and neighborliness he recalls in the Owens Valley. Plaintive pioneer songs, outrageous tall tales, Native American legends, and colorful cowboy poems inspire and amuse, personalizing the Western saga as they try to make sense of it. Stub Lydson frames that past in his terms, as he liked to remember it: when a future in farming in the Owens Valley was bright with promise and a man was free to roam in the Eastern Sierra wilderness. Missing from his account, however, is that later chapter, when the dream of a small farm ended with the sale of his Manzanar land to Los Angeles in 1924.

When Stub moved his wife and three daughters from southern California to the orchard subdivisions at Manzanar in 1919, developer George Chaffey's irrigated fruit-growing venture was in full production. The 22,000 trees planted years earlier were awash in spring blossoms and heavy with fall apples and pears; with the town's shaded homes and flower gardens, the Manzanar Irrigated Farms was a pastoral vision on the desert landscape.

The Chaffey interests had tapped into that enduring American ideal, ownership of a small farm, to promote sales of the irrigated parcels at Manzanar. For those who had missed out on the so-called free lands of the West, the "frontier" lingered in its mythic appeal—despite the 1893 pronouncement by historian Frederick Jackson Turner that the imaginary line of settlement westward had reached its end and was "closed." Until well into the twentieth century, the dream of creating a "garden in the desert" brought the Lydstons and thousands like them from the East and Midwest into southern California. By then, developers were transforming the region's dry hills and remote valleys into irrigated citrus colonies and agricultural projects—like Manzanar, the planned ventures of urban corporate owners, new rural satellites of distant cities.

Although Manzanar lacked the frontier past and gradual maturing of nearby Independence, it was, reportedly, close-knit and neighborly all the same. Those who lived there remember how everyone "helped each other out." Stub's gregarious and fun-loving nature quickly brought the Lydstons into the town's round of picnics, ice cream socials, and Farm Bureau meetings; friends and neighbors from all over the valley, he recalls, came to Manzanar to dance and socialize at the crossroads community hall.

In popular memory and history, the idyll at Manzanar was cut short when Los Angeles agents returned to the valley in the 1920s to buy additional land and water rights. The reality was more shaded. The past of Manzanar—and the Owens Valley—was neither so static as Stub's stories would have us believe, nor as idyllic. Expectations for the orchard subdivision, so bright in 1910, dimmed as the Manzanar Irrigated Farms acreage sold slowly and the anticipated hundreds of new settlers failed to arrive. Good years at Manzanar produced tons of prize-winning apples shipped out across the country, but late frosts and fierce winds left farmers with profitable harvests little more than three years out of five.

In 1916, 32 percent of the nation's population, or 32.5 million people, lived or worked on farms. That number declined rapidly in the 1920s, as industrialization, corporate capitalism, and an expanding market economy forced small, family-owned farm operations to adopt more entrepreneurial business practices or abandon agriculture altogether. By then, said one historian, "rural America stood deeply at odds with the urban America taking shape . . . The independent yeoman farmer, once the ideal American, became an object of contempt . . . to more cosmopolitan Americans."[1] Contrary to the widely held notion that Owens Valley farmers and ranchers mounted a united front in opposing City of Los Angeles buyout policies during the 1920s, most at Manzanar and elsewhere in the valley acted individually and in their own economic self-interests. Not uncommonly, community ties were sacrificed and friendships destroyed when those who accepted the City's terms and sold immediately were branded as traitors by others who had formed alliances to force higher prices.

Stub Lydston, center front, and his wife Nellie, to his right, with friends in the apple orchards at Manzanar, ca. 1920. *Author's Collection*

The Lydstons stayed at Manzanar as renters, growing apples and pears as before, until 1934, when they moved to Independence. Stub worked for the City of Los Angeles and later, as a school custodian, delighted new generations of schoolchildren with his humorous yarns. At Manzanar, a large remnant of the Lydstons' pear orchard survives after more than ninety years and is under the care of the National Park Service.

W.C. "Stub" Lydston—Interview

I first visited the Owens Valley in 1901. I was in Nevada, and in the fall that McKinley, our president, was shot, I came into the valley over Montgomery Pass on the narrow-gauge railroad. It was a mixed train carrying both passengers and freight—one passenger car, the rest freight cars. No meals served on the train, no sleeping accommodations. We started early in the morning and we got to Keeler about five o'clock in the afternoon. I was on my way to L.A. We made stops at stations along the way: Mina, Laws, Zurich—the station for Big Pine, and also Kearsarge, the one for Independence. We went to a place called Reward near the mine close to Owenyo. We didn't stop but just a few minutes. I recollect a small settlement there, a mining settlement. The next station was Keeler, which didn't look much like anything.

Well, we left Keeler the next morning on the stage. It was drawn by four mules. To the best of my knowledge we changed twice on the way to Mojave. It took twenty-four hours and the roads were poor. There wasn't any road to speak of. Later on, when the City of L.A. got the water from Owens River Valley, they had no transportation here so they negotiated with the Southern Pacific and they built the line from Mojave to Owenyo to accommodate the City [when it was building the aqueduct]. There was thousands of tons of material used to build the aqueduct.

I came to Manzanar in the fall of 1919, and it was really a wonderful valley—thousands and thousands of acres of fruit—apples, peaches, and pears, mostly. There was thousands of head of cattle in the valley. There were thousands of sheep traveling up, in the spring, into the high country and back again in the fall. The fishing here was somethin' wonderful. The legal limit at that time was fifty fish. I could saddle my horse on a Sunday morning, the only time I had to go fishing, and in a few hours, in any creek in the valley I could take fifty as pretty fish as ever you laid your eyes on. Now they restrict us to fifteen fish and they're minnows compared with what we caught forty years ago. Deer hunting in them days—you didn't have to travel to the top of the mountains to find a buck. They were down on the edge of the desert. The limit then, the legal limit, was two buck deer, and now it's cut in two, and you've got to walk your legs off to find one buck.

When I first came to Manzanar there was a store and a post office combined. A man by the name of Robert Bandhauer run it. At Manzanar they had a two-room school. They had a school at George's Creek, too. At one time there was a little school house at the old town of Reward. There was another one at the Fort, the Indian reservation, about 3 miles north of Independence. And locally that's all the schools we had here. There were settlers at the Fort and they taught both the Indians and the white folks. There was a small schoolhouse at Owenyo, where the broad-gauge and the narrow-gauge railroad met.

All our hay and grain from Manzanar was shipped out by rail, and a good part of the fruit went down by rail. Most of it was shipped from Lone Pine. For that reason we didn't have to transfer it from the narrow gauge to the broad gauge. There was no meat shipped in here. They bought their cattle off the ranches, they killed their hogs and dressed them and hauled them to Lone Pine or any other towns that was buying meat. We used to sell quite a few to the Natural Soda Products Company at Keeler.

We didn't have much amusement in Manzanar. In the summer time we was too busy, but in the winter time, about two or three times a month—Saturday night—we'd go down to what was called the Company Building there, a good big hall. We had the old-fashioned square dances, and all three of my daughters, they learned to dance down there. The wife was raised a Quaker, and they don't approve of dancing. We went down there after I'd got acquainted with the neighbors. I didn't feel like I wanted to get up and take another woman and go dancin' around the hall and let her set there, so I'd set them out. One evening one of the neighbors come along and requested a dance with my wife, and she says, "I don't dance." He looked at me and kinda smiled and took her by the elbow and says, "Daughter, you'll never learn any younger." And it wasn't no time at all until the wife learned to dance and she enjoyed it as well as the rest of us.

We had a Missourian there callin' the dances. He was a wonderful dancer but he was a little quick-tempered, and one night I went outside and set down on the curb. Another one of the boys come out and says, Well, Stub, there's no more square dancin'. And I said, "How come?" "Well, Charlie got his back up and says he'll never call another dance in the hall." "Well," I says, "he ain't the only man that can call a dance." This fellow looked at me and says, "Do you call?" I says, "I used to back in the state of Maine. I guess I haven't forgot it all." And he says, "Come on," and after that I had my hands full.

At the Fourth of July they most always had a little fun in the town of Independence. For instance, one Fourth of July was coming, and I was into Henry Levy's place there. Henry was the owner of the Independence Hotel—that hotel was built, they tell me, in 1876. Julian Eibeshutz was the grocer here, and he come in and says, "Henry, we're gonna have a little time the Fourth of July, and I've got a subscription list here." Henry looked at him and says, "Julian, I'll match every dollar you will." Well, Julian donated $500 and put it on the counter. Henry walks to his safe. He pulls out a sack of gold which is all the currency we had here at that time—gold and silver. He dumped it out on the counter and he says, "Help yourself." So Julian counted out $500 and says, "Thank you," and out he went. Well, Fourth of July day came and they had quite a swell time. They had a little barbecue. They had races for the Indians and [for] the white man. You doubtless know there was a reservation 3 miles north of Independence that's still there. They had a tug-of-war and all kinds of foolishness like that.

It was my recollection that in about 1920 or '21 the movies came to Independence to put on a movie.[2] One of their scenes was supposed to be a country fair, and they wanted a big crowd there, so they rented everybody, or hired everybody in the county to come to the fair. I took the wife and my three daughters and we went. And my recollection tells me we were there two days. They paid us four or five dollars a head for just walking around the fairgrounds there. They had quite a wonderful time here for this little burg.

I used to help on the ranches that was around Manzanar in the spring and in the fall. There was the old Shepherd Ranch near Shepherd Creek. I understand that was settled somewheres in the 1860s. There was the Kispert Ranch on George's Creek and the Albers Ranch which adjoined the Shepherd Ranch. The City bought them out. Across the Owens River, on the east side, the old canal run down there; that was called the McIver Ditch. There was ranches on the east side of the valley. The principal one was the old Skinner Ranch. It was a noted ranch, and they raised lots of grain, potatoes, and hay there.

I used to help take cattle into Templeton Meadow, also into Ramshaw and Big Whitney meadows. The largest amount of cattle that I was with belonged to [Fred]

Eaton, and he moved them to Centennial Spring which is about 12 miles west of Darwin, and also into Long Valley where Crowley Lake is now. One time when I was in the mountains with cattle, I was ridin' up Templeton Meadows along towards dusk—there was lots of little low brush there—and I spotted an animal in the sagebrush. My partner was ol' Dee Gill, a noted cowman in the valley. I said, "Dee, that ain't a coyote, is it?" Dee took a look and says, "No, that's a lion." He was one of the best ropers in the valley. Well, he got that lion in the rope twice, but his hide was so slick and so smooth he couldn't hold him. He run up the hillside and got up in a tree. Ol' Dee and I followed him up as close as we could. Neither one of us had any firearms with us and we just had to ride off and leave him. He was up there switchin' his tail and snarlin' at us.

I used to run a little trap line. The coyotes was just as thick as they could be. They bothered our poultry and our stock. I never was fortunate to catch a mountain lion, but I have caught lots of coyotes, lots of lynx cats, and them little bushy-tailed fellows that you don't pet or want to meet—what they call a swift fox. And up in the hills and along the river there was quite a few mink and quite a few pine marten. Some winters I'd pick up quite a little piece of change—I think about $400 was the most I ever made trappin' in one winter.

I recollect that the youngsters, they used to ride their ponies to school. There was lots of wild burros along the Inyo range, and on a Saturday the children would go over there, especially the boys. They'd round up a bunch of them little wild burros and run them over to Manzanar to an old corral. And Sundays the boys'd go down there and try to ride them. One Sunday I was there watching the boys, settin' on the fence. They had one little mouse-colored burro—he was kinda small. He looked like I could catch him by the tail and throw him over the fence. And he piled them kids as fast as they could get on him. Well, I got to razzin' them youngsters pretty hard, and one boy was a pretty good rider. The burro had throwed him two or three times, and he says, "Well, Stub, if you're so smart, you get on and try." Well, I had to do it. I got on him and stayed with him three or four jumps and then he and I dissolved partnership. And if ever you've heard a man get razzed, it was ol' Stub.

Well, I'll tell ya. The valley is nothin' like it was in the old days. Now days all we have here is fishermen, hunters, and tourists. There's no fruit, not much hay raised in the valley. In fact, all we've got left is the valley.

THREE

Truman Buff (1906–1996)

That's how I spent most of my time, among white people

Introduction

"I don't have any Indian stories to tell you," Truman Buff announced, when I spoke to him late in 1990 about an interview. Then eighty-four years old, Truman was an Owens Valley native and Paiute elder of the Fort Independence tribe. An accomplished musician, he had played in valley dance bands for over five decades, and after retiring in 1971 from the Los Angeles Department of Water and Power, he enjoyed studying Owens Valley history, was a frequent visitor at the local museum, and had been at work for several years compiling a Paiute-English dictionary.

When we met for the interview a few weeks later at his granddaughter's home in Independence, he again reminded me there would be no Indian stories. His insistence was intriguing: perhaps it was his effort, I speculated, to connect with *my* Owens Valley past through our mutual ties of friends, family, and music. Truman's far more complex perspective on his life became clear in the next two days, however, as he related the story of his remarkable journey through the twentieth century.

For most his nearly ninety years, Truman lived at the Fort Independence Reservation, 2 miles north of the town of the same name. The 356-acre reservation, established in 1915 by executive order from President Woodrow Wilson, was on land occupied in the late 1800s by U.S. Army volunteers were sent to protect white steaders from Indian raids. By the time Truman was born there in 1906, the federal government had unofficially set aside a portion of the former army post for the Independence-area Paiutes.

Truman's ancestors were among the nearly 1,000 Indians removed from the valley in July 1863, to a reservation 200 miles south at Fort Tejon. Those who later made their way back found their communal lands permanently appropriated by white ranchers and miners and their prospects for survival uncertain.

The Paiutes responded to the white occupation with a strategy of "flexible accommodation," or "cultural creativity," selectively using opportunities available to them in the white economy that allowed them to subsist and remain in the valley.[1] Men worked on road building projects, ranches, and farms, and women winnowed grain and worked as laundresses for the white families. New plans to remove them were abandoned as whites came to depend on the Indian labor that enabled the valley's young ranches and towns to prosper.

In a parallel life at the fringes of white society and largely hidden from it, the Paiutes held fast to the essential elements of their culture: community structure, language, rituals, and food-gathering activities.[2] The once-violent resistance to the whites took form now as the "pranks, lassitude, and carelessness that grumbling settlers ascribed to Indian character." A more subtle defiance was expressed in pride of work—doing a job better than whites, notes historian John Walton.[3] These strategies, however, went largely unnoticed—or were ignored—by the whites. As evidence of independence and self-direction, they contradicted a view of the Indians, carefully cultivated by reformers, as child-like, helpless, and in need of protection—an image that allowed whites to assume responsibility for the Indians' education, welfare, and eventual incorporation into Anglo America.

For nearly five years, between 1918 and 1925, Truman attended the Sherman Institute in Riverside, California. Founded in 1904 and still operated by the federal Bureau of Indian Affairs, it was one of 153 Indian boarding schools established nationwide by 1900 that effectively institutionalized white paternalism, often through harsh and repressive methods. In 1879, Richard Henry Pratt, superintendent of the first school in Carlisle, Pennsylvania, articulated its mission: "Transfer the savage-born infant to the surroundings of civilization," he said, "and he will grow to possess a civilized language and habit."[4] Education and immersion in Anglo culture, isolation from tribe and homeland, and the breakup of tribal lands were the government-sanctioned strategies Indian reformers used as they attempted to eradicate tribalism and "free" Indians to become true Americans.

In the long term, the price of Indian incorporation was the virtual disappearance of the modern Indian from public consciousness—and from history's narratives. No longer noble, savage, or an impediment to white advancement, Indians remained encased for much of the twentieth century in a past defined by popular culture and its mythic versions of frontier conquest. They were, said one historian, little more than "an interesting sideshow . . . to the main act of white history."[5] Still today, white Americans' versions of the Indian presence among them will often leave out the extraordinary diversity of a people whose cultures are as varied as the lands they once occupied. Adds one historian, "Traditional frontier history flattened out Indians, rendering them insignificant both before and after conquest."[6]

Truman Buff, 1990, at age 89. *Author's Collection*

In 1934, anthropologist Julian Steward declared that "Paiute culture has practically disappeared" from the Owens Valley. "[They] are more reticent and repressed than most Indians," he added.[7] Remarkably, the Paiutes did not disappear. Nor, as Truman Buff's life suggests, did their culture.

There are today 562 recognized American Indian tribal units, of which four are in the Owens Valley. In 2000, American Indians accounted for ten percent of the Inyo County population. At just over 1,800, they number about the same as their ancestors who first encountered white explorers more than one hundred fifty years ago.[8]

Truman Buff—Interview

I'll start from my birthday first, when I was born, November 29, 1906, out at the Fort Indian reservation near 2 miles north of Independence. Then a few years later we were in the town of Independence. We had a homestead up above town here, 120 acres. It was given to my grandad through the government. They built a home up on the creek there, just a little one. And so my mother spent a lot of her time—the trees are still there, the ones she planted. Yes, you take a ride up there someday, you can look at it, and see how they're not very big trees, but they got a history. So my grandfather was given 120 acres up there.

Jane Wehrey: How old were you when you lived up there?
TB: Well, I was around about six, I guess—seven years old.
JW: You didn't spend too much of your childhood out at the Fort?
TB: Most of my childhood was spent right here in Independence. See, my grandmother—both grandmothers—worked for people in town. They come from the Fort, and walked into town, to do their laundry. So my grandmother just went from house to house, working for these different people. But I was with her most of the time. See, my mother died when I was eight years old. That's how I got with my grandmother—that's [my] maternal grandmother. My brother, they separated us. Most of the time my brother and—my grandmother Maggie is the paternal side, see—they stayed out at the Fort. But we moved in here, and we'd go from house to house. I went with her 'cause I was only eight years old, but I couldn't do nothing. Grandma would stay overnight. [At one place] they used to let us stay over at the house, they had a little cabin, and then they'd feed us there. The Mairs, all the Brierlys, the old-timers—you heard all about them, that's how I got [to] know everybody. That's how I spent most of my time, among the white people. I used to play with the kids here in town. We used to go all over, fishing, stuff like that. Then, when I got around about twelve years old, I went to Riverside, to the Sherman Institute, in Riverside, California. From 1917 till 1923 I stayed there with that big Indian government school. And while I was there I was going to music school. I studied violin for about five years over there.
JW: I'd like to ask you about the property up Independence Creek here. What did [your family] do with that? Did they farm it?
TB: It was just idle. They didn't do nothing, just squatted, just sat there. I tell you what happened. My uncle, he kind of took command after [my mother] died, 'cause

we was all kids and we didn't know any better. And grandmother, of course, she didn't know much, or grandfather. They're not educated enough to get into this business, you know. So uncle took over. [He sold the property to] the City of Los Angeles in the 1920s.

JW: Do you know, why did he sell it?

TB: He just didn't want nothing to do with it. He was offered a price for it, to get rid of it. Well, there's nothing but rocks up in there. Then the City took quite a bit of that land, so the [Department of Water and Power maintenance] shops are up there today. They gave him the money for it, then he moved to the Fort. Then everybody moved and got situated, see. He started raising alfalfa, and he built a lot of things up out there. But [my uncle] was the only one in the family who knew what it was all about, 'cause he was raised in town here, too. He knew everybody. He was one of the smarter Indians. (laughter)

JW: What was his name?

TB: John Symmes. You probably heard of him. He was well-known. He went to school here. And you know, when they built that old [Pioneer Memorial Methodist] church? That was his, every Sunday he went to church. And the family, my grandfather and the old-timers with us, they helped build the church up there. See, most of my people, we're all, practically saying, raised in town. But later on, [in 1915], when they made that reservation and gave it to the Indians, everybody moved back out there again.

JW: What about your father? After your mother died, was he still living in the area?

TB: He was one of the typical Indians—you can't move him out. (laughter) He lived out at the Fort, but he stayed with my paternal grandmother. They had the house out there. So he spent all his life there. But he was just like my grandmother, he was another one that worked for the white people. He was a cowboy, he worked for the cowmen. Every summer, you know, they'd drive the cattle all up to Long Valley. And that's where he spent a lot of his time, working with those people. He worked for the Brierlys, he worked for the Partridges—all those pioneers.

JW: Was there quite a bit of agriculture out at the Fort after the people moved there in 1915?

TB: The Fort as a whole was only 140 acres, that's all. I figure they got about 5 acres apiece. Couldn't do [much], but they made quite a bit of money off that land—gardens, cultivating it, putting alfalfa in, 'cause you remember in those days, a dollar is worth a million dollars.

JW: Do you remember very much about the Fort, what it looked like when you were real young?

TB: No, all I remember was, the most attractive thing were those caves out there. See, when the soldiers came in [in 1862]—you know about that, when they made that a fort, in the gulley there, they had three caves where the soldiers stayed. Then we used to go there and play. That was our pastime. It's too bad they couldn't have saved those caves. It was up to the historical people; they should have saved it.[9]

Truman Buff, right, with brother Philip, ca. 1915. *Andrew Forbes photo. County of Inyo, Eastern California Museum*

There was one place where the soldiers stayed; they had some nice rooms made. They had kind of a bunk made out of the dirt, and it had a hole going up where the fire [was]—it was a chimney. We had fun. We even found some guns out there those soldiers left. Oh, you find everything. Where they used to have target practice, you could still see the markings of the lead.

JW: When you were growing up at the Fort, were you speaking Paiute with your family?

TB: I was speaking good Paiute. I used to talk to the old people.

JW: Did you teach your children to speak it?

TB: I didn't teach none of my children how to talk it, none of them. Just my brother and I, we were the only ones that really could talk. I'm making a dictionary—I'm working on that right now. But I don't speak it no more.

JW: The Paiute language that you were speaking, you said that it had some other languages mixed in with it—Spanish and Chinese? How did those words get there? Were you in contact with these people?

TB: That's right, working with them, like the railroad. You know the Chinese come in on the railroad. We had a bunch of them over there at the railroad, see. And my father used to work with them. Then they got to intermarrying into the Indians. But the Chinese seemed to be—well, they always had good organization. When they married these Indian women, they established them[selves] pretty good with the Indians. Where Mexicans, I don't know—some of the Indian guys married into that kind of family. The Mexicans had a lot of shoot-outs in this valley—stuff like that.

JW: Do you remember that?

TB: That's way before my time, when the Mexicans were still coming in the valley, mostly near Keeler and all, Cerro Gordo, a lot of Mexicans. [The Chinese] were quiet. Well-behaved people. And they produced a lot of young kids. So we had quite a few half-Chinese kids. I think most of them Chinese moved up to Benton. That's where they intermarried.

JW: Did you ever hear about the Indians getting opium from the Chinese?

TB: Yes, over here in the Chinese town. It covered about half a block right about over in there [the center northeast part of Independence]. They had dens, underground. They always had hideaways. The younger people—my uncle was young, living here. Two, three men his age, Indians, they used to go over and visit the Chinese. They'd go down in the den. The Chinese, they had the opium. But they were so organized where everything was just underground.

JW: What kinds of things did you do with your family when you were young?

TB: Fishing and hunting. 'Course, we had horses, too. I spent a lot of my time riding on the desert. I'd go all over. That was one of my hobbies.

JW: Did you go by yourself?

TB: A couple of the Indian boys—they all had horses. We used to go out. We got to roping, learned how to rope stuff. I done a lot of hiking. Most of my hiking was up in the mountains, the Sierras. I've been all through them from Mono County clean down to Little Lake—deer hunting, you know, and fishing. See, the reason why I'm in good shape today, like I said, I played ball among the white people for thirty years. And I took part in all kinds of athletics, whatever was going on. Most of my activity was in the mountains, hiking, go look for rocks, prospecting, all that stuff. We'd go up and look for pine nuts, the Indians would. I went out with my folks a few times, in the pine nut season. But most of my activity was going over the mountains—over the top of the mountains. During the day, when I'm doing nothing, I used to take off from the house. I'd get some funny idea. I'd say, "Oh, I'm going to go to the top of that peak today." I'd go and fool around.

JW: Were there trails where you were hiking?

TB: No, no, I made my own trail. There were a few times I got caught on top of some of these mountains, where darkness got hold of me. I couldn't do nothing. Sometimes I had to stay overnight till I'd get daylight. It's getting to the point now where there are roads right up in the mountains. Too many people, they drive right up.

JW: Did you and your family travel around the valley, to visit people in Bishop or Lone Pine?

TB: Well, about 1913, in Bishop, the fair used to be called the Harvest Festival—that's what they called it in them days. So my grandfather, he was quite a traveler—when I moved back out to the Fort, I stayed with him. So we used to go every year, up to Bishop to the Harvest Festival. He'd raise the vegetables and he'd take them up for exhibition. He used to get up at four o'clock in the morning, harness old Dobbin up. Then, "Well, here we go," and it's still dark. And we'd travel and we'd get to Big Pine about noontime, and he'd put his old horse in the—in them days we called it a livery stable. We'd stay there an hour, feed the horse, water him, everything. Then we'd go to Bishop, that was our destination. We'd be there by five o'clock that afternoon. So that's how long it took us to go from here. See, my grandfather did most of his shopping in Big Pine or Bishop. Then when the Mexicans had their celebrations in Lone Pine—that's September 16, I think, every year—he wanted to go there. Lone Pine took us about three, four hours.

JW: Did Indians from all over the valley go to the festival in Bishop?

TB: From all over the valley. Well, they called them pow-wows or festivals, or *fandangoes*, mostly *fandangoes*. That comes from the Mexican part of it. They had a great time. Of course, them Indians liked it so much—they'd put a bunch of willows all around and make a big fence where they'd dance, you know, at night. Then the Indians, whoever could afford it, they have a little booth, then they sell food. Just like a fair. During the night, that's when the dances started, the *fandango*—they danced all night. They'd have it a whole week. People from all over the valley, they'd get those big wagons—they haul heavy freight, stuff like that. Well, that's what they used; they'd load their family in and move up there. [They had] their little teepees and set them up. It was a wonderful thing to see.

JW: Did the white people come to those, too?

TB: Oh yes, they used to go. That was a main attraction. Even the people in [Independence] used to go up there and donate a little money for the Indians so they could start up their stands or whatever they got to sell. Oh, they were interested. They'd go up there nights, you know, when they'd start dancing. A lot of the old pioneers—that's how they'd learn to dance. They'd bring their family up there, dance all night. Like Pete Mairs, all his family, they used to go. That's why they all can dance.

JW: I'd like to ask you about school. Did you go to school here in Independence before you went to Riverside?

TB: Nineteen seventeen, that's when I went to Riverside. Well, the year before that I went to grammar school here for a whole year. Let's see, it was right down the street here. That's where I went. In them days Indians were—they didn't want to recognize them. They didn't want them with the whites in school, see. A lot of the old[timers]—you know how people have funny ideas. But the year before I went [to Riverside], of course I was with these boys all the time here, and I was living with them practically in town. So they had to call the parents together and say, "Well, are we going to let the boy in here to go to school?" So everybody says, "Yeah, you can bring him here." See? But the other Indians after that, they couldn't go to white schools. That's the way it was.

JW: When you went to school in town, were the teachers okay to you?

TB: Oh yes. In fact, I was kind of—I don't know—kind of a pet to the teachers. Like I say, I was practically raised among the whites. Everything I did, I stayed with the whites: baseball, music—

JW: You said you were the only Indian when you were in school. Were there other kids—Mexican kids or any other—

TB: No, nobody. They won't allow nobody else. My uncle, when he was living here in town, when he was a young lad, he went to school here, too. Him and I was the only Indians went to school among the whites. They kind of voted him in too. They just let him in.

JW: Truman, did many of the Indian children from around here go to the Sherman Institute?

TB: One year, the superintendent from Riverside, he come up to the valley to recruit the Indians. So a lot of them left here and went to Riverside. That's how a lot of these Indians got up higher, you know, instead of staying back, being backward.

JW: Were most of the Indians at the school from around southern California?

TB: Clear back from New York. I think we had a few Alaskans. See, I think we had about a thousand students in that school. They come from all over. That superintendent, he used to go out and recruit them, bring them. We had a lot of Navajos. There's quite a few of them from Arizona, they come to Riverside.

JW: What kinds of things did they teach you there?

TB: From the ABCs on up to high school.

JW: Did they talk about *your* background, your Indian background?

TB: No, they didn't allow that at the school. If they caught you talking Indian in that school, you were reprimanded.

JW: You've said that you studied violin when you went down to the Sherman School. Did you start having an interest in music when you were still up here?

TB: Well, we had a band. The Fort Indians had a band. They used to give a concert every Sunday afternoon out at the Fort then. People used to come out [all the way] from Manzanar. They'd come with the horses and buggies and have a concert, right out at the Fort there. I was just a little kid, but my father, he was in command of the band, he directed it. And my uncle, he was in it. Quite a few of the old Indians was in it, and I think they had three boys from Bishop—Indian boys. They had quite a nice band, a nice band.

JW: How did they learn to play? Did they have lessons?

TB: Well, somebody showed them, you know. They used to have a butcher shop here in town—Roepers, they had that. And this old man Roeper, he got interested in those Indians, and he's the one that went in and showed them. Then he got to be the conductor. That's how they got that band out there. And of course, it's just natural. I notice years later, it's just natural for an Indian to pick up something like that. That's why they just picked it right up—all the different kinds of horns. And Mr. Roeper used to go out to show them how to finger and stuff. "You do it this way, you do it that way, see?"

When I first started music, my grandmother had an old mandolin. I was working on that all the time, then all at once I got interested in [the violin]—but I couldn't afford a violin or nothing in them days. Finally, some people gave me one, and I says, "Oh boy, this is going to be my instrument." Then I got to playing fairly well.

They used to have old-time dances, that is, it's not Indian—they were like Masonic people, they were great for dances. They showed me how to [play] schottisches, all them old-time dances. We used to have a dance over at Aberdeen, I think once a month. We all had to drive over there with the horses, and they'd have it in that old schoolhouse. Oh, a wonderful time. That's how I learned, among them, all these old-timers—mostly it was the Masons. They're the ones that showed me.

JW: Then when you went to Riverside, you had more lessons.

TB: I had a little start on it, then I was there a few years. 'Course they had regular bands there. The government gave them schools all kinds of instruments, so I had my pick. All I wanted was violin for some reason. From there I got started. The conductor got interested in me. He says, "Hey buddy, you better stick with that violin." There used to be a lady come out to Riverside, she was a professional violinist. So after she heard me playing with the school orchestra there, she said, "Starting this Saturday, you're going to start taking lessons." She knew I had possibilities. I studied with her two, three years. I studied classical, I wanted to be a highbrow classical man. (laughter) Then I got a call for the job in Los Angeles. That's what spoiled my classical [career], I got into jazz. But I made money, and traveled.

In 1920, '21, I came home again for awhile, to see the folks. I stayed here about a year, and then I went back to Los Angeles. That's when I got my call to go to work. This white man got interested in Indians, see. He used to be in Bishop years ago, and when he went to Los Angeles, he had his own band. [It] was well-known all over the country. He was an arranger, a composer, everything else. He had one of the best bands on the coast in the twenties, thirties, but he got tired of it, 'cause he liked the Indians. The guy told me, "We got a band here, an all-Indian band," something novel, 'cause in those days, they didn't have stuff like that. That's when he got us all together, six of us. I traveled with him for two years, all over southern California, here and there. It was kind of a novel deal, the first time they had ever seen an Indian band like that, so we got pretty popular. I went up in Nevada and northern California and part of Oregon and Utah. Once in a while, we'd get in with—like that [1935 California Pacific International] Exposition in San Diego. They had a whole year of it. I was there for a whole year, but it was all Indians. They picked the Indians from all over the United States to come in. That's one of my longest stays in one spot.

JW: What were you playing in the band?

TB: I was playing sax. I dropped the violin. Violin was getting out of date about that time. I covered all the saxophones. I played them all. I had to, 'cause we got [different] music here, old numbers that Benny Goodman wrote [for dance bands] and all—we used that music, see.

JW: Did you meet people when you were out playing for them?

TB: I met all kinds of people. I met pretty near every nationality. We met quite a few Orientals, mostly whites and Hawaiians, and even some foreigners from Europe. First thing I heard when I was sitting up there playing: "Look at the Indian!" (laughter) It was a novelty.

When I was working with the bands, most of my travels were in northern California, Los Angeles, San Francisco, along the coast, one-night stands. We go one night here, one night there. And that was rough, I'm telling you, that was my downfall. I went hog-wild, you know how it is, drinking and everything. That's what ruined my life—but I'm still alive today. (laughter)

Then I'd come here and stay for a while—I stayed here for a couple of years in the '20's. Your mother [Mary V. Bandhauer] was playing and we got a little band here. So her, myself, and Les [Bandhauer], we stuck together quite a while. I'd come and go, but we had a nice band, and we played all over, up and down the valley 'cause we was the only band. That's why most of the time I was with the white people. That's why I was very unpopular among the Indians. They were jealous, seeing the Indian among the whites.

Same with playing baseball. I played in this valley about thirty years, every time I come home. I played with the whites. So I didn't spend too much time with the Indians. I think the most time I spent was in Riverside, when I was going to school. Then I came back here. I kind of settled down. But I still went out and played [in bands]. I'd get a call. I got married in 1930, April 22, 1930, in Nevada—that's where I met my wife.

JW: Is your wife Indian?

TB: Yes, she's part Irish. See, her grandfather's name was Callahan. [He] was some kind of a businessman in 'Frisco. She went to school in Carson City—that's another Indian school. Then when she got bigger, when she got out of school—they used to have a system where they'd take the girls, or the boys, and place them in jobs.

She spent about six years in Oakland, where she worked for some people there. In the meantime, she tried to get to school at the University of California at Berkeley, but finances weren't good, so she kept on working.

JW: And what was her name?

TB: Clara.

JW: Truman, do you remember much about when the aqueduct was built?

TB: Nineteen thirteen. My friend and I, we had horses, see. We traveled. We'd be gone all day long, traveling all over the valley here. That's when I first seen the aqueduct started at Aberdeen. Oh, they had the big old shovel. Yes, we'd go out and watch them. And I seen how they done it, and 'course, the old aqueduct machinery—they were all lumbersome, you know—they were funny-looking things, but they done the work. And years [later], I'd come home and I'd go duck-hunting. I followed that aqueduct coming this far, down below Independence. It was a wonderful thing to watch.

JW: Were any of the Indians here working on building the aqueduct?

TB: No, they weren't—I don't know. I think, for one thing, they weren't qualified, 'cause they didn't know how to [operate] the machinery. That was their biggest trouble. But they were hired once in a while like with a shovel or something, just as a common laborer.

See, the Indians in them days, they got educated. They'd go out with the white people, these old pioneers. They showed the Indians how to drive nails, saw [wood]—they just picked it up. So they built nice homes. My father, he was quite a carpenter. My uncle, when they built this [Inyo County] courthouse [in 1921], he worked on that. There was only two or three Indians worked on that whole thing. So he was one of the main Indians that built that courthouse. I used to go up there and watch them work.

JW: When you went to work for the Department [of Water and Power], what was your job?

TB: Running all the heavy equipment, bulldozers and all that stuff. I was all over the valley, diverting ditches and grading all the roads, digging ditches. That was my job. The last ten years, they put me on a grader, fixing the roads, so I went from Little Lake clean up to Mono County fixing the roads for the City, putting in new roads. But for fifteen years I was sent to Mono County to plow snow. We had to keep the roads open for the City—that was my job, and I come home in March.

JW: Oh, you went up there all winter.

TB: I stayed up there all winter, fighting that snow. I had fifteen years of it.

JW: Let's go back and talk about baseball. You said you had played—

TB: About thirty years of it.

JW: Thirty years! Was that all up here in the valley?

TB: No, here and there, but I started here. I was a member of a small team for a good many years, the Independence ball team.

JW: Did you start when you were real young?

TB: Ten years old. I started playing with the men's team, the big men, that's where I got my training. Then after I played for about five years, something like that, why there used to be some retired professionals come in. That's where I learned a lot of it. That's my experience.

JW: Were there other Indian people on the team?

TB: Well, no. These were all whites on the Independence [team], all whites. All the Mairs and the Clines—they were cowboys from the valley—they had their boys. And Roeper, the one that had the meat market. And the district attorney, he was our star, Jess Hession. And the Lawrences. We kept our little roster up pretty good. But like I told you, I was raised in here anyway. Then later on, the Indians out at the Fort, they had a ball team—all Indians, see.

JW: Did you go around and play other teams in the valley?

TB: We'd go play in Big Pine, Bishop. And they even had a team in Manzanar. That was a pretty good little farming community. They had quite a few people there—ranchers, you know. But they all sold out. They moved away, left the country.

JW: I'd like to ask you a little more about your childhood. What do you remember about some of the Indian customs, the ceremonies?

TB: When I was small, I was with the old people, that's where I learned the songs, the ceremonies, and watched them dance. That's why I was always interested in the old people, I listened.

JW: What happened when someone died? Was there a ceremony for that?

TB: That's right. When the person dies, the body would be put by the house. Sometimes it'd even be put for two or three days, and the people would come from all over. They just sob and cry. I don't know why they prolong it so long. And my uncle, John Symmes, he was the official casket-maker. After two or three days of that, then they go out and dig the grave, then another ceremony goes on for pretty near all day. They put the body down in the casket and the women, they do the dancing around the casket. It's quite a ceremony when they do that. The women all have to have white cloths, and they kind of wave them around. And then they sit down and rest after that dance. Then the singers—they have four, five singers, and they start singing. And over and over again, sometimes four and five hours straight. Then after that, after it's all over with, then they put the body down.

Now, the children, like me, when I buried my—what was it, my grandfather—just before they put the body in the grave, they made the grandsons like me and my brother jump over the casket. And they tell us, "Now you jumped over this grave. Now you go home." So we had to walk home, down to the Fort. "And don't look back." That's how they performed the burial.

And my mother. Now we get to my mother. She died when I was eight years old. She died of tuberculosis. And the medical ceremonies—they had her in Lone Pine. We had her down there for three months. They had a little Indian camp just the north side of town. I remember we moved from here, stayed there two, three months. And they performed [over] her every night. But she had a woman doctor. Usually, it's a man doctor, the medicine man. This was a woman, see. And it's every night, the same thing. Get up and stay up all night. And of course, they had to eat, different things they had to eat. See, the medicine doctor picks out a certain location. That's why they had it in Lone Pine. In the meantime, she was dying from tuberculosis.

JW: Were you there with her a lot of the time?

TB: I was, yes, I was there with them, and, you know, just a small guy. We had to go. Seemed like they'd start in the evenings. During the day they sleep, then they start again in the night, over and over. Actually, of course, after two or three months of that ceremony going on, well, she died anyway. But that's the way they do. I don't know. When they get sick, they depend on the medicine man too much.

JW: What about Manzanar, the relocation center—do you recall that?

TB: I worked at Manzanar when it first [started], yes, for a temporary job, building it. I was just hired by the government for a little while. I seen that Manzanar built from start to finish.

JW: They built that pretty fast, didn't they?

TB: Oh yes, everything was prefabricated. They'd take a whole house and just build three, four sections and just slap them together. And put tar paper over the house, that's all they done. That's why the Japs, when it was cold, real cold, they was awful cold [in] those barracks. That's why they were doing a lot of complaining, but it didn't do them any good. The government ordered them to stay right there. "You're in jail."

JW: What did you think about bringing the Japanese up here?

TB: Well, the Indians as a whole, they didn't like it. And the reason why, they say, "Why is the government giving the Japs everything? Why are they bringing everything up." That's food rationing days, remember, about that time. Why, they had the best things to eat in the world. Meat coming in by the truckloads everyday. Fruit coming in. When I used to go and eat with the Japs, they had three barracks [for] the restaurant, where the Japanese come and eat. You ought to see them eat—three, four different kinds of meat. And out here, we couldn't buy no meat. We was lucky to get a salami or something.[10]

JW: You said you ate with them. That was after the camp had started?

TB: After it was [partly] built. They charged us workers thirty-five cents.

JW: When you were eating with the Japanese people, how did they treat you? Were they friendly?

TB: Oh yes, buddy, buddy. I think we got along better, the Indians who worked there, got along better. They [the internees] were kind of bitter against the whites, that's what they were, you know. They were in jail, in other words. But we got along good with them.

JW: Even though there was still some resentment that they were there.

TB: Yes, but we resented the government worse, 'cause years back [during the Depression] the government used to give Indians rations. And that's what the Indians seen, the food coming in to the Japs, by the truckload. And here the Indians [used to] get five pounds of beans for one month and a bacon about that wide. And the crackers, those old-time what-you-call-them, big crackers. That's all—five articles they sent out every month, each Indian. That was a regular ration for the Indians, given by the government. And they used to bring in clothes, once in a while.

But I've been going to that [Manzanar] pilgrimage, you know, every year. I go all the time. I watch [the Japanese Americans] perform. They have dances. They got a dance similar to the Indian dance, like the ring dance. They call it a ring dance. They hold hands and go around like that. I go watch, and they say, "Come on in, dance with us." Couple times I danced with them. It's the same ring dance.

FOUR

Vic Taylor (1910–2001)

Water is everything

Introduction

A civil engineer and hydrographer with the Los Angeles Department of Water and Power for over forty years, Vic Taylor acquired first hand an encyclopedic knowledge of Eastern Sierra geology, water sources, snow conditions, and weather history.[1] With his wife Eleanor contributing, Vic talked with interviewer Richard Potashin in 1991 at the Taylors' home in Independence; describing that career took him back in memory to a lifetime of camping, fishing, hunting, and skiing among the Eastern Sierra landscapes he first explored as a boy.

Vic Taylor brings to his story an outdoor enthusiast's attachment to the natural environment but calls on the technical language of engineering to explain the hydrographic measurements, tunnel inspections, and snow surveys that Los Angeles carries out in the Eastern Sierra. With few annotations, those terms remain in the dialogue; while they may be obscure to the layperson, they come easily to Vic. Using them, he better conveys the extraordinary scope and complexity, and unerring exactness of water management in the arid West.

For nearly a century, Department of Water and Power engineers have been charged with delivering water from the Sierra Nevada eastern slope through the Los Angeles Aqueduct to southern California. Completed in 1913 and lauded as a marvel of engineering second only to the Panama Canal, the aqueduct was the first of the giant projects conceived and built in the first half of the twentieth century to capture, store, and transfer water in the West: among them, the O'Shaugnessy Dam of the San Francisco Hetch Hetchy project, completed in 1923; Boulder Dam on the Colorado River in 1936; and the Colorado River Aqueduct in 1941.

The Los Angeles Aqueduct still operates today as it did on November 4, 1913, when thirty thousand jubilant Los Angeles residents gathered at the last cascade-like segment to witness the first water arrive from the Owens Valley. Flowing the entire 233 miles by gravity, it tumbled down past the waiting crowd. "There it is, take it," Chief Engineer William Mulholland said, his five words a portent of the uneasy, symbiotic coexistence of city and valley now entering a second century.

The aqueduct and other western water installations trace their origins to the early-twentieth-century Progressive initiatives of President Theodore Roosevelt. The Reclamation Act of 1902 legislated federal assistance for irrigation projects in rural areas, but the "greatest good for the greatest number" policy that produced it soon was applied instead to metropolitan growth. Municipal ownership of utilities, bureaucratic efficiency, and a scientific approach to the conservation and beneficial use of resources were the new instruments of social progress and national prosperity,

Vic Taylor in the Owens Valley, 1976. *Taylor Collection*

and implementation of this agenda was entrusted in large part to engineers. Hailed as the early twentieth century's new heroes, they transformed the nation's landscape with their highways, dams, bridges, and skyscrapers, symbols of a modern, urban, technological dynamic, in American society.

In his 1878 *Report on the Lands of the Arid Region*, Major John Wesley Powell described an imaginary line through the nation near the ninety-eighth meridian, or about halfway into the Dakotas, Nebraska, and Kansas. Beyond it, he said, was the West. There, except in the northern Pacific coastal belt, average annual rainfall is less than twenty inches, the amount needed to grow crops without irrigation. "Aridity, and aridity alone, makes the various Wests one," author Wallace Stegner declared in 1987.[2] Yet, argues historian Richard White, "the West that Americans recognize in the twentieth century is their own work."[3]

Vic Taylor's accounting of his work in the Owens Valley leaves room for both views. Singular technological achievements that joined engineers and public policy in the early 1900s have sustained cities of millions where topography and climate would otherwise have limited populations to thousands. "Maybe we shouldn't [have] put 20 million people and 6 billion acres of asphalt in the middle of a desert,"[4] ventured a *Los Angeles Times* columnist in 2003.

"And what do you do about aridity if you are a nation accustomed to plenty and impatient of restrictions and led westward by pillars of fire and cloud?" Stegner asks. "You may deny it for a while. Then you must either try to engineer it out of existence or adapt to it."[5]

Vic Taylor—Interview

Originally, my grandparents came up to the Owens Valley in 1910, and they homesteaded 160 acres down by George's Creek. Then my folks came up and they bought 40 acres from my grandfather. So it was June of 1920 [when I was ten years old], that we came up and built a house on that 40 acres, and we lived there for four years. The ranch is up on the hill—you notice where all that green stuff is going along there?

Richard Potashin: Yes.

VT: Well, that's where all the ranches were. We were down at the south end of that, towards Hogback Creek. My grandfather had an apiary up there. He had, oh, a couple hundred stands of bees. He made all comb honey, you know, with the little squares. Then once a year, they'd get those all cleaned up and they would bring them up here to Kearsarge [Station] and ship them south. Then they'd put in a large order of $1,000 or something like that from Ralph's Grocery [in Los Angeles] and lay in a year's supply of foodstuff.

RP: So your grandfather came up primarily to get involved with the bee business?

VT: Yes, there was quite a bit of alfalfa around George's Creek and Hogback, and that makes very good honey, the blossom from the alfalfa. Then there was a lot of buckwheat brush down in that area, too, which makes good honey. He had a little orchard, too.

Before my father came up here, he was teaming. He had a couple of teams, great big old Percherons, and he was hauling pumps out to the various [oil] fields around Los Angeles. So he sold those and came up here. He was going to farm this little 40 acres, but he no more than got up here than a Mr. Claude Van Norman, who was in charge of this aqueduct district [for the City of Los Angeles]—not the whole aqueduct—he came up to the ranch one day and wanted Dad to go to work for him. Dad said, "No, I'm going to try farming for awhile." So [Van Norman] kept talking and said, "Well, if you could just help us out for the rest of this summer, that would really give us a good boost before you get to farming." Dad said, well, okay, he'd do that. That was in 1920, and he worked for them for twenty-six years. So he never did any farming on the place at all, other than just a little garden farming—corn and stuff like that.

RP: So your parents came up because your grandfather had already settled here?

VT: Yes, and my mother's health. Her health was very bad, and she felt so much better up here after a visit with my grandparents that they decided to come back and live.

RP: There were quite a number of ranches then?

VT: Oh yes, as you came north, there were some nice ranches down here west of the aqueduct. The biggest one of those, I think, was called the Winterton [Ranch]. I know we got a horse from there when we first came up in 1920. They had apple and pear orchards and alfalfa fields. It was a beautiful, big ranch. When you came north from Hogback Creek [on the west side of the valley], there were several big ranches along there, too, and some of them very nice. The first one down there was the McGovern Ranch, and then up around George's Creek, there was the Kispert Ranch. Then, north of that, the Albers Ranch. Then you came up to the Strohmeyer Ranch, and they sold that out to Abernathy, who in turn sold to the Department of Water and Power. Then you got up to Manzanar, to the OVI—the Owens Valley Improvement Company—subdivision. But those big ones were 200-acre ranches down there, something like that.

The OVI had come in there and they divided the area up into 10- and 20-acre parcels, most of them. So each parcel had a family on it. Manzanar was a beautiful little community down there. They had more high school kids going to the school at Independence than Independence had. They had their own grammar school, too, at Manzanar. Then about 3 miles south was where the George's Creek school was, right about where you cross the aqueduct on the highway. The little white schoolhouse sat right in there. There were those two schools down there.

RP: Do you know much about the Owens Valley Improvement Company, who organized that or where they were from?

VT: They put in a very good concrete pipe irrigation system to go to all these lands, and then they would sell you 10 acres of land, and you were allotted so much water. They delivered the water to you from Bairs Creek and Shepherd Creek. They had the rights on those two creeks. And then they had what they called a *zanjero*, one that distributed the water. So when you wanted some water, you contacted him, and he would go up, and through the pipe system one way or another he would get that water down onto your land. The Japs used that [pipe] system later when they took over that Manzanar area.

RP: Was the ditch system also the domestic water supply, or were there wells?

VT: No, each little farm or ranch had their own water supply. If they were close to George's Creek, they took water right out of the creek, but all the rest of them had little domestic wells.

RP: At that time, was there any electricity servicing the area?

VT: Not up to our place. Along about 1923 or 1924, the Department of Water and Power ran a power line from down by the highway up to this stretch of land that runs all along there, where the farmhouses were. Yes, just about the time that they were selling out—most of them in there sold along about 1924, sold to the City.

RP: Are you talking about the subdivision in Manzanar?

VT: Yes, everything down there. We moved from George's Creek to Lone Pine in 1924, probably August, September.

RP: Can you tell me something of your impressions of growing up at George's Creek?

VT: Oh, you were just free to do anything you wanted and roam all the fields up there. I fished every day I could almost. The limit was fifty [fish]. I managed a time or two to get fifty, and then they changed it to twenty-five. But twenty-five was even too many. Ten is about right. I think it's down to five now.

RP: Did you help with the bees or any of the ranch work?

VT: No, I didn't like bees. You know, the bees swarm, they cluster onto something. My grandfather would give us a dollar for finding the swarm, and I would go watch him gather them in. Those things would start buzzing around me, and pretty soon I just took off. Of course, a dollar was quite a bit of money. Talking about money, they had all of these orchards at Manzanar—apple orchards, and peach and pear orchards. Well, I never did pick any peaches or pears, but I picked a lot of apples. A packing company would come in here at Manzanar—there was the little [town] area, the store on one corner, and the town hall and packing building, which was quite large, on the other one. And then across the highway from the store, there was a garage. It was a two-story building, the town hall was, and that would turn into a packing building during the fall.

And these guys with their wagons would go out to all these farms to bring in the fruit, but they had to have somebody picking them. Well, I think I must have been eleven or twelve then, probably 1921 or 1922, and they wouldn't hire me because I was too young. But they said, "You can go with your mother." She was picking then. They were paying seven cents a box. So I did that, and there were a couple or three days—weekends, it had to be—that I'd make as much as $7 a day, and that was a fortune then. [It] would go down under her name, you know, but I kept track of the number of boxes that I had picked.

I could climb around those trees so much easier than she could, without a ladder. You had this big bag hanging around you and you'd just reach in there and pick them—beautiful Winesap apples, most of them. They had an Arkansas Black, too, that was a real good-looking apple, and then they had a Spitzenberg apple that was a pretty good-keeping apple, but most of it was in Winesaps.

RP: Most of the labor for the picking was local?

VT: Yes, they'd just come down and sign up. The guys with the wagons, now, I don't know whether they were working for the packing company or themselves, bringing the apples in off the orchards on their own. But at Manzanar, the orchards ran all the way up to where this alfalfa field is on the west side [of the highway]. Then the main part of the development went to the east side of the highway and sort of followed an earthquake fault line along in there. You get above that fault and the water table was higher than it was down below it. I did a lot of work for the Department [of Water and Power] on that, is the reason I happen to know something about it.

RP: Did you or your family participate in the packing activities as well?

VT: No, my father was working for the Department every day, so he was not available, and my mother—Well, she did work in the packing house sorting apples some, but she could make more money by going out and picking them off the tree, so that's what she did most of the time.

RP: And that activity lasted about how long? How long would you and she be picking?

VT: The Department, after they bought it all out down there, they kept the orchards going. They had a superintendent by the name of Johnny Gorman. So, in 1929, I worked down there again—that's when I got out of school. But that's about when the Department had to—See, we had quite a drought then, 1929, 1930, 1931, 1932. That was a pretty severe drought, so that's when the Department decided to do away with the ranches, take all the water off of them and let them dry up. The old houses that were around on the places, they went in and tore out the windows and the doors and then they burned them.

RP: So from the time the Department bought up the Manzanar area, in 1923, 1924, you say, until about [1933], they were still maintaining the orchards and still producing fruit commercially?

VT: That's right. And they had another one that went along with that. The Red Mountain Fruit Ranch up here [near Big Pine] was operated along about the same scale, and in 1932 they took the water off of that also, so those orchards all started drying up too.

RP: Can you recall, what was the feeling about that change of ownership [at Manzanar]? Do you recall how people reacted to that?

VT: Most of them were so happy to get their money out of it. You see, if they could have counted on a crop of apples every year, Manzanar would have been a very lucrative area. But like these frosts we get—I don't believe they could count on more than two years out of five. They would get a good year and it would carry them along, and pretty soon a frost would come along and they were just barely on the borderline of getting by. So when they were offered, say, fifty or seventy-five dollars an acre, most of them were real happy to take it and locate over where it was greener.

These good friends of ours that I mentioned, the Albers, they had a big cattle ranch down there. They ran about four hundred cattle this side of George's Creek, and they had a pretty good orchard in there. Well, they sold out. These land agents from various areas in California knew that the people had some money over here, so they came over and enticed them to come take a look at some lands. I know in this case, they took the Albers up to Lake County and everything was green, and they thought, boy, anybody ought to be able to make a living up here. And they had close to $100,000 that they had gotten out of their ranch down there [at Manzanar], so they bought two ranches and they both went broke.

RP: So there wasn't a great deal of animosity or anger about the City's policies in that area?

VT: No, I would say not. In fact, I know of some areas down there, or ranches, that were not too desirable for the Department to buy, and three or four of these ranchers would get together and they would have a [petition] against the Department of Water and Power to make them buy.

RP: Oh, really?

VT: Yes. It wasn't a very prosperous community. It was a nice community. It was really a beautiful place down there, with all those orchards and the lane roads running every half-mile.

RP: How close-knit a community was Manzanar?

VT: Oh, at that time the Farm Bureau was very active and they kept things going very well. They had meetings periodically and they would have dances in the lower part of this town hall. After midnight, then the ladies would serve sandwiches and cake and coffee and refreshments in the upper part of the hall. I remember us kids, we thought it was great, you know, when they'd have a Virginia Reel and we'd get out there and dance around with these big people.

RP: You mentioned the drought around 1929 to 1931 or '32. Exactly how did things change? What were the impacts of that?

VT: Just about like we're seeing this year, everything dried up.

RP: How did it affect the people and the local economy?

VT: Well, the Depression came in there, too.

RP: In other words, the Depression hit this area like it hit most other areas?

VT: Well, I'm not sure that it did as bad as other places. I guess if a person stayed here he had a job. I think that's the way it was, that everybody around here was pretty much employed. It seemed like it was all pretty steady, static. I couldn't get a job, though, from the end of that semester when I was at Glendale Junior College. I went down there for one semester, and then I got sick and had my appendix out. So when I came back up here in 1930, I was going to go to work and get some money saved up. But you couldn't get a job if you wanted to hire out for twenty-five cents an hour. So I did the next best thing that I could. Since I was a kid down there at Manzanar, I had set out a few traps—coyote traps—and so this half-uncle of mine and I got together and we set out quite a string of coyote traps. We had two old Model Ts, so we covered everything from the Alabama Gates up to the [aqueduct] intake, and even mountain roads up there.

One time we went clear into George's Creek Lake. It sits up at about 11,000 feet, and we'd go up there and trap for marten. They're a pretty high-altitude animal—say 9,500 to 11,500 feet. They do well in rock piles where they can catch these rock rabbits and mice and whatever. They're illegal now. You can't trap them anymore. Well, we did better for marten than coyote. At that time, we got as high as $40 a pelt for the little guys. Where a coyote, you'd get a dollar, or a dollar and a half, and bobcats were less than that, generally.

RP: Was that the bounty on them?

VT: No, you'd just catch them and skin them and dry the skin and send them to a fur company. They would make almost anything out of the coyote skin. At that time, these necklaces on coats were very popular, and a coyote skin came around like that. But you didn't get much for them, just to make a few bucks, enough for gasoline. Coyotes were quite plentiful then because nobody bothered them. They are one of the hardest animals to trap, a coyote is. But when they're so plentiful, they were pretty easy to trap. In fact, we caught over a hundred of them that year.

RP: Was there any regulation back then of trapping at all?

VT: There was a season. It was during the cold months of the year. That's generally about when you trap coyotes, and cats, too, because that's the only time that the furs are prime. But there were more animals, because it always came right back to the food [supply]. A lot of rabbits would come out, and consequently, the coyotes would come out to get the rabbits, and that's the way it works. The biggest harvest of animals in the valley here came during periods when the furriers were paying the most. In 1977, '78, '79, along in there, that's when prices were up. We had a lot of people trapping then but it didn't seem to hurt the population.

RP: You say your father began working for the Department around 1921. What are some of the things he was involved with [in] the valley here?

VT: He was working on the end of a shovel or he was doing some kind of concrete work. See, after they built the aqueduct along in this open [unlined] section they had a dredge in there and he worked on that as a crane man. They had the engineer and the crane man and an oil man. He had really the only dirty job of the works because he was [out] there when it was cold and blowing and ice freezing all over him with his raincoat on.

In fact, I worked for about a month on that as an oil man before I went to work for the Department on the survey party. That was in 1931. Once I got a job with them—that was during the Depression yet—I wasn't about to quit work for anything and try to go back to school. So I took a course in civil engineering. It was a six-year course from the International Correspondence School. I started working for the Department as a laborer, and when I quit I was a registered Associate Civil Engineer with the State of California, so the course did some good.

RP: Yes, I'd say so. Can you tell me where you were in your survey work and what you were planning for?

VT: Well at that time, when you worked on the survey party for the Department of Water and Power, you worked all the way from Mojave to Mono Lake. Anything they had to survey, if they bought a piece of property from some rancher [who] was selling 40 acres or whatever, immediately we had to go out and from some well-established point tie the corners in and put iron pipe markers in there to show the extent of the land they had just purchased. And, oh, it was just all kinds of different jobs that would come up. We did a triangulation signal one time from Little Lake to Big Pine, across the valley. We would go up on a peak over on this side, not high but where you had good clearance from there across without picking up too many heat waves from the valley floor, or from there to a point farther south in the valley that you could see. And you had to bring it in line and then triangulate across there. It took us a year, I guess. It was varied work and lots of level work.

All the wells, all the test holes, they all had to have an elevation on them so they could make hydrographs for the water level in the wells. The Department of Water and Power has probably got the most complete water record here in the Owens Valley of any place, I'd say, in the United States. They've got a really fine water record. They could tell you anything you want to know about the water.

RP: Were there a large number of wells at that time in the valley? Was groundwater pumping like it is today?

VT: Almost the same [number of] wells, only they've been replaced by newer wells. They started putting in wells before 1920, and then they just kept drilling and drilling.

RP: Do you remember a springs around the Independence area at that time that was still flowing, Heinz Springs?

VT: Well, Heinz Springs, it will flow. I've seen it flow and then I've seen it dry up and flow and dry up. Pumping will affect that. When they pump, Heinz spring will generally dry up. Then there's two springs down here [near Independence], one on each side of Mazourka Road. Those will fluctuate. They're just this side of that big fault line, so the water is backed up there. Springs that were flowing [a long time ago] that are not flowing now, is that your question?

RP: Yes.

VT: Gosh, they've been on and off so many times in the last sixty years that it would be pretty hard to say.
RP: Not only as a result of pumping, but drought periods as well would dry them up?
VT: Yes, just like vegetation, it responds directly to the precipitation.
RP: What about the Owens River below the [aqueduct] intake in the twenties and thirties? What was the river south of the intake like then?
VT: Just about like it is now, if they've got the gates shut off tight up at the intake. There isn't much water. There's a few little springs [that] come up along in different places, and [the water] would pool up and form kind of a tule pond and it wouldn't go very far. Yes, about the same—willow trees all along the bed of [the river] because it's not too far to the water table, you know, anyplace along there, and those willows will get right down to it. In fact, if they got rid of all the willows, they'd have more water running down. But one thing [the City] used to do is open the gates more often and waste the water down into Owens Lake. When they would do that, it would flush all that old stuff out, you know? And boy, the fishing [in the river] after they flushed it out was just super.
RP: Oh, really?
VT: Yes, and then as the ponds receded, the fishing just kept getting poorer and poorer and then there was no fish. But I don't know where those catfish hang out when there's no water being flushed down there, but they just seem to come right back up.
RP: Do you have any recollections of Owens Lake at the time you were growing up?
VT: Yes, I have a very good one. We came up here in 1920 in that old Model T. We could see the Owens Lake down at Cartago, and by golly, there was no end to that water, looking out across there, although it was probably only about [one to two feet] deep. And I think it's 19 miles from Cartago up to where this end of it was.

In 1921 I went into the mountains with these Albers brothers with their cattle in the spring, and we'd stay all summer up there at the cow camps. The cattle were driven up Cottonwood Canyon, and where the old sawmill is, you could look back down and see this big body of water. When we came out [at the end of August], I looked out over there and here [the lake] is all white, the whole thing. The water had evaporated and there was no surface water showing, or very little, you know, just spots here and there. I'll never forget that. When I came out, looking for that great big lake of water, it was all dried up. It was salt crystal.
RP: But you did see it when it was completely covered [with water]. How close to the highway was the water?
VT: Oh, it was way out there, probably just about the way the salt shows now, only it was covered with a little bit of water. I don't think it was a whole lot deeper when we first came up in 1920 than what it is right now. Because, see, the evaporation off of Owens Lake is about four to five feet a year, it's that much. So, if there was a foot on there, it wouldn't take long during the summer to be dry.

RP: After your survey work, what did you get involved with, Vic?
VT: In 1936 I transferred over to the hydrographic section with the DWP, and I stayed in there until 1948. Then I transferred back to the engineering section until I retired in 1972.
RP: Could you tell us about what you did in the hydrographic division?
VT: Yes, hydrographics is the gathering of water records from streams or wells, springs, anyplace there is water. They make up a hydrograph, which is time versus the fluctuation. So, at any given time, they can go back on these records and find out what the flow was in some certain stream or they can find out what the elevation was on any one well.
RP: So every year, you'd have to go out and—
VT: No, you'd keep them up every two weeks. You'd go out and measure the water level in the well, and then you would plot it on these graphs. Then, at the end of the year, you'd connect all these points at the time, and it would give you the water surface elevation all the way through the year.
RP: And you also were involved with gauging the springs, too?
VT: Oh yes, every place there was water the Department had a measuring device on it. They measured all the water flow and springs. Wherever there was water, they were interested.
RP: You also did a lot of readings on the Owens River, I guess, too.
VT: Well, yes. You see, the records on the Owens River go back farther than the Department of Water and Power because the army kept records on the Owens River [in the 1800s]. In later years, [the City] had a measuring device and metered sections up there [near Aberdeen] where they took the water of the Owens River and put it into the aqueduct. Just downstream, they had a meter bridge go across where you would take sections and go across that to get the flow. Then, above that, at Charlie's Butte, there's a bridge and that's one of the oldest meter bridges there. You know where it's at there, that swinging bridge?
RP: Yes, I've seen that one. Vic, were you involved with measuring the snow too?
VT: Yes, the first snow survey I went on was in 1935, on the first of March. We had courses starting from the south, two of them up Cottonwood Canyon, then in Big Pine Canyon we had three courses, and then Rock Creek, we had three courses. Then we'd get up to Mammoth and we had two. On the Minnaret Summit, right where the ski hut is now, we had a course go right across that area. That was the highest one we had.
RP: Now what do you mean by courses? Could you explain that?
VT: Well, beforehand, say during the summer, or when they originally started this, they would go up there and they'd take the line that they wanted to measure the snow on. And then every fifty feet they'd put a marker. But when you went back in there later, all you had was a tape because the markers were all down under the snow. So you'd start at one end, and measure. At that time, there was only two of us. You had to ski in there—well, like Big Pine Canyon, I'd put the skis on there at the

powerhouse at the bottom and go all the way up to the Second Lake. That was where our upper course was.

RP: So it entailed quite a bit of danger and risk.

VT: Yes, Big Pine in particular. That's probably prone to avalanches more than any other canyon in the Sierras. I've seen the whole thing come down on both sides, the north and the south.

RP: Can you describe what you'd do then?

VT: Oh, you'd leave at daylight—they measured the water with these steel snow tubes, and they're waxed inside. They use a ski wax so they're real slick. With this scale that we weigh them on, it's calibrated in inches of water for that diameter of a core you take out. You take the core, the snow sample, and then when you put the tube on there, it measures just the snow that you bring up and out, and that's measured in inches of water for that diameter tube.

Now they do the same thing with their snow graphs that I was telling you about with the hydrographs. They plot all that and then they correlate—the snow survey is made up on top of the mountains, see, and there's so many inches of water up there. Well, they've got a measuring device down at the bottom and that gives them any [stream] flow they want, the maximum flow at the time or it gives them the annual flow that went through that measuring device. So that is all plotted up, you see, and you get a graph on that, too. So after you start, then you've got the average, and then they just keep working up that average. Now, say from 1930 until now, the normal [run-off] is pretty well established.

Eleanor Taylor: You know what used to be dangerous about that, sometimes they would go in the snow for days and a storm would come. So I would sit down here, and he wouldn't get out when he was supposed to, and you never knew what was going on. It was real dangerous.

RP: How did you feel up there while you were doing this?

VT: Oh, I loved it. I'd have done that every day. You'd ski in—well, down at Cottonwood it was roughly 8 miles each way to where our upper course was. Coming down was pretty easy, but going up sometimes, that was kind of a hassle. And you could have good snow conditions and you could have rotten snow conditions.

RP: Vic, had you skied a lot before this?

VT: No, this friend of mine, Ed Parker, was a hydrographer and he kept wanting me to go in there with him. So they finally worked it so I could, although I was on the survey party, and that's how I got started skiing.

RP: What was the skiing equipment like then?

VT: Oh, at that time, the skis were the best we could get. They were Northman skis and they had to come from Sweden. There was very little ski equipment in the United States then. And they used an eight-foot ski. I think that was to their advantage with this pole that they rode, the long pole. They didn't use ski poles. They used one long pole and when they wanted to come down a mountain, a steep mountain, they'd get astraddle of it and the slower they wanted to go, they'd sit back on it, see, and use it as a brake. That's the way they got down, and turning [was] the same way. But these old eight-foot skis, the binding on them was the biggest problem. You know, the most important thing in skiing is to have control between your foot and that ski. You didn't have good control.

One time this partner of mine and I were coming from Cottonwood Golden Trout Camp down to our snow survey cabin at the old sawmill. At that time, they had these mortised skis—that weakened them when you would take almost half of the wood out right under your foot. About half way down I came up onto something—the ski went up here and my weight was down here, and all the weight came right in the middle and it broke, right in front of my toe. [We were] on a slope and so we figured, well, we had three good skis, but we had four legs. So, the two outside skis, we kept them on. The middle ski, well, the guy [in front] would lift up his heel and the other one would slip his foot in under there and then the weight would come down and hold it. By the time we got down, we were getting pretty good at skiing with three skis.

RP: That's pretty neat. You mentioned a snow survey cabin up there. Did you have those in every canyon?

VT: We had access to them in all the canyons where we had snow courses. At Cottonwood, we had one there. It might be there yet, I don't know. Then we'd go from that to Golden Trout [Camp], and we had use of the Golden Trout fishing cabins up there.

RP: Were some of those built strictly for snow surveys?

VT: Cottonwood was. They put a real fancy one up at Mammoth. The snow would get so deep there that you couldn't get in the door. So they had a tower that went up, maybe a four by four tower with a ladder on the inside. So you could get in and then go down the ladder to the lower part, the building.

ET: You know, Vic might not tell you but our son is the head of the [DWP] hydrographic section in Bishop now. He goes on these snow surveys. They do it the easy way in one of those snow cats.

RP: They just motor up there and take their readings and back they go?

VT: That's right.

RP: When did they stop using skis?

VT: I never got in on the easy stuff, so it was after 1972.

RP: You said this survey was usually done March first?

VT: No, when I first started, they were making them four times a year, the first of January, February, March and April. They got a—well, we'll call it the normal [snowpack], pretty well established, so then they started making them [just] in February and April. The one in February was to give them a forecast so they could kind of work up their leases down here, how much water to allow the lessees. Then the April one, that was final. That told them what was there. It was quite a bit of skiing. In fact, that's how Dave McCoy got started.[6]

RP: So Dave actually worked on the snow survey group?

VT: Oh yes, he did a lot of surveying. In fact he became hydrographer at Long Valley, and so [in 1938] he put in a little ski lift of his own over there at McGee Mountain after the original guys had given it up. The original men that put that lift in there were Tex Cushion—you've probably heard that name?

RP: Yes.

VT: He had the dog teams up at Mammoth. And I think Jack Northrup, who had Northrup Aviation, was in on that at first. There were three or four of them, and it was just a temporary thing to kind of see how it was going to go. They pulled out and Dave started with some little portable ski lifts that you could put on a sled and slide up the hill. You'd just go up there and grab onto the rope and up the mountain you'd go. And then from McGee Mountain he moved up to Mammoth Mountain [in 1941] and he did the same thing there, with a portable lift first, and then it just grew.

RP: Did he have any kind of operation going on here in the valley, too?

VT: No, the first one here in the valley was when I put one up in Onion Valley.

RP: Oh, tell me about that.

VT: In 1941 we had a big snow year. So [Eleanor's] brother-in-law and I, we set up a rope tow in Onion Valley. We used a Model A Ford [engine] just like Dave used. The first thing we did was get so much snow that we couldn't even get in there. So we tried for the next [year]. But the road was bad and the county wouldn't do anything about keeping it open. 1952, I think was the last year that we tried skiing up there.

RP: So you actually ran a commercial operation?

VT: Yes, we had to get a Forest Service permit and had to get this damned expensive insurance.

RP: How many people would you have on a weekend?

VT: Oh, our best weekends we might have had maybe 100 to 150, something like that. Then we were thinking of chairlifts. To get a good road in there, you had to give them something more than rope tows. I know I made a survey from Onion Valley back up that stream that comes in from the south to Robinson Lake, and I think there was an 1,800-foot drop and then whatever the distance was back there. It was a pretty good drop. We wanted [the Forest Service] to move the wilderness area [forest] boundary line. Just in this one canyon. That's all we wanted, just back up that one canyon. We had actually gotten the permit on it, but they wanted it shut down for some reason or other. I don't know just what happened. They got it closed down, anyway, and that went back to the wilderness area.

RP: So there wasn't any organized opposition to that?

VT: The Sierra Club was bitterly opposed to it.

ET: Vic and three of these boys in town here built that nice ski hut we had up there. Then a snow slide came and demolished it.

VT: That was, well, I'm going to say 1985, 1986. It had been a long time since a snow slide like that one had come out of there. There were trees that were taken out that were this big around. Before I picked that location in 1931, well, you get familiar with these mountains and you can almost tell where snow slides and avalanches and everything else—where they come down.

ET: That ski hut, two summers I went up there and ran a little restaurant up there.

VT: We had that in the winter also. We had a counter in there and we'd serve hot stuff. You get these canned Dinty Moore stews and soups and—

ET: I cooked a lot of breakfasts.

VT: Lone Pine had an [operation] up at Whitney Portal, too, just rope tows.

RP: They had a rope tow there? How long ago was that?

VT: That was along in that same period, about 1940. They put it right in an avalanche chute coming off of Lone Pine Peak. Oh, it came right down through there. After they got wiped out at the bottom three or four times, they decided that it wasn't a good thing to do. It was a pretty nice slope because the avalanches kept the rocks and trees and everything trimmed out down there.

RP: Most of the people that were involved with the little operation that you had and the one in Lone Pine, were these primarily local people or people that came up from Los Angeles?

VT: Well, see, the first ones in the area were [at] Deadman [Summit] and McGee Mountain. Then people down here could see that there might be a future in ski tows. So they started these little ones up, just rope tows.

RP: But it drew mostly local people?

VT: Yes, you could say that, but the Santa Monica Ski Club, which is a big organization, they liked this [one at] Onion Valley so well that they just about took it over. Every weekend they were up here in force.

RP: Vic, were you involved at all in the Mono Craters project [to bring water] from the Mono Lake Basin down?

VT: I did a lot of work on it in later years, but I wasn't in on the job when it [started]. Let's see, it ended in 1940, I believe. Of course, everything had to be mapped before any projects got started up there. So the first thing they did was to go up there and set up a big camp—many, many cabins in there—and they called it the Cain Ranch. They made surveys from there. They probably had—I'm just going to guess now—a hundred survey parties. They had to cover all of Mono Basin and the route from East Portal to West Portal that the tunnel was going under. But after [the tunnel] was completed, when I was in the engineering office, we'd go through there on inspections.

RP: Through the whole 11-mile stretch of it?

VT: Yes, several times I've been through the tunnel. We'd go in at the West Portal and come out the other portal. They had a jeep, a diesel jeep. Now apparently, [diesel] doesn't manufacture carbon monoxide or dioxide. That's the reason they didn't use a gasoline jeep in there to tow the buggies. There were two of them and they had everything on these buggies, in case anything happened, you know, you could take care of it. There was one [inspection] we went on, we left just so much water going down the tunnel, and we put two or three boats in there and went the 11 miles in the boats.

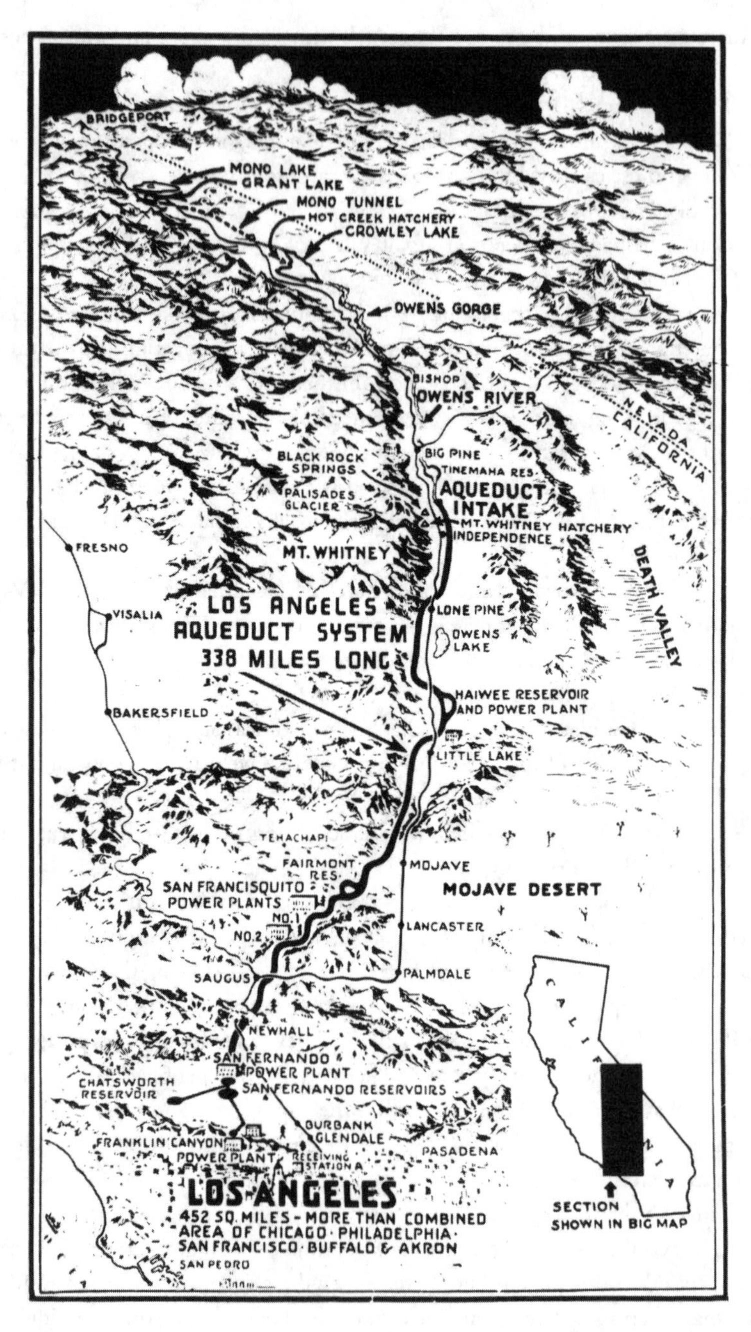

The Los Angeles Aqueduct system, ca. 1940. *Reprint Courtesy of the Los Angeles Department of Water and Power*

You'd go along, inspecting all except the bottom part. A hundred second feet [of water] would float the boat all right, and that's all the water you needed in there.[7]

RP: Then what did you use, just flashlights?

VT: Yes, some of them were big, big flashlights. That [aqueduct] tunnel down at Soda Springs, below Little Lake, my dad worked on that in the twenties. They had crews then, you know, just labor crews, and they'd have to go in there and clean these tunnels out. There's an algae that gets in there, and builds up these little barnacles and things around in the tunnel. It can cut the flow from—say the maximum flow is 500 cubic feet per second, and it can cut it down to 425, something like that. Their safety factor down at Little Lake was that they wore these candles. You've seen miners with those?

RP: Yes, a little candle.

VT: Well, when that candle started flickering or going out, that was time to get out of there, the carbon dioxide gas was getting in there pretty bad. They didn't have any instruments to measure it. Now, up here at the Mono Craters tunnel, to check the gas, they had a huge blower, just like our air conditioner, you know, only it's ten foot in diameter, and they had a Ford engine driving it. Then one of the jobs I had at that time was to take a couple of young engineers up there and we'd test the gas that was coming out, where this blower was putting it out. We had regular instruments up there. Until that gas got down to a certain percentage, nobody could go in there, so it was a safety factor.

RP: So the whole tunnel was arches of steel—it was encased in steel and concrete?

VT: Yes, the steel ribs, they called them, were in there.

RP: What was your feeling going into that tunnel? Was it kind of spooky?

VT: I didn't like it the first time, but, heck, when you once get in there and everything is dark and you quit thinking about it, all you're looking for is cracks. Some places the water would be squirting out under pressure, about like a hose. The normal flow through that tunnel is about nineteen second feet—nineteen cubic feet per second is what that amounts to.

RP: Measuring the wells as you did, from the time you started to what we have now in the valley, the controversy over groundwater pumping and stuff, was there a time or a period where [the groundwater] got drawn down considerably?

VT: Yes, before I went to work for the Department, we had a drought that was four years, 1929, 1930, 1931, 1932. Nineteen thirty-three came in and it was a big year. It would have started in December and continued all winter, big storms.

RP: In those dry years here in the valley, I guess they would cut the allotment for water to some of the lessees, wouldn't they?

VT: Oh yes, they did. At first, it was kind of a disagreeable thing. That is, when they were going to have a dry year, they didn't make any provision for it beforehand and they just cut the lessee off. They'd cut his water supply way down or maybe clear off. Well, that didn't set too well with [the ranchers], especially if they had put in a crop of alfalfa, because it takes maybe three or four years to really get maximum harvest out of it. That's what brought about this agreement where the Department of Water and Power will leave 50,000 or 75,000 acre feet of water in the valley up through here.[8] So how it's distributed, I don't know, but they wouldn't dry the valley up anyway.

RP: Right, so the people that have the leases would always have some irrigation contingency.

VT: Either that or they got their lease with the agreement that there were years when they wouldn't have it which wasn't a very smart thing to do.

RP: Were you also involved, Vic, with actually installing any wells?

VT: Oh, yes, drilling them and installing them, [although] there was a long period in there when we didn't drill any wells. Some of the original wells they drilled right close to the aqueduct and generally up above the aqueduct. And then they had a huge compressor plant right down here where Mazourka Road crosses the aqueduct, and they had an air line going both ways and they pumped all their water with air. They would put the air down in there and bring the water up and it would go right into the aqueduct. That was their original system. And those wells were all, I think, nine to twelve inches. They were small wells. Now, in later years when I had anything to do with it, our wells were all eighteen- and twenty-inch wells.

ET: He picked some of the sites for these wells.

VT: Oh, yes, and then the Department hired a geologist. I was just an associate civil engineer. So they hired him to come up here, and heck, some of the sites he picked weren't ten feet from the sites I had already picked—just from looking at the area, you knew what might have happened underneath in the years past, where the [ancient Owens] lake might have been. If you got into that sand and gravel aquifer down there, you could follow it all the way along. That's the reason these wells all follow right along here in a line. That was probably a lakeshore as the water came down off of the hill there and deposited first the boulders. And the clays and stuff like that were carried clear out into the middle of the lake. Then there was one place where there would be lots of good water-bearing stratum, you know, sand and gravel, and that's where you want to get in to get your [ground]water.

RP: What was the feeling amongst the valley farmers, ranchers and stuff towards the DWP employees?

VT: I don't think there was any hard feelings there at all. [It was] just a job, that's all.

RP: And were people who worked for the city also very close socially?

VT: No, I think it was all pretty much together.

ET: Everybody had their friends whether they worked for DWP or not—

VT: Yes, I don't think that came into it very much. Maybe not as much as it does now.

RP: Vic, you mentioned that they would open the intake gates and flood the river channel. You referred to it as "wasting the water." Can you recall how often that happened?

VT: Yes, they only did that when there was a surplus of water [to put in the aqueduct]. And they spread it out here in the flats and in the river and everyplace, because there was a surplus of water.[9] These lessees would want water spread on their lands, you know, because then they got irrigated for nothing. Their first lease was based on a dry lease, and I think it cost them maybe twenty-five cents an acre per year. There was no water furnished or anything, though. So when they had the opportunity to have some water spread, they grabbed at it and got their lands irrigated. It would just be, "Here's ten second feet of water, use it." Kind of a pasture is about all that was good for. [But] it could save us from paying somebody to go out there and spread it.

They used the old farmers' ditches [to spread the water], too. See, the farmers had this valley pretty well covered with an irrigation system [by the late 1800s]. Their first one was there at that reservoir—Pleasant Valley Dam. That's where the old-timers took out their water. Owens River Canal, that's the one I'm thinking of. And then it came way down south of Bishop and put water out. Then the next one down would probably be the Bishop Creek Canal, and that took in a big area in there. And for spreading, these things were perfect, because you could put all the water you wanted in this top one. If it overflowed, it would go down and be picked up in the next one. And you could spread out of that one. It made just a beautiful spreading system. Those old farmers, they must have dug those all with horses and mules. That's all they had at that time.

RP: Vic, in the time you have spent in the Owens Valley, can you kind of generalize on what are some of the positive changes you have seen occur here in the valley during your life?

VT: Well, my being an outdoorsman and hunter and a fisherman and a trapper, everything has gone negative, I think. We don't have what we used to have. What has brought it about is probably too many people up here in the valley. Whether it's the hunting or the fishing or whatever, there's just too many people. And the camping—in the old days, you could go up there on any creek and just put your tent up and camp, no restriction whatsoever of any kind. Now you've got all this rigamarole to go through to camp up there. You've got to get a permit. So as far as I'm concerned, it has kind of gone to hell.

RP: What about the valley's environment, in general, between the time you first came up here and now?

VT: Well, there was quite a bit of change—when I came up here in 1920, there was still a lot of water being put onto the lands here. Of course, as far as the environment goes, you're changing things completely with water or no water. Water is everything. But I don't want to get into who is right and who is wrong, whether the Department is right or wrong on that water deal.

What regulates everything is what we're getting right now, this precipitation. That regulates your vegetation growth, and consequently, your animal population. And it's all surface [water], whether it's spreading or whether it's normal rainfall or snowfall or whatever. Everything is how much water you get in the valley.

FIVE

Emily Roddy (b. 1911)

It was a railroad hotel, made of box cars—everything was box cars

Introduction

The boxcar town at Owenyo, where twelve-year-old Emily Roddy, her mother, and young sister went to live in 1923, was the transfer point between the 1883 narrow-gauge railroad into the Owens Valley from Nevada and the Southern Pacific standard-gauge extension built from southern California in 1910. Emily's mother ran the hotel at Owenyo Station, and Emily and her sister helped with the cooking and cleaning. When she was older, Emily worked at Manzanar packing fruit.

Her conversations with Richard Potashin in June 1992 and March 1993 are grounded in these two milieus and brim with the wit and contagious sense of fun that have endeared her to friends and neighbors in the Owens Valley for decades. Leaving behind her beloved yellow Mustang, she moved recently to a Bishop nursing home, where she still tells stories of Owenyo; their rich details of dust, bugs, and colorful workers suggest it was there, and not the orchards and shaded lanes at Manzanar, where her youthful identity was forged and her deep sense of place in the Owens Valley took root. Moving between the two locales, she recounts the interplay of economic necessity between them in her life as she struggled to make ends meet. That struggle mirrored an often contentious alliance of western railroads, agricultural interests, and the expanding urban centers they served in the early decades of the twentieth century.

By 1890, more than 72,000 miles of track lay across the land west of the Mississippi, much of it in short lines like the 300-mile Carson and Colorado Railway built in 1883 from Mound House, Nevada, to Keeler, near Owens Lake. Railroad financiers, unwilling to put major routes into areas of unproven growth potential, instead installed feeder lines to serve specific industries.[1] The Carson and Colorado, built as a narrow gauge to carry mining ores out of the valley and over steep mountain passes, gave the isolated valley a first rail link to outside commerce and society. Described by one pundit, it was "a passenger train, freight train, and a milk train . . . but in order to economize, one engine is made to pull all three."[2] With tracks and stations on the east side of the valley, however, far from the towns and ranches, the line did not sufficiently benefit farmers. Still missing was the link to southern markets that could ease a prolonged economic slump.

Like other industries, the investor-owned agricultural ventures that appeared in remote areas of the West after 1890 depended on efficient rail transportation to urban markets. At Manzanar, it was clear that the Chaffeys' fruit-growing venture had little chance of success without a rail line south. With their plans for an electric-powered railroad embroiled in litigation with Los Angeles, subdivision moved forward only as the Southern Pacific "Jawbone" line from Mojave, built to supply the aqueduct project, was nearing completion. With the "Jawbone" open, Los Angeles officials enthusiastically predicted, the narrow- and standard-gauge lines, linked at Owenyo and both under the Southern Pacific seal, would make "this agricultural and mining region tributary to Los Angeles."[3]

Two decades earlier, Southern Pacific and its arch-competitor, Santa Fe, scrambling for the lucrative business of urban growth, lowered fares and set off a new westward migration. With tickets going for as little as a dollar, thousands of Midwesterners flocked to southern California to experience its temperate climate and see for themselves the renowned orange groves and sparkling beaches. Many stayed on, and by 1904, the nearly tenfold increase in Los Angeles' population over the previous two decades had sent worried officials to the Owens Valley in search of new water sources.

Known as the "Octopus," after the 1901 Frank Norris novel of the same name, Southern Pacific's voracious network of political influence in California was challenged by Progressive reformers in the early years of the new century.[4] The growth in Los Angeles seemed assured to build the line into the Owens Valley, both from the aqueduct construction and the valley farm trade. But the handsomest returns by far were indirect: now supplied with a new source of water, growth in Los Angeles was assured for decades to come.

At Owenyo, the clamorous, twice-daily transfer of freight and passengers Emily describes gave ranchers, mining operations, and soda ash production in the Owens Valley access to southern California markets and transportation links for nearly four decades. But as Emily's story suggests, it was a cobbled-together system that even in the early years was showing signs of strain. Nationwide by the 1930s, declining farm prices and new modes of transport had already diminished the economic and political influence of both the railroads and the farmers they had served.

Emily Roddy, 2001. *Author's Collection*

Just out of view as Emily concludes her story are the last days of Manzanar as a fruit growing enterprise. By 1927 nearly all the agricultural land in the Owens Valley was in Los Angeles ownership. Fruit production at Manzanar continued into the early 1930s, the apples, pears, and peaches that Emily helped pack sent out on the Southern Pacific in crates bearing a City of Los Angeles label.

Emily Roddy—Interview

We came down on the train from Berkeley to Mojave and up from Mojave [to Owenyo]. I was so sick at the time I didn't care if I ever saw Owenyo or any other place on the face of the earth. If I could have got on the train and gone back I would have. We were dressed Berkeley-style: dresses up to here and socks up to there. We got off the train and went to Lone Pine and all the girls were dressed in Levi's and they laughed at us and called us flappers and we hated it.

Richard Potashin: What year was that?
ER: Nineteen twenty-three. July the first. The hottest time of the year. I thought I knew where I was when we came out of cool Berkeley and into this hot valley. I was twelve years old.
RP: Why did your family come here?

ER: I was born in Berkeley. My father and mother were separated. My mother was taking care of a little sick boy for Mr. Weaver, a mail clerk that worked on the railroad. He had the run from Mojave to Owenyo and back, so we moved up here because this was where he stayed the longest. That is how we ended up here.

RP: You said when you first came over to Owenyo you stayed in a tent cabin over on the east side.

ER: We rented a house in Lone Pine and then in about a year we moved over to the east side of Owenyo maybe 2 miles or so out in the desert. A tent right to the floor. It had to be built because there was no place to stay in Owenyo.

RP: I bet the wind blew out there.

ER: You bet it blew.

RP: You were kind of out there alone.

ER: There was nothing else—a lot of [salt] cedars. Just before we moved there the [Quakers] had lived there. All those squares were where different people had lived.[5] They had water, there is a big ditch out there, and right where they lived there was a place about so wide and so deep for water to go to different places. We lived there for a while and then we moved into Owenyo—uptown, you know. We could get a house, a boxcar house.

RP: You had to buy it?

ER: No, it was furnished by the railroad. I think the railroad people got free rent, and they got ice free, I know—and coal. They had two boxcars and then they built between the two boxcars about twelve feet wide and then divided it in half. That boxcar and one family got the front room and that boxcar and another family got the back room, and then the two middle rooms were bedrooms. Some of the places had put cardboard up on the ceilings—you know, heavy cardboard over the top. It was framed in so bed bugs loved all this. They would walk along the ceiling and just drop down on you. People coming in from Mexico—wetbacks they called them—they had a bunkhouse right close to the ticket agent's house, and they brought in bed bugs. [The railroad people] would get rid of them and then they'd bring in some more. So Southern Pacific would fumigate and you had to leave for a day.

RP: So it was bad enough to fumigate.

ER: With cyanide. It killed everything. They put some out by this bunkhouse and some of the water [had] some cyanide in it and [these] goats ran up and started drinking it and dropped dead just like that. Ada [Cline's] father lost quite a few of his goats that day. Ada and I would go to her house and we'd sit there on the bed and it would make us so nervous. [We] used to kill them by the dozens.

RP: I've heard so much about the boxcar school.

ER: Oh, we had a lot of fun. First, we had an elderly teacher. She said she was about sixty but I'm sure she had passed that a long time ago. But she was quite cute. She had her hair done up in a big pile on top of her head and then she put white and pink and blue pearls all around on it and then flirted with the guys on the work cars. Then we got a nice lovely young teacher, Miss Campbell, but we took advantage of her because it was her first year of teaching school.

RP: Did the teachers live at Owenyo?

ER: They built a room kind of on the side of the boxcar for her. It was just one room. She had to go to the outhouse out in the back past all the houses because the school was very close to the railroad track.

RP: So how many boxcars actually made up the schoolhouse?

ER: Just one. We had school desks down each side, and the teacher's desk was at the back and the black board was on the front. Oh, they had a wood stove, and the teacher had a wood stove in her place. We were all comfortable. I mean plenty warm. Of course in those days you didn't have air conditioning. You just had windows. So I couldn't say you were just exactly comfortable all the time.

RP: How many kids were going to school?

ER: I'd say a dozen, mostly the Clines and the Meyers.

RP: Can you tell us a little bit about how your mother got involved with the hotel there?

ER: Well, we had been there I'd say, four or five years at Owenyo. They needed somebody to run the hotel so she volunteered to do it. The railroad didn't pay her any wages.

RP: Did the railroad own the hotel?

ER: Yes, Southern Pacific owned it. We were just thankful that we made a living.

RP: You had room and board.

ER: Oh yes, because we lived right there. It was made of boxcars—everything was boxcars. They built on the kitchen and Mother had her own room. Then in the back they had a little room with a huge icebox. A man brought over fifty or seventy-five pounds of ice a day and put in it. There were bedrooms on each side of the building. In the middle was the dining room. It was a huge dining room, the length of the box-car and quite wide. We kept it open for anyone who would come and dance or play the piano. They really enjoyed it. We had Ada Brown and her husband come up from Olancha and bring cakes, and people [came] from Independence, and they would have hay rides and dance and everything. Most country people didn't come out that far. When they would come from Olancha or from Independence, that was a long ways in those days.

We just had no drinking. Never. If anybody even thought about drinking they were sent away. But everybody had a wonderful time. In those days people were poor. We didn't care. It was Depression days and they needed some place to have fun. We would put stuff on the floor—I think it was soap chips or something to make it slippery to dance. The piano and phonograph was our music and the battery to the car was our radio for Sunday programs. We didn't have electricity. The next day we had to wash the floors. We'd wet it with a fire hose and put soda ash on it with great big old brooms that the railroad supplied, and we'd scrub real good—and the kitchen, too, and then flush it out with water right out the back door. We kept that floor just beautiful and real clean.

RP: So some of the passengers would stay in the rooms there at the hotel?

ER: Sometimes. Usually, when they came down [from Reno], they'd come in to eat and then they transferred to the Jawbone [broad-gauge line] and went down to Mojave. If they came up from Mojave they ate and transferred on up to Mina [Nevada]. I don't know if they ever stopped any other place. Of course, a lot of people carried baskets of food then—you know, sandwiches and things. But we had a lot of customers. We had sometimes a hundred and thirty, forty, or fifty passengers that we'd feed when the train came through. Many times there was no way through the valley except by train. Oh, there might have been one or two cars that braved it.

One time the moving picture company had a whole crew coming up, and they called and said what they wanted for breakfast. We had eggs and bacon and ham, and we had toast, stacks of it, and then they called and said they weren't coming. Mother wrote and told them they had to pay for it, and they did.

We never stopped working. We had the passengers and we had the fellows that worked on the platform, transferring things—they transferred hay, soda ash, and mining things. A lot of the fellows [who worked on the railroad] lived in the bunkhouse, so they ate at the hotel, too. And then we had to cook for the work crew, when they came up from Bakersfield. There was eight meals a day that we cooked. I made all the pies, and that was a lot of pies for passengers and work crews. You can't imagine this big old coal stove, going all the time, how hot it was. They were big meals—big old platters that long with meat. It was family style and they ate all they wanted.

When the wind blew—you know how it blows here—you couldn't see out of the windows because that soda ash was so white. The cracks in the hotel were pretty wide, so we put the plates [on the table] upside down and put a cloth over them, and then when we put the food on, people didn't get much dirt. It was not so bad in the summertime, but in the wintertime they had a stove—a huge old stove in the dining room, and we would keep coal in it all the time to keep it warm. Of course, in the kitchen the big cook stove kept it warm and there were no stoves out in the bedrooms. You were on your own out there.

RP: How much was the room?

ER: I don't know what Mother charged. Not very much. I know I had to clean the rooms and make the beds. It was about sixty cents for a meal. I remember because we had one guy who walked out all the time and never paid. Mother would never argue with him, so one day he started to walk out and I said, "You forgot to pay." And he came back and gave me a $10 bill. So I took out all the rest of the money he owed and handed him back a little bit of change. He didn't do that again.

RP: Did she make enough on the meals to cover all the food expenses?

ER: No. We had a real rough go of it. I had to go to work and so did my sister. I would get somebody to take care of my children, and I would go clear over to

Manzanar and work in the packinghouse for twenty-five cents an hour. I would pack until they ran out of apples, and then I would run out in the field and pick them and bring them in. Mother had to carry on the whole day without us while we were working, and we would come home and take care of the children and wash clothes and get to bed at twelve. Get up at four, iron, and then take off and go to work. The cars we drove you would never believe. They were antiques, I can tell you. It was pretty hard times. It went through the valley. Hobos would come through. There was no place for them to go and eat. Sometimes we would have five or six out in the back. We had a picnic table out back in the shade, and they'd sit out there and we'd take them their plates. Sometimes if we could we would put them inside but the railroad men didn't care for that—and the passengers didn't either. So we couldn't turn them down. You can't turn people down when they are hungry and way out in the country.

RP: Let's get a better idea on the running of the narrow-gauge line. When did it arrive from Laws?

ER: The [narrow-gauge] train came up from Keeler to Owenyo. And here comes the Jawbone, the broad gauge up to Owenyo [from Mojave]. And it backed around at this Y and [went] back down to Mojave. But the [narrow gauge] went on up to Mina [Nevada] and then broad-gauged again. All the way up [through the Owens Valley] they had stations, you know. The narrow gauge would leave from Keeler and arrive [at Owenyo] about the same time the Jawbone did, so they could transfer, because the platform was wide and they had to transfer from this train to that train. In the morning it came up and transferred and in the afternoon it came down and transferred. Passengers coming down from Reno could transfer here and go to Mojave and down [to Los Angeles on the broad gauge]. It would come up [from Mojave] in the morning and back through at night, and they had Pullmans on at that time.

RP: Were those just on the broad gauge?

ER: The broad gauge had Pullmans. That was maybe 1927 or somewhere about that time. Very nice Pullmans.

RP: Now there were also freight trains that came up too?

ER: Oh yes. We had freight trains come and bring things up, and we also had work trains come up and stay for weeks at a time repairing cars. They kept the work cars out right along by the school there. The reason I know that is we had that teacher—she didn't do much teaching—she kept looking out the window at the guys.

One time I was going to Mojave and I got the red velvet treatment. They put me in a little room that had all the mirrors around it. The narrow gauge didn't have all those curtains and things. And going from Owenyo to Laws was something else. That was like riding a bucking bronco. I'd stand there at the hotel door and watch to see if the train was coming from the north so we could start putting the food on the table for the passengers, and you could just see the wheels jumping up and down off the track.

But they sure had nice porters on [the Mojave line]. We had a problem with the white men and the black men. The porters were black, and the white trainmen wouldn't sit at the table with them at the hotel, so we would set tables in the kitchen

Owens Valley railroads, ca. 1938. In 1900, Southern Pacific acquired the narrow-gauge railroad built in 1883 from Nevada to Keeler. In 1910 it was linked at Owenyo with the new Southern Pacific standard-gauge extension, the "Jawbone," from Mojave into the Owens Valley. *Map by Carl Fallberg, in* The Slim Princess, *by John Hungerford. Reprint courtesy of Golden West Books*

and give them good food and they appreciated it and they were very nice. The passengers that came through, I don't remember them being fussy, but some of the workmen on the train were. They acted real nasty but we said we don't care. We would just give the porters the best food and that would make the others kind of aggravated. The porters were very, very nice gentlemen. Polite. They had to be, because of the job they were in. They never caused any trouble at all.

RP: The porters would have to sleep over, too?

ER: The white workers wouldn't let them in the bunkhouse. They slept in their Pullman car. In fact, sleeping in their car was a better place because it wasn't as dusty when the wind blew and the bunkhouse was like the rest of the places. It had cracks in it and bed bugs.

RP: What about the section gang? That was mostly Mexicans?

ER: Yes. Mostly wetbacks, as they called them, that came in.

RP: Did they have to eat in separate quarters, too?

ER: The Mexicans had a bunkhouse for them, and the other men had their own bunkhouse. They had a single boxcar—some of the Mexicans that worked over there lived in Lone Pine. There were a few boxcars that had families in them. There was one man—very nice people—he had about nine kids and he had a double boxcar.

RP: You were talking about the transfer platform and about the problems that these men had with the soda ash burns.

ER: Oh, it was terrible. All of them usually got burns around here where their shirts were tight and around their ankles where they would sweat. But Johnny Lange lost a whole bone in his nose from breathing it. Nobody wore masks because nobody knew about it. It seemed like it was bad enough on the body when they perspired, but when they wore something tight it was worse.

RP: Was it when they were transferring it on the conveyors?

ER: Any time. Because the bags broke open. And the dust was terrible.

RP: I understand that later on they put it in a bin, where they dumped the soda ash, and then they had a conveyor belt?

ER: It was a building, quite high and quite big, south of the depot. I'm not sure how they put the soda ash in there. They put it from the narrow gauge into this building. It was a big pipe-like thing, kind of flexible because they had it hooked on the building, and they blew it into the [broad-gauge] car. They thought that would be quicker than to get it across [the platform] with the sacks. It was a mess, I'll tell you. You couldn't hardly see when it was going. It was just white everywhere. Terrible! With the wind blowing towards the south we got plenty of dust anyhow, but when it blew to the north we got it from [Owens] lake and Keeler and the conveyor, too. You just couldn't see outside.

RP: Were there instances where people suffered respiratory problems from either the dust off the lake or problems with the soda ash?

ER: Well, the transfer of soda ash and dust, people got sick, but they didn't know what was their problem. They could hardly breathe at times. I never dreamt that I would get anything the matter with me from breathing that dust. We just breathed it, that's all. Nobody told me I was supposed to get sick from it. I didn't, until later when I realized I was having pneumonia and pleurisy.

RP: Did they transfer the hay by carts?

ER: They had to because they couldn't lift it. It was baled hay.

RP: And how did they transfer other freight over [to the broad gauge]?

ER: I think they did it out by the highline, as we called it. South of town, they used to have the train go up on the tracks right up on that thing, and then they put the other cars underneath, and they opened the bottom of the boxcar, and [the freight] dropped down into the boxcar below. We used to walk down there and wave good-bye to the passengers—big deal.

RP: So the narrow gauge was on the top; otherwise if you had the broad gauge on top, those cars would be bigger and half the load would fall on the ground.

ER: That's right. The narrow gauge brought in the ore from Keeler, but the broad gauge took it out. There were trains switching back and forth in front of the hotel nearly all the time. Then when the engine was put away, went to Keeler or whatever, they would push the boxcars. They had great big iron crowbars they used to stick under the wheel and move them along the track until they got it out of the way, and then [they'd] push another one in its place. There was three or four men doing it—there were a lot of men out there on the platform going back and forth all the time. Those iron things as I remembered were about that wide and that long because there was a space that big between the platform and the boxcars where they put them. The cars were right close. The broad gauge pulled up here, and they would transfer [the freight] in carts from this side to [the other]. You could hear them all day long. The platform had cracks in it, so it was pretty noisy.

Down where I told you the highline was, they had two little buildings that they were going to use for the car whackers, but they never did.[6] The red light girls came up from Keeler and used them. They were about as big as this front room. I was over at Ada's, and I'm walking down the track, and I see these fusees burning. You know, what they put out on the highway.

RP: Flares.

ER: A fusee means accidents [on the railroad], so they would put one of those out, then of course the guys would see them. [The girls] always came on payday. I never did see it before, and then all of a sudden I see all these men going down that way, and boy, I thought it must be a car fell off the highline. I'm walking down the track, and Winston Churchill—he was one that worked there on the platform—he comes along. He says, "Where do you think you are going?" I said, "I'm going down to see why the fusee is burning." He said, "Oh no." I said, "Oh yes I am. You aren't going to tell me what to do." He grabbed me by the arm and said, "You're going back to town. Go home and talk to your mother." But Mother never tells me anything, so I came back to talk to Ada. She said, "Oh, you sure didn't go down there did you?" Wouldn't I have been embarrassed if I had!

RP: Emily, could you recall, did the mail come into Owenyo for Lone Pine and other towns in Owens Valley there?

ER: I think they took the mail that went to Lone Pine off at Lone Pine Depot, and at every station they delivered mail. That was the only way you could get the mail in or out of the valley at that time.

RP: Was there one car that was set aside for the mail?

ER: One car, the mail car. We had a mail clerk. Flem, I think, was his name. Boy, was he good looking! He couldn't stay sober for anything, and he had the run from Owenyo to Laws. He got so drunk at Laws, coming down, he stood at the door and said, "Whoopee!" and [threw] mail out the door. So when he gets to Owenyo there's no mail—no sacks available to transfer to the broad gauge. They wondered where the mail was, and he didn't know where it was. So everybody got hand cars and went up the track, and they spent half the night looking for it. We went as far as we could. I think we went practically up to the mountains to get the mail. Some people probably never did get letters. You can imagine the air from the train blew it all over the country.

RP: During your time there in Owenyo, were there still quite a few ranches around? How did the valley look to you?

ER: Oh, the valley was beautiful. Years later, after we ran the hotel for a while, I lived in Manzanar and that was beautiful over there. We moved down by the store. In Manzanar where it says Reward Mine on the highway, you know, where the road goes over east—there was a service station and a wickiup on that corner, and Bandhauer's store on [another] corner and a packinghouse on the corner [across the street]. I worked at the packinghouse and lived behind [it] about a block west. Johnny Gorman had a great big house across the street with a beautiful veranda. He had a small rock wall going around his driveway with iris and all, and it was a beautiful old place with oak trees.

Everybody told me I was losing it because I kept talking about the wickiup where we went and had ice cream. They made this little hut just like they do in Hawaii. In the center they had a post and a table around the post and then it had benches around and it was just real cute. They took the big alfalfa field and just moved part of it and put this in there, and you could go and buy homemade ice cream with different fruits in it—it was just beautiful. You could have any kind you wanted, so that was a big treat to go out there.

You know how they had those little stands. Just every so often, maybe every mile or so down the road were places where they had apple cider. Everybody sold grapes, peaches, pears, corn. You could buy anything you wanted. It was beautiful, delicious. Everything.

When I worked in the packinghouse they had a six-inch cull belt, and those apples were so big they wouldn't go down that belt. They had a trough with posts and cloth rope wrapped around like that, so as the apples come down slowly they roll over. They kept on rolling over so you could see if there was a wormhole in them.

If you saw an apple with a wormhole you put it over in the cull belt and it went out the back in a pile. That cull belt was stuck most of the time because the apples were over six inches wide.

When I first worked there, those apples were coming at me, you know, and I wasn't used to it, and oh, my stomach was sick and my hands were swelling from grabbing those big apples. I stood there and I kept getting greener and greener. Finally next thing I knew someone had ahold of me and was taking me away from there and laying me down. Oh, I was sick. My arms were swelling. I was packing these big apples. They would just keep a-rolling at you all the time. They were hard to do, and you had to wrap them, too. They had those wax-like papers that you put them in. You would do two at a time and put them in a box for them to be shipped. They had beautiful apples at Manzanar. Everything was big at Manzanar.

RP: How many other people worked at the packing operation?

ER: I think there was about five of us on each side of the conveyor. They were women. I remember there were all women on that. The men were doing the picking at the time you were doing that.

RP: How did you get a job there at the packinghouse?

ER: I had to. I was starving. I had two little kids. I had got married and my husband was gone with somebody else, so I got a job there at the packinghouse. I made twenty-five cents an hour.

RP: What time of year are we talking about when you first got hired?

ER: In the fall—let's see, it must have been around 1930 or '31, something like that. I started out on apples and then [packed] peaches too. I picked peaches too. Peaches were on about the same time. I know that they were rushing the apples so they could get to the peaches before they got too ripe. If there were no apples in the packinghouse then I had to go into the field to pick. So I would go up on a ladder and pick and then you come down off the ladder, and you carefully open this big canvas bag about so wide you had around your neck and let the apples go into a box. The big old peaches would be so big, they would just peel them off, they would be so ripe. Many got too ripe and they couldn't ship them and they gave them away. People could take all they wanted. My sister like pickled peaches and we had pickled peaches till they run out of our ears.

RP: Do you know who ran the packinghouse and who employed you?

ER: I forget his name. I don't know what he did but he was in the office.[7] Anyhow, I was always fast as everything. When I did anything I did it to the best of my ability. So I packed real fast. I picked real fast. He had to go to Red Mountain [Fruit Ranch near Big Pine] and pick pears, and find out why the packers were missing so many worms in the pears. And he said, "Emily could go up there because she is the fastest girl we got." I will never forget it. We went up there and we picked pears, packed pears. They had so many worms in them from Red Mountain that they were complaining about shipping them by boxcar, and they said when the pears got there the worms were sitting on the pears thumbing their noses at them.

RP: So the same company that owned the packing shed at Manzanar also ran the one at Red Mountain?

ER: Evidently. They had a beautiful house there at Red Mountain. Boy, it was a two story—a porch all the way around and all white, you know, and everything. They had a dining room. We were treated royally.

RP: Did you stay there?

ER: No, we came home every night because I had little kids to take care of. There was a lady in Lone Pine that would watch them for me in the daytime and then I'd pick them up and go back to Owenyo. When I got done at the end of the month I didn't have any money, but we did have it pretty nice because we canned apples and we canned peaches and pears. They let us have all the fruit we wanted. We were eating better than a lot of other people. We had big piles of these beautiful apples that maybe only had one wormhole in them, so we canned like mad. I must have had at least a thousand quarts of food canned all the time. We would get together, the ladies and I, and get these double boilers going just for canning. We would put the jars in a pressure cooker and then play cards while the pressure cooker was going. Then we would get up and put some more in. All night long we would do this. It was too hot in the daytime to have the stove going.

RP: The fruit that was packed at the Manzanar shed, was it shipped out on the train or was it trucked out?

ER: As far as I know they put it on a truck to take it out, and I never paid much attention to where they went with the trucks. It was taken to the railroad—the Manzanar station, I believe, and shipped out. See, the narrow gauge went up to Manzanar. The station was there by the railroad track right straight across from that Manzanar Reward road on the west side of the track. It wasn't anything big. It was just a boxcar. Then they finally had to bring in refrigerator cars to keep the fruit from going bad.

RP: Since that was the Depression I guess women working wasn't such an unusual thing. How did you feel about working then?

ER: Nothing ever bothered me. I look back over my life and I thought when we lived in Owenyo we had nothing. But like I told you we made entertainment ourselves. I was poor, real poor, but I never worried about being poor. I just did what I had to do. I had to work to support my children and I did. Then my husband came back and we lived there at Manzanar. We had turkeys and chickens and a couple of sheep.

During the Depression they would bring old trucks up to Manzanar [from Los Angeles]—a whole truck load of young boys, young fellows, anybody that would want to come, and they would bring us some vegetables. I don't know if they did that for anybody else. They did it for us because we gave them meat which they didn't get down south. Those boys had a ball. They would pick apples and fill that truck and then they would take the truck down and give the apples to the poor people in Los Angeles.[8]

Last run of the "Slim Princess," Laws to Keeler, April 1960. *County of Inyo, Eastern California Museum*

RP: Now who was bringing these guys up?
ER: It must have been the City of Los Angeles, to give them employment, and maybe also to give people down in L.A. food that were hungry and stood in the bread line.
RP: Some kind of welfare or social thing.
ER: I think it was a welfare deal sent them up. The trucks were plenty raunchy, many of them, but the fellows loved it at Manzanar. They would bring their sleeping bags and sleep in the packinghouse—they didn't have sleeping bags in those days, they had blankets. So we would give them things to eat and they loved it.
RP: Now the City of Los Angeles had already come in before this time and bought up the land around Manzanar and the agricultural community that was there earlier on in the teens and twenties. The City had the land, but they leased it out to the farmers and leased out the packing operations to this particular company.
ER: I don't know how they did it, but the City didn't own a lot of the land at first because I know people that lived there in a place where they put down a pump. They pumped the water out, so that dried the person below on either side of them and they had to sell. Some of the ranches stayed for awhile. There was quite a bit of fruit left—it was just all over in different places. But then when I finally lived in Manzanar [in 1932–33], the orchards were going fast. They weren't being watered. The City didn't keep them up. It was a shame because it was beautiful up there. Big old trees and birds and everything. You could go across the aqueduct like you are going east and clear on the other side of the aqueduct was alfalfa fields.

When we worked at the packinghouse, one of the guys, Johnny Gorman, he drove the City truck. He worked for the City of Los Angeles and he would pull up about noontime, and we would all run out and jump in the truck with our lunches, and he would say, "Are you going out to eat your lunch again?" And we would say, "Yep, we are going over to the aqueduct to eat our lunch." So he would drive us over to the aqueduct and say, "I'll pick you up in about an hour. I have some work to do." He knew what we were going to do. We all dropped our lunches and jumped in the aqueduct and went swimming there at Manzanar. He'd say, "You didn't swim in the aqueduct, did you?" "No, we didn't swim in the aqueduct." [9] It was telltale, our hair was wet. We laughed at what we were doing, but boy, he was here on time every day to take us over there.

SIX

Concha Lozano Salas (1915–2003)

We were a close bunch of people, a lot of good people

Introduction

When Connie Lozano was growing up in the 1920s in company housing at southern Inyo's soda ash processing plants, the Mexican communities clustered there and in nearby Lone Pine accounted for a third or more of the area's population. A hub of mining, commerce, and transportation since the 1860s, Lone Pine from the start had been a colorful amalgam of Mexicans, Indians, Anglos, Chinese, Chileans, Basques, Germans, and a dozen other groups. Spread across the southern Owens Valley, they labored at desert mining camps, railroad stations, and soda ash operations, worked in stores and livery stables, and managed herds of sheep and cattle.

The town also boasted a high per capita ratio of main street saloons, back street breweries, and other pleasure houses, where paydays—or pay dirt—could quickly turn the ethnic mix volatile. The regular shoot-outs and street brawls cemented an image of Lone Pine as a "loose" place in the minds of more sedate Anglo residents in Bishop and Independence. That unfortunate label hung on well into the twentieth century, obscuring a historic cosmopolitanism, unique in the valley towns, and now enhanced by legions of foreign tourists.[1]

In 1994, Connie talked with interviewer Richard Potashin at the home in Lone Pine where she lived with her husband Silvestre; it was a cozy place, filled with plants, wind-chimes, and family pictures. By then a great-grandmother several times over, she recalled a life circumscribed by economic uncertainty, yet comfortingly ordered around her close family, church, and the community's Mexican traditions.

The husbands, fathers, and sons of the Mexican families constituted the core of a labor force that processed tons of natural soda ash, or sodium carbonate, a derivative of the saline brine and dry beds of Owens Lake used in glass manufacturing, metallurgy, petroleum refining, and cleaning products. The first plant at Keeler, built in 1887, and later those at Cartago and Bartlett, employed hundreds of workers. But as Connie recalls, fluctuating demand and advances in processing methods closed down operations intermittently, often for years, forcing workers and their families to move on to another plant or find new work altogether.

Her memories of girlhood are replete nonetheless with sweet pleasures: Sunday ice cream, fruit from Manzanar, high school graduation. She recalls the annual festival of Mexican Independence Day, one of the valley's largest and most exuberant. Mexicans, Anglos, Indians, and the other groups came from distant towns, ranches, and mining camps to join the celebration. Memorable too, were the outsize western movie star heroes—John Wayne, William Boyd, Gene Autry—who filmed on location in the nearby Alabama Hills and were regulars in Lone Pine hotels and cafés where young Mexican women cooked and cleaned.

The mix of cultures and races in Lone Pine was a more authentic rendering of western communities than popular movie images of predominantly Euro-American frontier towns suggest. Always a meeting ground of diverse peoples, the West nonetheless remained firmly in the hands, economically and socially, of its white settler families and businessmen, who took for granted a superiority of race and privilege—God-given, some believed—that made few distinctions among their subordinates.[2]

In general, Mexicans in Lone Pine occupied a respected, if not entirely co-equal, place in the community. Those from the area's early ranching families or with ties to the *californios*, descendents of the first Spanish colonists in California, were likely accorded more deference by the Anglos. Others traced their presence in the valley to miners, their roots in the arid, silver-rich Mexican state of Sonora.

An estimated ten thousand Sonorans went to the California gold fields in 1849, equipped with little more than superior mining skills. Their success inflamed anti-Mexican sentiment among the Anglo Forty-niners—who wanted California gold to stay in American pockets. Physical intimidation, discriminatory laws, and high taxes on their earnings forced the Mexicans out; dispersing into the state's Central Valley, most took up farm labor, while others crossed the Sierra to prospect in the Owens Valley.[3]

By the 1930s, the Mexican population in southern Inyo was a mix of long-time families, recent immigrants, and so-called wetbacks, or illegal workers. Connie's father, Mike Lozano, had crossed legally into the United States, just ahead of the first wave of migration from Mexico that brought 460,000 Mexicans into the Southwest between 1920 and 1930 to fill post-World War I labor shortages. At the end of the twentieth century, Latinos were the largest minority in the nation and had replaced Anglo whites as the largest ethnic group in California and in both the City and County of Los Angeles.[4]

Connie Lozano Salas, ca. 1937. *Gonzales Family Collection*

Concha Lozano Salas—Interview

My father came first, in 1917. He worked at Saline Valley, where they had that salt tram, but he didn't last very long because he said it would rain or snow up there, and the only one that had a decent place to live was the cook. Then he came down here in the valley and that's when he started working in Cartago, at the soda ash plant, in 1917. His name was Mike Lozano. He was from Jalisco, Mexico.

Richard Potashin: And he came into the United States when he was a teenager?
CS: Just a young man. At that time, they only paid two cents to get across the bridge and they were free. They came right through the border, I think by Texas some place, because it was in Chihuahua, in that area. They never had to get any papers or nothing at that time. And then in 1917 that's when the world war was going on, and they called him to serve. He was drafted, but they didn't take him because he was from Mexico.
RP: What year were you born, Connie?
CS: October 22, 1915, in Los Angeles. My father used to work in the fish cannery in Wilmington [in Los Angeles harbor], and my mother lived right in L.A. She used to cook for boarders. When my father went to Cartago, he decided to bring my mother and me up here. At that time, we didn't have a car, but we rode on the train with all our furniture and trunks. They put it in a freight car, and we rode in the passenger car.
RP: When you came up here, it was a little different from Los Angeles.
CS: It didn't bother me, I was just a little kid. I grew up in the desert. Wherever they made a home, that's where we were and we were happy. When we were going to stay longer, when the job was going to stay open, we'd always try to have chickens so we would have something to eat. Before I started going to school, I was always with them, close to them.

We traveled quite a bit. See, at that time, the jobs were not really just at Cartago. The [California Alkali Company] plant closed down for a while.[5] It was kind of a depression, I guess you would call it, because my dad worked picking grapes in Fresno, which was a big experience for me. We were camping out under a tent. They were picking grapes, but in the afternoon all the families would get together. They had stoves outside, where they cooked, and we used to get together and play out there, the kids.

Then he went to work at I.D. [Inyo Development Company, a soda ash processing plant] in Keeler. Some of the foundations you can still find there. I used to go to Keeler School while we were at I.D. from the time I was in the first grade to the third grade. We lived there until they closed down, so then my dad moved back to Cartago.
RP: Can you tell me a little about where you lived at Cartago?

Gathering trona at Inyo Development Company soda ash plant at Keeler, California, ca. 1925. *County of Inyo, Eastern California Museum*

CS: In 1917—the early part—it was a tent, half of it. It had wood on the bottom and then they had a tent on top. They had nice homes when we came back [in 1924]. At that time the plant was going full-blast. From the fourth grade to high school I stayed there. That was really my home town. So we had a nice place, and we had a garden. My dad worked a lot of hours there. He was a foreman for a crew.

RP: He was in charge of sacking soda ash?

CS: Yes, where they sacked.

RP: Now when he first started there, did they fill up the bags with machines, or did they have to do it by hand?

CS: They had to do it by hand, by shovel, and they had to sew the sacks.

RP: Do you know how many men he was in charge of?

CS: Well, sometimes he had seventy, maybe a hundred men. Because sometimes they put him in charge of not only the ones sacking, but the guys who worked on the furnace. The way they worked the furnace, they had to haul the rock from the marble quarry at Dolomite. That was the lime rock they used to heat the furnace. They used little cars, like mining cars, you know. They'd load [the rock], and they had to use an elevator, and they'd take it up there on top. The cars had the [belly dump] bottom that opened and all the rock would fall in there and it would burn. That was what made gas for the furnace there at the plant.

RP: So he was in a pretty good position there.

CS: Yeah, he worked there for a long time, until they closed down. That's when our Depression started coming in, and there were no jobs and he had to work for the

WPA [Work Projects Administration]. They got $15 a week. And we lived on it. It was a lot of money in those days.

RP: What type of work did he do with WPA?

CS: It was on the road, doing road work, in the county here.

RP: I've heard that Cartago was a very nice company town after 1924, well laid out. And you had a park.

CS: Yes, the men had a baseball team, and they used to play other towns—Bishop and Independence and all that. The company fixed our place really nice. We had a store, a post office, a mess hall, and a clubhouse for the men—the higher-up men. Then they had bunkhouses, and they had another set of little bunkhouses on the side where all the Mexican people used to bunk.

RP: Did everybody pretty much have the same type of house construction?

CS: Well, on one side it was all the same houses. On the other side, there were bigger houses for the bosses. But the homes for the families, they were really nice. In fact, there are some here in Lone Pine yet.

RP: Did you have indoor plumbing in these houses?

CS: No, we didn't. There was only a long kitchen, and there was kind of a front room and one bedroom, and a screened-in porch. Me and Lupe, my sister, had the bedroom, and my folks slept in the front room. When [the plant] was going full-blast, the company did put in—at first it was wooden toilets, and then afterwards they put in regular flush toilets and showers on the outside, away from the house, and so many houses had the right to use them, for the shower mainly.

RP: How were the houses heated, with wood or coal?

CS: They had coal. The company would bring in a boxcar of coal—a gondola, they would call it—and it would cost fifty cents for a big bag of coal. So that's what we used to heat the stove. And then we had our grammar school. And we had a movie house. We had silent pictures. If you knew how to read, it was fine. If you didn't you just watched the picture.

RP: Did you learn to speak English there?

CS: Well, I started school in Keeler and I learned it there. In those days they didn't have kindergarten, or anything like that. First grade and that was it. My folks didn't know much English either, so they couldn't help me. I just learned it.

RP: You said you had a store [at Cartago].

CS: It was called a commissary, and the people that worked there [at the plant], they'd buy books with stamps in them. You know, like welfare, they have those little stamps? Well, they'd say, "I want two books of ten dollars," and they would take it out of your check. And you went in the store, you bought whatever you want, then you just paid it with the book.

RP: So you did most of your shopping at the commissary?

CS: Yes, we did, because my dad didn't know how to drive, and we didn't have a car, so everything was bought there.

RP: Did you order things, like from mail order catalogs?

CS: Yes, we had the Sears catalog, and my mother used to do a lot of ordering, and it would come on the train. The only time that my mother and us would go shopping, maybe once every two months, we would take a passenger train. In the morning the train would go up from Mojave to Lone Pine. And my mother and sister and I would walk up to [the stop at Cartago] and catch the train into Lone Pine. There was a rooming house there on the corner in Lone Pine, Lottie Dearborn's. So my mother used to ask to rent a room, a front one, and my mother would pay her two and a half dollars, I think. She didn't want to charge my mother—they were friends—but my mother always helped her out.

And then we'd load everything. We'd go to the drugstore, buy everything we needed, put it in that room. We'd go to the butcher shop, and we'd buy all our meat there, bring it into the room. We'd go to the other kind of a general store—Morgans had it at that time. It had everything—saddles, harnesses, and cans and yard goods. So then across the street, they had a rental car, they called it, and Felix Castro had it. So, when we got through shopping and everything, my mother would go tell him that she wanted to rent a car, and he would come and bring us from Lone Pine to Cartago with all our stuff.

RP: That was convenient!

CS: Before the rental place there for cars, there used to be a horse livery. There was a lot of ranches here at that time—Spainhowers and Lubkens—oh, a lot of them. And water was great at that time. Lone Pine Creek was loose and it just came right through town. Locust trees were planted all along those streets, and it was a regular town with a boardwalk all the way. It was really western, but the people, I don't know who they were, they decided they wanted to make the town look better and they took all the western atmosphere out of it. Then later is when they started putting it back again, making it look like an old town. What changed their tune is when the movies started coming in, then they wished they had left things alone.

RP: Right, left it western. Were the roads at that time still dirt?

CS: All dirt roads. In Cartago, we had a friend that had a car, a touring car, but he didn't have a top on it. My mother and I and the other family all piled into the car, and we'd go to Manzanar and bring pears and apples from over there. At that time Manzanar was a regular little town. They made apple cider and they shipped out pears and all that fruit.

RP: You didn't have to pick them yourself, did you? You just bought them?

CS: We went and bought them. They just had them already there. I guess their first-class pears they shipped out, the Bartlett pear. And then they had red apples, too. They were good, the Delicious apples. And they used to talk so much about the school there, and they had a slaughterhouse. We never went right into the town, we just went where they used to sell [fruit], right along the highway. When it was time for the apples and pears, we'd take a run over there, every year, and we thought that was great.

RP: Now, you had a garden there at Cartago?

CS: Oh, we grew everything. We had a big patch of alfalfa. And then we had pigeons—and turkeys. We used to sell turkeys sometimes to the mess hall and the commissary. And we had chickens, and we had about four goats that I used to milk every morning and afternoon. That was my job.
RP: Did you sell any of that milk?
CS: No, we kept it there for the house, we used it all. And we had rabbits.
RP: And you sold them?
CS: It was Depression days and it helped. I used to go in [to Lone Pine] when I was going to high school and get orders from Safeway and the Mount Whitney restaurant. There where Dean has the drugstore used to be a Chinese restaurant. They made that chow mein, but instead of pork, because they couldn't get it, they had rabbit. They'd buy three and four of them—tender, the young ones—and Safeway used to do the same thing. So I'd get the orders for my dad and he'd get [the rabbits] all ready. In the morning, I loaded them up with me on the bus. And then I used to tell my principal, Mr. Hoffman, if I was going to be a little bit late, because I had to deliver these rabbits. It was fine. He was a very good man, and he let me. And I had to walk with all these bags and everything, take them to the different places and collect the money. Twenty-five cents a pound, that was all. Half was my allowance, for doing the work.
RP: Did you get together with other families at Cartago very much? Did they have dances or any other activities there?
CS: Oh, yes, the people would get together and make dances. Like the Mexican people used to celebrate Cinco de Mayo and Sixteenth of September, and they'd get together and make a party at the school or at home, wherever they could. There were some Mexican people that knew how to play the guitar and the violin. And then sometimes they'd have—you know Truman Buff from Independence? In those days he was just a young man. He was in a band, and they were hired to come and play.

We passed the time real good. And the families—like in my home, my mother liked to make a lot of *tamales* [at Christmas], and everybody would come. She'd put up a Christmas tree, she'd buy presents for all the kids. And they used to make *bunuelos*, they call them. That was a fried tortilla, and you put sugar and cinnamon on them. She'd make just pans full of that. Then we used to get a lot of Mexican chocolate at that time, and she would make a big kettle of that and everybody would dip the *bunuelos*.
RP: Oh boy, that sounds good.
CS: We had a wonderful bunch of kids in those days. We had some kids living on a ranch outside of Cartago, and there was another white family who lived in another little house there, and they used to come and play with us. In the middle of the night they'd take off for home—not afraid of anything. Or my mother would say, "Well, you kids can't go out like that. You don't know what bug or coyote might get you," and she would put a blanket on the floor, and say "Here, you guys lay down there."
RP: There were a lot of Mexican families at Cartago, I gather. Do you have an idea of how many lived there?

CS: Oh, let's see—I imagine about thirty. And white families. And two nice fellows—one was from Canada, and the other one was an Argentinean, very nice people. They worked there, and they were real friendly with everybody. You know, that town was a very close-together-knitted family there. We never had any problems, there was no such thing as somebody stealing. Never. Everybody would watch for each other.

RP: Connie, do you remember priests coming to the town?

CS: Father Crowley was one that used to be there. He knew my mother real well before she passed away. When he heard that she was real sick and was not going to make it, he went down there to Cartago and stayed overnight with us and took care of her. There was [another] father—he was the one that used to come in and give us catechism once a week. And all the kids, we'd get together on one porch and the priest would come there and teach us. And then we had missionaries. They had their big vans, and in the back they had the altar all fixed up. We all had to stand outside the van. This way they always allowed [the priests] to come in and give services there at Cartago.

RP: Connie, did your dad work a five-day or six-day week?

CS: Five days a week, Monday through Friday. When he was a foreman, he was on call all the time.

RP: Was the plant running around the clock, in full production?

CS: Oh yes, twenty-four hours, three shifts.

RP: Now, did your father have any problems with discrimination and racial comments at the plant?

CS: No, my dad always got along with everybody. My dad was a real fair man. He had blue eyes, red hair—a real light complexion. The people from Jalisco, they're all white. You go down there and you see a lot of these kids that are blond, blue-eyed, and you hear them talking Spanish, it sounds strange. My mother was different, she was dark. She was from Chihuahua. She had more of the Indian, the Mexican-Indian.

RP: Did your father ever talk about the working conditions in the soda plant? Were they very harsh conditions? Was it very dusty?

CS: No, he never complained. He was never sick.

RP: He never had problems with soda ash burns?

CS: No, a lot of them did. A lot of [the sackers] used to have it. It used to affect them, because they would rub it in and then they'd get infected. Sometimes he'd just come home real white, but it didn't bother him. Never.

RP: How about the dust storms on Owens Lake?

CS: No, not on the lake. It had water in those days. But we used to have some terrible winds here, terrible. At Olancha, Cartago, that wind would hit you from the mountains, and it was really, really bad. Some of the houses were knocked off the foundations—they weren't made like they are now. They only had blocks of cement all around. But it moved them, moved the houses. Trees, great big old trees would fall down, and the sand would hit you.

But it doesn't bother me about that soda ash. Some of them say, "Oh, gee, that dust can kill you." See, where we lived at NSP [National Soda Products plant in Keeler], there's nothing left. But when my folks lived there and the dust storms would come up, my mother would put wet towels on the door and the windows, and it would catch the soda ash. But still the houses weren't insulated like now—just clapboards, you know, one-by-twelves and that's it.

RP: So it would come through between the boards.

CS: But then the next day, if the wind blew all night, we could draw our names on the floor, the dust was so thick! But we never got sick from it, never felt any bad effects from it. I'm still here.

RP: You're going pretty well. So after Cartago shut down in 1932, you moved back to Keeler—to NSP this time?

CS: Yes, my dad worked over there in the soda ash plant, too.

RP: Was he a foreman over there, too?

CS: No, just a regular peon, a worker, the same thing, sacking again.

RP: Can you tell me about what the housing was like at NSP? It sounds like it was more primitive than what you had at Cartago.

CS: It was only a kitchen and another room, and they had outdoor toilets there. Then the guys would add—maybe they could get some old lumber and they'd make like a garage deal in the back, another extra room. The parents made their bed there and they let the younger people stay in the house because it was warmer. See, we only had a wood stove. Saturday and Sunday, the guys would get their trucks and they'd haul wood from the [Owens] river. That's where all the wood came from.

They had a commissary too—they used to feed the guys there. And they had a little park that had swings, but there was no grass. Nothing grew there, not even sagebrush. On Sundays we'd walk to church into Keeler, and Father Crowley gave the mass over there. Then after that, there was a little general store, Annie Gandera and her husband had it, and we used to buy ice cream or candy, or whatever they had, and then we'd all walk back to NSP.

RP: Did Father Crowley conduct services every Sunday there at Keeler?

CS: Yeah, every Sunday he'd give mass over here in Lone Pine early, at nine o'clock, and then he'd go down to Keeler. And I think Saturdays was the day he'd go to Death Valley. They didn't call him Father Crowley; it was "The Desert Padre." And he didn't wear the black, he wore khaki with the collar around here and then these breech pants, and he put the other thing [leather gaiter] on top of his shoe and it made it look like a boot. That's the way he used to dress. But he was very good, a very famous father.

RP: Now what was the social life at NSP?

CS: They had dances there, a lot of them. Especially the Mexican people used to. They used to have some big, big deals going on there—dances for Sixteenth of September. They used to bring the mariachis from L.A. A lot of people went from Darwin, there was a lot of Mexican families in Lone Pine, so they'd come out.

And the stations and railroads, like Owenyo and Kearsarge, and Lone Pine Station and Cartago had them.

RP: Were the Mexican families kind of put together at NSP, too—did they all live in the same area, generally?

CS: Yes, they did. And the people from town, and from Cartago, used to go down there and visit, to NSP. They had friends over there. We were a close bunch of people, a lot of good people, all friendly, all got together.

RP: What are your memories of going to high school in Lone Pine, Connie?

CS: Well, I graduated in '36, and we had a very nice school, some very good teachers. Oh, everybody was involved in baseball. And they had a lot of good football games here. Everybody mixed. There was no such thing that somebody was mad at each other because he was a Mexican or he was a white.

RP: What was your graduating class size?

CS: I think there was only twenty.

RP: Did you have a special party for your graduation?

CS: No, nothing. In those days there was no money. I'm surprised I even have a picture of the class. I wanted a graduation ring, and I couldn't afford it. So what I did, my mother would give me twenty-five cents every day to eat. She wanted me to eat lunch in town. Well, instead of that, I'd sneak a sandwich and bring it and saved my twenty-five cents to get me a silver ring for graduation, which I still have.

RP: What did you do after high school, Connie?

CS: After? I got married. To my first husband, Charlie Gonzales. He was working for the railroad as a section hand, over there by Cartago. I was married with him for twenty-one years, and I had all my kids. We had a big wedding here in Lone Pine, at the Santa Rosa Church. November 2, 1936.

RP: Did Father Crowley do that ceremony for you?

CS: Yes, he was the one that did it. And all my children were born here in Lone Pine.

RP: What about after you were married—did Charlie continue with the railroad?

CS: No, he went to work at Bartlett [at Pacific Alkali Company]. He was a sacker, too.

RP: Did your father move back over to Bartlett from NSP later on?

CS: Him and my sister. My sister worked in the office.

RP: Was your dad again at the foreman level?

CS: No, just another worker there.

RP: Okay, so the town of Bartlett was much smaller than Cartago?

CS: Oh yes. See, there used to be a plant there; it was called Kuhnerts. And then that folded up [in 1928], but they [still] had the houses. Then [Pacific Alkali] took over the houses, and they charged $25 a month rent. But we didn't have electricity until Pittsburgh Plate Glass came in [in 1944]. They were the ones that had the lights on. Before that it was just kerosene lamps and wood stoves.

RP: That's in the '30s and '40s, so that's kind of late.

CS: Well, after the lights went on, but even before that, the school bus used to pick up forty-one kids from Bartlett. They used to call it the "producing town." (laughter)

Then PPG built a lot of new things in the town. They improved it real good. They got the water running right straight from the well to the homes—indoors. And we had a swimming hole. We had a lot of fun there. We all had our kids. They'd play baseball in the evening, and they liked to watch the train go by, the passenger train, then there was a freight train. The track used to go right over near the houses. The guys on the train, either the conductor or the caboose man, always threw candy for the kids, and they'd stand right near the line and wait for the guys to throw candy. Or else they'd run under the bridge and hear the noise of the train go by. But finally, I guess it was too much money they were putting in that place, and they closed it down and they just gave it up. That was about 1964.

RP: So how long did your husband work there, Connie?

CS: My husband, this one now, he worked there sixteen and a half years.

RP: How about Charlie?

CS: He was there about eighteen years, I think.

RP: Did he advance in that time?

CS: No, he just was a sacker. When he first started there to work, his wages was only thirty-five cents an hour. And they only worked six hours.

RP: Were there times where production was pretty slack, and he didn't have much work?

CS: Pacific Alkali used to lay off fellows in the wintertime. But when PPG was there, they worked all around the clock. They did a lot of new ways of working there, that they could produce a lot more. So that's the reason.

RP: Now Connie, did you ever work at the soda plants?

CS: No, I never did. They had laundries and motels [in Lone Pine], and I worked at the Dow [Hotel] for sixteen years—where I met a lot of people, a lot of movie stars. Oh, we had Gene Autry there and his helper—they'd leave a note: "If you're the maid for this room, would you wash these socks and shirt for me?" And the next [day] I'd have money on the pillow. I didn't ask them, they just left me a tip. At that time I was only making a dollar an hour, and I was doing thirty and thirty-five rooms myself. There was three of us girls working there, and we had to do the towels and wash everything.

RP: The extra money was welcome.

CS: We had a lot of movies going on then. One bunch would go, another would come in. I knew all those guys. I knew Cary Grant and Douglas Fairbanks. I went [to watch] when *Gunga Din* [was being filmed]. And they had the Spanish Garden [restaurant], which was where all the movie stars went. Very nice guys. They never said "Well, I'm a movie star, we don't talk . . ." No, they were friendly. [People in Lone Pine] didn't go overboard about them, they'd just say hi or something like that.

RP: Pretty common around here—

CS: In fact, some of those guys said they liked to come up here because nobody bothered them, that they could walk up and down the streets and nobody would say anything to them.

RP: People tell me there were a lot of bars in Lone Pine in the '30's and '40's.
CS: Oh, there was. Let's see, the Sierra used to be one. And then there was Nogales, and the Mount Whitney bar, and the Spanish Garden. There was one called the Nugget, and Mr. Ed's. The Nugget was the one that was really wild. They had a lot of fights. They'd knock each other out the window and everything else, but they all survived. The next day they were shaking hands. And then, they had Penney's and Safeway, and a little waffle shop, really good, a nice little place.
RP: Did you go to the movies here?
CS: Oh yes, we used to go to Pierson's movie house. We lived in Bartlett at that time, and Sunday was the day we all came in and brought the kids to the show. That's when we were sitting there watching a movie and all of a sudden they gave the news of Pearl Harbor.
RP: That brings me to another question. Connie, do you remember the day [in March, 1942] when the caravan of automobiles came up to the camp [at Manzanar]?
CS: Oh yes, I remember that. We saw them when they went by. We were still living in Bartlett. And then another thing, they used to grow their vegetables [at Manzanar]. I remember we used to go to Bishop, and you'd see those fields with lettuce growing—in December—carrots, a lot of green stuff that they were growing there all the time. And we'd think, oh no, winter's coming, we don't grow any more, it's going to freeze. They had huge old pumpkins, all that. Mostly it was for their own use. Those Japanese knew how to do it. They're really good growers. I don't know who used to bring it, but they had [some of the food they grew] on display in one of the stores here.

Sometimes we'd be in town, and at first they used to bring them in to go shopping. See, they had a guard who would bring in so many people—ten, and another one had ten—and they went into Safeway and got some things they wanted there, then they'd go in Penney's and buy clothes. And the guard was with them. They never raised any trouble, never tried to get away or nothing. They were good people. My sister was working at that time at Penney's. [She] used to say how they were so polite, so nice to attend to and everything. But then there were some people here in town that didn't like the idea. Somebody said, "If they're going to be prisoners over there, they shouldn't bring them to town." But there were never any problems.

SEVEN

Owen Cooper (b. 1916)

We maintained the individuality of the towns and the newspapers

Introduction

Newspaperman Owen Cooper recalls more than fifty years in the Owens Valley publishing business in this 1991 conversation with Richard Potashin at Cooper's home in Bishop. At Bishop-based Chalfant Press, publishers of newspapers, books, and magazines in the Eastern Sierra for over one hundred years, Owen Cooper managed book production, oversaw printing of the Chalfant Press papers, and was co-publisher between 1942 and 1982. Advancements in technology transformed the publishing business, he recalls, and went hand-in-hand with the social, cultural, and economic changes he also saw taking place after the 1930s in the small Owens Valley towns. There and across rural America, a rich local life and deep attachments to place and community were giving way to the more impersonal and fragmented connections of an urbanized society-at-large.

"The known horizon and the familiar walls are the stuff of community," wrote historian Robert Hine.[1] He'd likely heard of Jim's Place, a popular main street café in 1920s Independence where Owen Cooper dispensed sodas, and locals and travelers gathered for hearty food and good times. It was a humble place, a "small, familiar world . . . inexhaustibly rich in the complication of ordinary life."[2] According to the ancient Romans, the *genus loci*, or guardian spirits of place, watch over and protect such places so infused with meaning and memory.

By 1931 the isolation of the Owens Valley, palpable in Owen Cooper's early descriptions, had eased as the last segment of highway between southern California and Bishop was paved. New waves of fishermen and campers, moviemakers and nature enthusiasts, heading across the desert to the Eastern Sierra's scenic wonders, stopped along the way for gas, lodging, and food, and helped revive the struggling Owens Valley economy.

The leadership group formed in 1936 to promote the Owens Valley as a tourist destination included, not coincidentally, George Savage, editor of the valley newspapers. In frontier outposts, newspapers had appeared early, often before essential services were in place. Looking ahead to future business, they targeted "audiences at home and elsewhere with the message of the town's possible prosperity," even as they "held together" raw communities of disparate people in the face of isolation, Indian conflict, and crop failure.[3]

Owen Cooper describes how the four newspapers he printed and published did both. Extolling the region's recreation opportunities, they also kept the scattered population of the county tied together in a community—one already brought closer by an ingrained conservatism and distrust of outsiders among many residents. Reader favorites were the local columns. Written in an eclectic assortment of styles, they reported on family reunions, bridge parties, vacations, new cars and babies in Benton, Darwin, Cartago, and other distant hamlets.

Owen recalls a rapid transformation at Manzanar, from close-knit farm community and rural landscape to a temporary, mass-produced barrack city of ten thousand people. The announcement in the March 6, 1942, *Inyo Independent* that a "reception center" for uprooted Japanese Americans from the West Coast would be located in the Owens Valley alarmed and angered local residents. In the same issue, news editor Savage had inserted a carefully-worded editorial urging acceptance of the camp as a patriotic duty. Over time, his words were successful in their calming effect; more telling, however, was the requisite promotional message they also contained:

> What may seem to many to be a liability has every possibility of being turned into a real asset. Needless to say, we should consider it our patriotic duty to cooperate with the Army and the department of justice[*sic*] . . . We do not know how many Japanese will permanently be placed here. But we do know that those who are here will offer a large reservoir of labor for certain needed and proposed projects of present and future benefit to this region . . .[4]

Inside the camp, the inaugural issue of the internee-produced *Manzanar Free Press* appeared on April 11, 1942, just three weeks after the first displaced people had arrived. From a two-page mimeographed sheet the *Free Press* grew to an eight page newspaper supported by Owens Valley merchant advertising and printed by Owen Cooper at the Chalfant Press plant in Bishop. Unfailingly upbeat in its reporting, it promoted school activities, social clubs, and sports programs; notified residents of jobs and relocation opportunities; and listed births, deaths, and sons in military service. Not reported was the riot of December 6, 1942, that left two internees dead after Military Police opened fire into an angry crowd gathered at the camp police station.

Owen Cooper and his partner sold the newspapers to a Santa Monica, California, company in 1982; subsequent new owners in 1996 dropped the Chalfant Press name, carried on the mastheads of Owens Valley newspapers since pioneer Pleasant A. Chalfant founded the *Inyo Independent* in 1870. In 1999, Owen Cooper left his quiet Bishop neighborhood to be near his family in San Diego.

Owen Cooper in graduation portrait at Owens Valley High School in Independence, 1933. *Owen Cooper Collection*

Owen Cooper—Interview

I was born on my grandparents' home place on the corner of Melrose and Normandie in Los Angeles. I lived most of my younger life in the town of El Segundo. My father was a night foreman in a machine shop for Standard Oil Company, and I spent time at my aunt's place in Manhattan Beach, and in Redondo Beach, visiting around in that area. I used to ride the old red cars up over the hill and down. I can remember how fast they ran and how they swayed back and forth on the track, because they were traveling at a pretty good rate of speed for that time.

My father was a great fisherman and every summer we would come up into the High Sierra and spend time around Mammoth Lakes—Twin Lakes, and June and Gull Lakes, and Grant Lake. We had spent almost every summer in that area. In 1926 we decided that my dad would quit Standard after eighteen years, and we looked for a place to settle down. We picked a corner of June Lake Junction where the road left [Highway] 395 and circled around June Lake and that loop. We planned on opening up a garage/service station and a little cafe. But when they went to file on that property, they found out that a man by the name of Guy Carrington had filed on it the day before, and he put in the Carrington Service Station and a little lunch counter there. So my folks came on down the valley and they found a place in Independence, a little cafe, and they made a deal to buy that place. We moved up to Independence in 1927, and they operated that, Jim's Place, until my father died of cancer.

Richard Potashin: Now you were born—?

OC: Nineteen sixteen. Made my first trip to South Lake up above Bishop in 1919. I was three years old. We had to back up almost three-quarters of the way because the old Model-T Ford wouldn't go up. You know, the roads at that time, the switchbacks, they didn't give you a good, gradual curve; they just went up the mountain. With the cowl tank [in front], it wouldn't feed and you'd run out of gas and have to turn around and back up.

RP: It was a rocky, dirt road?

OC: Right. And all the roads at that time, they were all one-way with just little turnouts. We used to cross the desert, the Mojave, on our trips up here, and at that time there was nothing but two little ruts. It wasn't until you got up by Aberdeen that they had a cement strip—I've forgotten now, it was about four or five miles long. But I can remember, coming across the desert you'd see the dust of another car coming, [and] you'd have time to pull out so that you could get out of the two ruts over to one rut on the side to let the other car come by. And very seldom did you ever make the trip from L.A. to Bishop and up to the lakes in one day. You always got up to Red Rock Canyon and you'd pitch a tent and get out your sleeping bags and get up early the next morning and make it on up to Bishop and the lakes.

Back in those days almost every year you had a series of cloudbursts, and the rocks and everything would come down and wash across the road, all across the desert. And I've seen boulders as big as a cabin just slowly moving in the mud. We got caught in one, one year coming up, and they had Caterpillar tractors there and they would hitch onto our car and pull us through some of the worst part of it.

RP: Were there a lot of travelers when you were driving up, a lot of people that would stop and camp along the roads?

OC: Oh, there wouldn't be very many. I'd say maybe out of Mojave if you met three or four cars all the way up to, say, Little Lake, you'd be lucky, because there just wasn't that much travel in those days.

RP: You moved up to Independence in 1927 and you finished grammar school and then started high school there?

OC: Right. The grammar school was just one building. I think it was divided into two sets of classes, because I know that that was the hardest thing I had to get used to was having three grades in one room—three different grades. Because, when I went to school in El Segundo, there were about thirty-five, forty kids in one class, but that was just one grade, and everybody was studying the same thing. The other thing that was rough on me was because I came from what they considered Los Angeles. It wasn't Los Angeles, but I was a flatlander, and they all hated the City of L.A. because of the water situation. So I was the scapegoat because I was a new kid from Los Angeles. I'd have to watch out or there would be some guy picking on me all the time because of being a flatlander. You have to live here about twenty-five or thirty years before you're considered a local.

RP: Right, before they ease up on you.

OC: We took a lot of teasing, but eventually we made a lot of friends.

When I was in school, they had quite a bit of action over at Kearsarge, the [train] depot. I used to go over there and work helping the man that had the coal, grain, and the hay business in Independence. I used to bale the hay and shovel the coal. All that stuff came in by train, and then we'd go over and haul that out of the depot back to Independence. Just about everybody there in Independence burned coal. I don't remember what we did to the coal, but I remember being just covered with black when we got through. The hardest job for us kids, because we weren't too big and husky, was unloading bales of hay. They were a hundred pounds apiece, and we'd get a couple of hooks in them and then would have to work our little tails off getting them down, and haul them and then stack them up two or three high, you know, in the flatbed truck. And that stuff would get all in your clothes, it would be hot and you'd be sweating, and you itched like mad.

Then, speaking of that type of stuff, after I had graduated from Owens Valley High, the first job I had was at Manzanar. I and several of the other kids, we got summer work there picking peaches, pears, apples. They had beautiful orchards there at Manzanar, and Consolidated Produce had their own packing plant there. We would be on these big twelve- or fourteen-foot three-legged ladders, you know, and you got this bag hanging over your shoulders. When you get the thing filled up, you just unhook it and the bottom goes out and you get your fruit dumped in the boxes in a hurry. Well, we'd be up on top of one of these ladders, and the guy in the next tree or a couple of trees down would haul off and throw a peach or a pear and knock you off the ladder. You'd be unbalanced anyway, with fifteen, twenty pounds of fruit in that sack hung around your neck. A wonder we didn't get killed.

RP: So the orchards were going pretty strong, even in the '30s there?

OC: They had beautiful peaches, pears, and apples, [and] they were shipping a lot of fruit out of there. That was quite a little town back in '22, '23, '24, and there were lots of ranches all around in that area.

RP: I imagine the fruit was shipped out by rail?

OC: I don't remember whether it was shipped by rail or by truck. I would imagine that they probably trucked it from Manzanar over to Lone Pine depot and shipped it from there, because the main line ended at [Owenyo, the station after] Lone Pine and then from Owenyo up was the narrow gauge.

RP: When you were out there picking fruit as a kid, do you recall many houses or ranches still there, or people living in the actual town?

OC: No, at that time I can't remember any around. Just the packing plants and the orchards was just about all that was left. But I know, boy, at the end of a day, especially if you were picking peaches and sweating, that fuzz from the peaches would get on your hide and just about drive you nuts until you could shower and get rid of it.

RP: How many seasons did you do that?

OC: I don't think it was more than one or two seasons, because shortly after that, why, I don't remember whether the packing plant burned down or was torn down. And then the City cut out the water and the orchards began to die off.

RP: So to your best recollection, the orchards probably ran maybe until 1935 or so?

OC: No, I don't think after about '33 and '34, because I remember later on after they had cut off the water, we used to play "ditch" in the middle of the night, with our cars running through the orchards in both directions with our lights turned off. I can't remember that anybody smashed into another one—

RP: That was a popular sport?

OC: It was like Russian roulette. They were going as fast as you could go down between the rows of trees, and the other cars would be going the other direction. It was just pure luck that—that was after having a few beers.

RP: Your parents bought the cafe, Jim's Place—was that right next to Mairs Market?

OC: That's where the [Still Life Café] is today. It doesn't look the same. The front part on the south side was a big, long soda fountain. I used to be a soda jerk. On the front was a candy counter, chocolates—hand-dipped chocolates—and all that stuff in cases, and I used to get around there and help myself. Then, on the north side of the building there were long booths, tables and booths, and on the south side of the building it was one big, long lunch counter. And the kitchen was in the back. On the south side near the front of the building was a small shed and it had a carbonating machine that pumped, with the CO gas, to make your carbonated water for your sodas. You'd go forward for slow feed—I mean, forward gave you a real hot shot that stirred up the foam, and then you brought it back and it would come out slow and fill up. I used to make root beer floats and sodas, sundaes, and milk shakes. Back in those days, there was no such thing as a bottle of Coca-Cola. I guess maybe they had it, but we always bought drums of the Coke syrup and then transferred that into gallon jugs, and you'd mix your Cokes, cherry Cokes, chocolate, and lime-lemon Cokes, mix them in the little original Coke glasses. You had all of your sizes and shapes of glasses in the back counter, and you were always washing and drying glasses.

RP: And they served lunch, dinner, breakfast, everything?

OC: Yeah, at that time I'd say you had thirty-five, forty people in there at a time. Because at that particular time, they were building the City [of Los Angeles headquarters] offices in Independence and they were doing a lot of construction work and everything. You had all of the truck drivers when they were putting in the Mono Tunnels. They were all stopping there, and you had all of the regulars out of the [Inyo County] Courthouse. It was a busy little place.

RP: Who was Jim?

OC: That was Jim Miller. He was an old-timer there, and he was well-known, so they just named it Jim's Place.

RP: So your cafe had a pretty popular following and reputation.

OC: Oh yes. We had a Chinese dishwasher, his name was Sun Ki Gee, and he was not a low-class Chinese. He was well-off. He ran an importing business. He had a family in China that he sent money to all the time, but he said in the big city, because he was Chinese, they didn't treat him very good, and so that's how he came up. And I don't remember exactly how we got to know him, but we hired him.

So we'd close the place up to the public, say at a certain time in the evening, close early, and then invite all the local regulars, gangs that worked up in the construction and everything at the new City offices, and we'd just turn the kitchen over to this Chinaman, and he would put out the best five- or six-course Chinese dinner that you could ever buy in the most exclusive restaurant. Prior to that he would import all kinds of stuff, these delicacies, thousand-year-old eggs, you know? We'd invite all these people in free because they were all good, steady customers. Well, they'd have a regular party. They'd be singing and playing the accordion or some other musical instrument. You don't see that kind of get-together and friendliness that was in those days. Eventually, when we got rid of the restaurant, he went down and went to work for Mr. Dow that owned the Dow [Hotel] in Lone Pine.

RP: You started in the printing business while you were in high school. You started working with the *Inyo Independent*—was that George Savage who ran it?

OC: Well, I started for Ward Parcher. He had the paper there in Independence at that time, and I started working part-time. Then George Savage and Bob Sanders bought that, and right out of high school, I started working full-time, ten hours a day, five days, six days a week, whatever was needed, at twenty-one cents an hour.

Sun Ki Gee, seen here, ca. 1948, worked at Jim's place in Independence in the 1930s. *Author's Collection*

RP: And the *Inyo Register* was being printed up here in Bishop. Was that another owner who was doing that?

OC: That was Bill [W.A.] Chalfant.

RP: Did you know him very well?

OC: I knew him by name, but after we bought [Chalfant Press], why, every morning I'd come in to work and we were doing a lot of changes, he'd kind of scratch his head and look at me and say, "How's the reform movement going today?" You know, because here I was a young kid and he was an old-time editor and publisher for umpty-nine years, and I was throwing away a lot of stuff and he didn't approve that we were getting rid of it. He figured in a pinch we could go back to doing all this stuff by hand, and that was foolish because it's just out of the question that you would do some of the stuff in the old, slow, costly way.

If you've ever read *The Story of Inyo* [by W. A. Chalfant]—I've never read it myself, I started a few times and just never got around to finishing it—but I guess he spoke his piece, of what he thought of the City of Los Angeles and what they did to this area. When you look back to all the green, lush valley that this was at one time and what a desert it's turned out to be today. I know I've gone out hiking with my dog out in the Laws area, and a good share of that used to be swampland. You can tell by looking at it that they had roads, embankments built up, so they could go from one road out to a ranch. And that was raised because the rest was all swampland.

RP: When you were working there at the *Inyo Independent* in—I guess the late '30s it would be—was it a local paper reporting primarily local news?

OC: It was strictly local.

RP: And did you also have those kind of satellite reporters from outlying areas?

OC: I think they just handled most of the stuff by telephone and by mail, people [who] gathered the news, or wanted something in the paper. Later on, they hired correspondents and they were paid so much a column inch for the space that they were submitting. They had correspondents in all of the little towns: Olancha, Cartago, Keeler, Darwin, Death Valley, Tecopa, Shoshone, all the little places.

RP: The *Inyo Independent* then bought the Lone Pine paper?

OC: Right, there was a *Progress Citizen* in Lone Pine. We bought that paper, and then eventually we bought the *Inyo Register*. We were printing the *Inyo Register* in Bishop and we were doing most of the typesetting and everything for the southern papers in Lone Pine and bringing the type up to Bishop. They had the press up there and were printing the paper. And then they bought the Mono paper, the *Chronicle Union*, and then the *Mammoth Herald*. Eventually we put in a big four-unit Web press and we moved all the equipment and everything into a new plant in Bishop down on East Line Street. But we maintained the individuality of the towns and the papers. We featured the Lone Pine stories and the main news on the front page of the Lone Pine paper, Independence on the front page of theirs—in other words, the inside of the paper was the same on all four papers, but we changed the front page so that it pretty much gave each town a share of the news, and that was their paper.

Then, when the new owners took over [in 1982], they said, "Hey, we're big city people, we're not for this little town stuff." So they made it the *Inyo Register* and they dropped all the others. And now they've got an *Inyo Register* that has mainly Bishop stories, and they just kind of let all the other towns fall by the side. In the old days we were there to serve the public and do everything we could to increase tourists and put on deals to honor all the sportswriters from all the metropolitan newspapers, give them free liquor and meals, butter them up, because they sent all the fishing and hunting stories, "Dateline Bishop." They don't do any of that stuff now.

RP: So the paper then was really actively involved in promoting the area.

OC: Right.

RP: I wanted to go over your involvement with printing the *Manzanar Free Press*. You said that you set up the type and printed the paper.

OC: They had their own editors and advertising people, reporters and all, and all they did was submit copy and layouts for the ads. A woman linotype operator there [in Lone Pine] and I set the type and made up the pages and printed the paper.

Advertising the Owens Valley's newspapers, ca. 1960. *The Inyo Register*

We printed it three days a week, and it ran all during the war. They would want special editions of the paper, sort of pictorials with more photographs and stuff, and we would run eighteen and twenty thousand copies on each one of those extra specials. They were in addition to the normal paper—that was right around 10,000 copies each regular edition.

RP: Did you ever go in and actually spend time with the newspaper staff at all?

OC: No. I knew them from talking on the phone to them, and I'd met them, but never spent any time or anything. They handled the whole thing and submitted the copy and everything.

RP: Who brought the copy down to you in Lone Pine?

OC: I think some of the camp personnel, not the Japanese. I think it would mainly be the truck drivers.

RP: And you dealt with Roy Takeno, I guess?

OC: He was one of the editors there.

RP: And how would you rate the skills of the staff and Roy as newspaper people?

OC: They were real professionals. I said before, when it came to laying out an ad, if we had had the lithography equipment that we have now, we would have been able to just photograph their ads and reproduce them, because they were artists. You could look at any of the typefaces and know exactly what type they meant, whether it was italic or cursive letters or Roman block letters. They did a job. They really knew what they were doing. They would submit a dummy for each page of their paper listing the stories, and when that type was set, it would match exactly. They could compute their copy exactly, right down, I'd say, to the line, and so you never had any trouble making up their pages because everything would fit.

I would go to work—leave Independence around eleven o'clock at night and drive past Manzanar and the big tower. They would turn their spotlight on me, and the next tower would pick me up until I had passed the last tower, to make sure that nobody got out or in the car as I went by. And I'd put together their paper and get it printed; usually it was right around 6:30 or seven o'clock in the morning. I'd finish and I'd climb up on a stack of paper and go to sleep, and then the office gal would wake me up about eight o'clock or 8:30, and I'd go ahead and do my regular shift. All during the war, I would average between eighty and eighty-five hours a week. I can remember my partner Todd Watkins would write a story, and while I was running the linotype and setting the type up, I'd look over there and he would be sound asleep with his head on the typewriter. And I'd wake him up and he'd write another story.

We were setting this stuff for the Jap paper and everything in Lone Pine. Then we bought a Ford panel truck, a wagon, and we'd take all those galleys of type and bring it up to Bishop. They had the bigger newspaper press up here in Bishop. First we were running an old, very crude cylinder press, but it was hand-fed. But when they started increasing that run to eighteen and twenty thousand copies, we switched to a smaller press that was mechanically fed that would run about three and a half, four thousand copies an hour. We had to go to that because you can't stand there and hand-feed big sheets of paper. But we got to the point where we just had to tell them, "We can't put out any more of these special editions." We could keep the three times a week [paper] going, but there was only myself and Todd and an office girl during the war. And then, when you're already doing eighty hours a week. Of course, they had the money, the government was furnishing the stuff.

RP: How big was the paper, the *Free Press*?

OC: I don't think any of them were more than about eight pages for their regular editions. But their special editions, they were around, I think, eighteen to twenty-one pages.

RP: And it was all printed in English? There was never any Japanese or anything in the paper?

OC: No, nothing but the names.

RP: Now, did you deliver the papers back there, or how were the papers taken back up to the camp?

OC: They had a flatbed truck, a stake truck, that was in town every day for supplies, and the driver would drop off the copy and then he would pick up the papers and deliver them out to the camp. The only time I went in to the camp was to deliver special scrip and invoices and stuff that they would request. The government would call up and say, "Hey, we've got to have requisition orders and we've got to have twelve copies in twelve different colors of paper." Well, during the war, we were unable to get all this stuff—you know, you were on allocation. I'd say, "Hey, there's no way I can get this." "You just be ready. A truck will deliver it Friday morning." And they would requisition umpty-nine reams of twelve different colors, and we'd print it. Period. Everything came from government requisitions. If you had to have a special weight paper or something and you couldn't get it, they'd say, "Don't worry, we want it, we will furnish the paper." And so you got everything. You were practically told, "We don't care how tired you are, it's got to be done and you've got to do it. You're the only print shop in the area, so do it."

RP: So you handled most of the printing needs of Manzanar, would you say?

OC: We printed purchase orders, requisition orders, we printed all of the camp scrip. And then, with all their graduations, maybe we'd have five hundred, seven hundred individual orders of fifty cards and fifty envelopes and fifty little business cards. It kept us busy doing a good share of the stuff from Manzanar.

RP: Owen, how much did the camp contribute to the local economies of Lone Pine and Independence?

OC: I think that camp kept Lone Pine going during the war. I think if the camp hadn't been there, there would have been a lot of businesses in trouble, because of all the employment it created. Just like with the printing, it accounted for a good chunk of our business. It was guaranteed government income, and a lot of it was just that extra push that kept us going.

RP: You figured that they might have accounted for maybe 25 percent of your overall business?

OC: Yes, I would say.

RP: Another question is, did the copy have to go through some type of government channels, a censor or something like that, before it could be sent out?

OC: I believe it was approved, but I never, ever saw anything that was censored. I mean, it could have been censored out there. We didn't see it—nothing came there that was crossed out or anything. Whatever came to us was the final copy, and I don't think there was any need to censor the stuff because mainly it was all camp news. There was news of other relocation centers and all, but those papers weren't circulated outside; they were the camp newspapers. It was a complete little city of over 10,000 people.

RP: When you were in the camp, did you ever shop at the [co-op] store or anything like that?

OC: No, I never bought anything directly in the camp. I think I got one of the workers to buy me a pair of Florsheim shoes for about five bucks when they were twenty-five or thirty or thirty-five retail. The only thing that I got regularly from the camp is each day that they came in to pick up the paper, they'd always send a lug box of fresh vegetables in that we'd all share, because they grew just about everything out there.

RP: You told us the story about the riot, about where you almost got caught in the middle of that.

OC: Oh, I had to deliver several cartons of this camp scrip, which was as good as cash to the Japanese. When I got to the guard gate, they wouldn't let my wife and son go in. They had to stay out there in the guardhouse and I went in alone. And when I got there, there were hundreds of Japanese, and all speaking Japanese, just a yakking away and milling around. I didn't know what was going on and I couldn't locate the MPs. I was at the headquarters, but all the MPs were out putting down fights and stuff. It was just before the riot, and there were little disturbances going on all around the camp. Finally, a couple of the MPs came back to the headquarters and I got all these cartons unloaded. I couldn't just leave them, you know—there had to be somebody to sign for them and put them in a safe place. And when the MPs got back there, why, the crowd started clearing out when the jeeps pulled up. Here I looked back of where all this crowd was and here's a trench along there and here are the soldiers lined up there with—I don't know whether they were machine guns or rifles or what, but I could see soldiers lined up there facing us. I was glad to unload the stuff and get in the truck and get back out of there.

And then it wasn't too long after that, the riot broke out. You never knew exactly how many people were killed, but quite a few, I imagine. Because you know with the government and the Army, you never hear exactly what's going on. It was pretty hush-hush, I think, the number that were killed out there. And all of them—I imagine a good share of them could speak English, but all of them that were around there, they were all jabbering sixty miles an hour in Japanese and I couldn't find out anything where the MPs were, you know. So it turned out nothing happened, as far as anything happening to us, but I was glad to get back out of the camp.[5]

EIGHT

LaVerne Reynolds Zediker (1919–1996)

I was what they called a real good cowgirl

Introduction

The real West and the mythic West are "engaged in a constant conversation," says historian Richard White; "each influences the other."[1] LaVerne Zediker joins that conversation with these recollections of growing up on a ranch near Manzanar and working in the family stock-raising business. It was work she loved, she explained to interviewer Richard Potashin in 1993. Cattle drives and the backcountry packing outfit she owned with her husband took her into the high meadows of the Sierra, and the movie companies filming Westerns at the ranch near Lone Pine brought her behind the scenes in the making of a mythic West, where real cowboys rubbed elbows with the actors who played them.

For most of the twentieth century, an idea of the American West, imagined as a land of big skies, open space, majestic mountains, and unfettered freedom, found its way into the American psyche and around the globe. The dominant figure and quintessential hero of this landscape was LaVerne Zediker's male counterpart, the cowboy. His lean frame, rugged countenance, and trusted horse embodied the mystique of individualism and manliness associated with a popularized western past, as his mythic stature seemed to grow in direct proportion to his ubiquitous presence in Western dime store novels, films, TV series, toys, and advertising. By 1958, filmmakers were cranking out a Western movie every week, and thirty of the prime time shows on TV the following year were Westerns.[2]

Missing from this West, though, was the cowgirl—or cattle-woman. She was all but invisible, left out of accounts that extolled the adventures of the trappers, explorers, miners, and farmers who pushed westward and settled the nation's new territories. More innocuous female images took hold instead, modeled after nineteenth century notions of women's traditional roles brought West with the household goods and farm tools. Best known was the "Madonna of the Prairie." A saintly, hard-working helpmate in a masculine milieu, she tended family and hearth and brought to the rawness of early settlement a civilizing influence and sense of moral order. The "loose" or notorious woman was her antithesis, the prostitute or dance-hall girl, a woman who defied convention and sometimes the law as well. "What a mystery she is," said one historian of the cattlewoman. "How have we missed her all these years?"[3]

But women like LaVerne Zediker, and her mother before her, have lived and worked on ranches and cattle spreads since stock raising began on the plains and in the mountain West early in the nineteenth century. Deserted wives or widows, or simply the adventurous and free-spirited women managed and owned the business of stock raising and did their work, too—the calving drives to summer range, selling, buying, and breeding.

Traditionally a family enterprise passed down through generations, profitable stock raising has remained dependent for one hundred or more years on inexpensive and unimpeded access to the West's "free range," now nearly 270 million acres of range and forest grazing lands overseen by the Forest Service and Bureau of Land Management. The Taylor Grazing Act of 1934 that brought grazing on more than 100 million acres of publicly owned land under federal management also divided up the range, creating the leased allotments now granted to cattlemen under renewable permits.

The dispute over livestock grazing on public lands is an old one. Opponents argue that despite increased fees, reduced herd sizes, and new restrictive measures, the federal government in effect still subsidizes the nation's cattle ranchers at a cost of about $124 million annually.[4] More to the point, they insist, is the toll grazing has taken on the land itself, to the detriment of recreation and other uses of it. But without access to those lands, ranchers counter, production drops, beef prices rise, and local economies are bound to suffer.

In the Sierra, the expansion of Sequoia National Park in 1926 and designation of Kings Canyon in 1940, the creation of the John Muir Wilderness in 1964, and new restrictions effective since the 1970s have gradually reduced summer grazing areas available to Owens Valley ranchers. The environmental ethos of the late twentieth century, together with the legions of urban backpackers and hikers in search of a pristine wilderness experience, has engendered an influential lobby committed to shrinking still further—or eliminating altogether—stock in the Sierra canyons and meadows that LaVerne describes.

Up the winding road into the hills behind Lone Pine, near where LaVerne and her family ranched, the landscape is breathtakingly scenic—a panorama of snow-capped peaks the backdrop to mammoth clusters of weathered granite outcrops strewn across

LaVerne Reynolds Zediker, at her family's ranch near Manzanar, ca. 1935. *Country of Inyo, Eastern California Museum*

the desert brush. "Symbolic landscapes," geographer D.W. Meinig has called those places familiar for the imagined pasts they represent.[5] The scenery in the Alabama Hills *is* familiar; cowboys and Indians of countless Western movies have ridden dusty trails among the towering rocks as the cameras rolled and the West came to life for moviegoers around the world. The majestic peaks and wide blue skies star in TV advertising, too, for SUVs, beer, cell phones, and soft-drinks—consumer props of modern life set in an Old West landscape. "It looks like they built these mountains for the movies," said one film director of the Owens Valley scenery. "Maybe all of America looks like this," a British fan recalls thinking about the Lone Pine Westerns of his boyhood.[6]

Laverne Zediker—Interview

My grandmother was born at Panamint City. They always said that she was the first white child born in that area and that the Indians came around to see the white papoose—the pale-faced papoose. Her folks were miners and were one of the first at Panamint City. They came across Death Valley in a covered wagon.

Richard Potashin: That would have been probably the 1870s, since Panamint City was going about that time. An arduous trek. Do you have any stories about their time there?

LZ: No, I don't. I think my grandfather was always a miner, and I think he also worked cattle. Most of those older ones were miners, and then they went into ranching. There never was very much said about him, you know, whenever I was around. I know he passed away fairly young. [His family] originally came from England. [His] name was Aaron Reynolds. My grandmother's name was Annie Bastian.
RP: Were there other mines in the area where [your dad's] parents worked?
LZ: In the Darwin mines, and all of those along the White Mountains. But I think he spent quite a bit of time after they moved here to the valley in the Cerro Gordo. My dad [Fred Reynolds] even as a young fellow worked there. I don't know how much, I think it was just one or two seasons, in the winter, because the summer was when they worked the cattle mostly.
RP: Do you know the year your dad was born?
LZ: Eighteen ninety-five, in Independence. That's where my dad lived all his life. He was a cowboy, one of the old, real cowboys. He started following cowboys around, I guess, when he was eight or nine years old. He went with the cattle as soon as the guys would take him. You know, in those days they started working young, the hard way, but I think he was about ten or so before he really got to go back up into the mountains with the cattle. He worked for a cow man [first], and when he and my mother were married, they started collecting their own, the hard way.
RP: A few here, a few there?
LZ: Built up, yes. He worked mostly for the Mairs brothers, Ray Mairs and Pete Mairs. And then he worked up until he was foreman for the Mairs, and took care of their cattle, taking them to the mountains.
RP: Do you recall some of the areas where the Mairs took their cattle?
LZ: Yes, because they were doing it from the time I was going. They started out in the Rock Creek area—the Big Whitney area—which is the northern part up in back of Lone Pine, in there. And then when that went into wilderness, we were shifted on down to what is called Templeton and Brown Meadows—and Horseshoe Meadow. But from the time he was going up, until, oh, I guess I must have been eleven or twelve when they got put out of the Rock Creek-Big Whitney area, they run them in that area for all those years.
RP: Now what year were you born?
LZ: Nineteen nineteen, in Independence.
RP: And how many children did Fred and Hazel have?
LZ: Just me. I was the only child, and I was with my dad all the time. I was what they called a real good cowgirl. My dad said I was better than any cowboy when it come to knowing what to do and where to be and everything. I was my dad's boy/right-hand man.

I went to school till I was in the third grade in Independence, and then we moved to Manzanar and I went clear through the eighth grade. There was two of us graduated from Manzanar—by then the school was getting smaller. When I first moved to Manzanar, it was a two-room school. There were classes and the two teachers, but I think it was the next year when I was in fourth or fifth grade, we didn't have so many, so it was just in one room all the rest of the time. You know there was a big apple-packing plant there [across from] the Bandhauer store and the post office and the gas station. And when it was harvest time, these transient followers of the packing plant came in with their kids. And we just hated that because those kids didn't care about anything; they'd just come into school and disrupt it. They'd cuss the teachers and wouldn't pay any attention, because they knew they were only going to be there maybe a month at the most. We just dreaded those kids coming. And some of them would be so mean. Oh, they were mean, you know, because they weren't supervised. Their folks were working, picking and packing, and they were just running. I can remember one batch of them making the teacher cry. And we thought she was really tough, that [she] could handle any kid.

RP: That would have been towards the fall?

LZ: In the fall, and then they'd be there maybe a month and be on their way.

RP: Where did these families stay? Was there surplus housing, or did they set up tents?

LZ: I can't remember where they lived. I know it was all right around the packing shed there. The school was right up from the store. There was a street that went right on up from where the store and packing plant was. It wasn't too far to the school.

RP: Where did your family move to at Manzanar?

LZ: The first place we moved into was what was called the Albers Ranch, and it was an old, old house up on George's Creek, up quite a ways off the highway. We were there for several years, and then we got to move over to George's Creek into this newer house. I don't know what year that was. There were alfalfa fields and everything in Manzanar—it was pretty good-sized—and quite a few people living there, either raising hay or the fruit.

RP: Originally, Manzanar was drawn up as a subdivision type of situation. So were the ranches all kind of uniform acreage?

LZ: No, and they were just scattered, not really a pattern to them. It was centered mostly around town, or what they called the town, and the orchards were pretty well planned out. But when you came to the alfalfa ranches and those scattered out away from the orchards, why, they were different sizes and kind of not plotted out very good. And, of course, where we lived, on George's Creek, that was all meadow pasture where we run cattle. We did raise wild hay there too.

RP: So your father owned the acreage?

LZ: No, it was all leased. It was City leased.

RP: The City had already come in?

LZ: Oh yes. The City started coming in when they built the [Los Angeles] aqueduct. In 1913 was when they finished it, I think. Well, they had started scaring people, that they weren't going to have any water, and they were selling their ranches and everything to the City. So, by that time [1927–1930], the City pretty much owned everything in the valley, with a lot of [the ranchers] leasing it back and then real unhappy that they had sold. But the City did that so they could get the water rights.

RP: Do you have an idea of how many families were living at Manzanar when you moved there? Was there still a sizeable community?
LZ: Oh, maybe twenty to thirty families, I guess, on scattered ranches. At that age you're not paying that much attention. Since they closed that all in for the Jap camp, why those roads are gone from the overgrowth. I'd like to go and hit each one of the streets, and I could just almost tell you who lived where.
RP: Did you ever pack apples at the packing house?
LZ: No. I stayed away from those kids. We went through it as a class a couple of times, just for school, so that I can remember seeing those conveyor belts and the women standing there, picking those apples over and wrapping them, you know. Gee, they could wrap those so fast! Beautiful apples. They really raised beautiful apples. They had pears, too, but the apples were the main thing.
RP: On George's Creek, the irrigation water was from the creek itself?
LZ: Yes.
RP: There was some restriction on water?
LZ: Not at that time.
RP: And your father had quite a few head of cattle over there?
LZ: Along with the Mairs'. As he gradually built his herd, he run his cattle with the Mairs', and took care of all of them. In fact, the only time Mairs would come was when it was beef selling time. He'd come with my dad and with the beef buyers, but the rest of the time my dad run it like it was his. Nobody had a better foreman than that—they could just trust him and know that he'd take as good care of them as if they were his.
RP: So he would buy calves from local ranchers?
LZ: Yes, that's the way he started, by getting the calves that people didn't want. And he and Mom would hand-feed them. My dad took care of the Schabbell cattle in the summer, too. They'd run their cattle up in the mountains, in the same area. Of course, he was range manager in the mountains, so he took care of keeping the cattle spread out. You know, you kept them off of the main meadows all the time during the summer, so there was quite a bit of moving cattle because they [wanted] to stay there. And you couldn't understand why because the feed was so good up in the higher meadows and what we call stringers. They're little canyons with streams and little meadows. They had natural springs and stuff in the canyons. But they'd come back down into the big [meadows], and you tried to save that for fall, so that when you started bringing them in you had the feed for them, to hold until you could bring them out.
RP: So it was a real effort to try to keep them up there.
LZ: There was nothing like it. I loved that. I miss it.
RP: When did you first go up in the mountains with the cattle?
LZ: I was three months old the first time my folks took me up into Onion Valley. Of course, the next year I was older and went up into Big Whitney. My dad carried me in front of him on the horse. I think I was about five or six when I got my own horse, with my legs out like that. We took my girls up, too, when they were pretty young.

RP: What was that like, to be up there as a kid?
LZ: Oh, it was special, real special.
RP: So your father was the range manager. He managed a lot of different herds?
LZ: Well, they all run together, see, so you just knew the brands and stuff, because they were all mixed.
RP: Then you'd have to sort them out later on, I guess?
LZ: In the fall they sorted them and parted them out.
RP: When you'd drive the cattle up in the summertime, how many hands would you need ? I guess it depended on the size of the herd?
LZ: Well, Mairs had a pretty good herd, along with my dad's. We usually had about eight cowboys to take them in.
RP: And how many head of cattle are we talking about?
LZ: I think around 1,500, give some, take a little. I'm sure Mairs had at least a thousand head. It took about three days from the mouth of the canyon where they went in to get back into the Whitney and Rock Creek area. Then they'd spread the cattle out up there. And when we got transferred, we were taking them in at Cottonwood Canyon. The cattle then were coming from Manzanar. The Mairs had leased a lot of the Department of Water and Power [land] there, and it would take us—let's see, one, two, three, the third day from Manzanar into the canyon itself. And then it would take us two days into parts where we spread out our camp.
RP: The main grazing areas?
LZ: Yes, and that was hard, hard work.
RP: Was there a certain established trail?
LZ: Oh, they were regular trails. They were used for the tourists, too, for the packers and everything. I know we had that to contend with, that we were wrecking the trails, in the latter years. The first years, people weren't so particular. That was mostly Forest Service that complained about that because they went strictly tourist, you know, and just were trying to ease the cow man out—which they have pretty much—and they were the ones that [said] we'd have to go back and kind of clean up the trail. I can remember my mother being so mad where she said she was going to take a broom and sweep the trail for them. I mean, sure, they knocked rocks into them and everything, but the Forest Service didn't keep them up that much, as much as we did, but they were the ones that really—
RP: Imposed some additional restrictions on your operations. And that affected your productivity?
LZ: Oh yes, they just gradually have been getting [the cattlemen] smaller, cutting them down on their permits and everything.
RP: Early on there weren't very many restrictions on that type of thing?
LZ: No, because most of the rangers that worked this area as I was growing up, they were old, rough guys that had just worked up to their jobs through hard work, the same as all the rest, and they more or less just kind of watched that nothing got too hurt and that the cattle were kept spread out so it would balance the feed. But when

my husband went to work [for the Forest Service], he graduated out of high school and came to work up here. At that time, they could work, I think it was eight years, and then they'd take an exam and they could then go on higher into the Forest Service if they wanted to. And there were a lot of them that went to work at that time he did, and when it got to their seventh year, they passed a law or something that they had to be college graduates to be in the ranger area. And those college graduates, all they knew was behind a desk and a book, and all of these [other] fellows had been out in that country and knew it, knew it all. And they all quit. There were about four of them in his area that worked with my husband. They were really provoked about it so they just quit.

And from then on it was entirely different. Well, some of them couldn't even ride a horse, and that was all horse area. You had to ride horses and pack mules to get in and out of there, and they had to learn that. So they didn't really know anything about the running of cattle and everything, but the cow men had to go by what [the rangers] thought they were doing wrong.

RP: You said that it was about a three-day trip from Manzanar to Cottonwood.

LZ: Right, down below Lone Pine and into the canyon a little ways, above the power plant there [into] what we call the "Worm Hole." Well, [it was] the end of the road to that area, and we shoved them up and let them work their way up during the night. A lot of them would just really go, and just keep right on going. They knew where they were going. But there was always those tail-end ones that didn't want to and would be waiting there in the morning when you came, to be pushed on up.

RP: Oh, I see. So you would just camp for the night and allow them to wander around?

LZ: Right, it would be afternoon before we'd get there on that day, and we had a camp there. Then the next morning we'd go and get those that were waiting, no further than where we had pushed them.

RP: Were there other camps along the way as you went down from Manzanar?

LZ: Well, the first night we stayed in a field below—it used to be Bonhams, that housing area just north of [Lone Pine] on the road that goes to the depot. Then the next night was at the old Jack Hale place, down on past the RV park [south of Lone Pine]. They used to have a big tank and the train would fill up with water there all the time, and we were in that field right below where there's sort of green on this end of [Owens] lake, and that was our second night. Then the next night was up into the canyon.

RP: You'd have to cross the highway at some point, wouldn't you?

LZ: Yes, we crossed it right at the Alabama Gates [aqueduct] spillway there.

RP: And of course there wasn't much traffic in those days.

LZ: Towards the latter part it was kind of rough, you know, really dangerous. And you'd get a cowboy up there on both ends to slow [the traffic], because it was narrow. We had to cross right there at that bridge, and you'd be surprised how [the cars] just wouldn't pay any attention to the cowboy trying to slow them down. Then it got to where we had to get a highway patrolman to be there to slow them down at those places. And the same further down. Let's see, where did we cross back over onto the west side? I guess just a little before we got to Cottonwood, we crossed over and then started up towards [the canyon].

RP: And, say with eight cowboys, how were they placed?

LZ: Well, they'd just kind of spread themselves out along, from the front end on down through, with somebody in the back.

RP: You were in the back?

LZ: My dad and I were always in the back. And my mother. She buffered, too. We just all did. We were the tailenders, to be sure. Eat the dust. Because those cowboys, they'd take off right quick to get the lead and along the sides.

RP: And when you set up camp at some of these places, like the Bonham Meadow, did you pitch tents or did you sleep outside?

LZ: No, we just slept out. And we always had a cook. He'd be ahead, you know. Like there he was in a truck until we got up and had to put all the stuff on pack mules. Then he would take the pack mules and go on ahead and have camp kind of set up and food a-goin'. We had to. It was long days, and you didn't want to cook. Of course, during the summer [up in the mountains] when we were moving cattle and everything, there was just the three of us. And sometimes, well, Pete Olivas or Leaky Olivas [from Lone Pine] would be with us for the summer, just to keep their horses up there, and they'd help. But then my mother and I'd have to come in and cook when we got in from working all day and moving cattle.

RP: So you spent the whole summer up there?

LZ: Oh, all my growing up I never was in the valley in the summer.

RP: And the other cowboys would just leave?

LZ: Yes, they came and went to their different jobs. They were just to go in and then they'd hire them again in the fall.

RP: Did you have a permanent cabin up there?

LZ: The one we had the most years was at Templeton [Meadow].

RP: Do you know the history about who built these cabins?

LZ: Well, most of the cattlemen themselves kind of in the early years built them, in each place that they were. Now, like the one at Big Whitney, I really don't know who built that because I was just real young there.

RP: Now, the cabins weren't restricted to certain families' use, were they? If you were in the area and were grazing cattle—

LZ: Well, if your permit was for there, that really was your cabin to stay.

RP: And the Forest Service issued these permits? And the rangers would be up checking occasionally?

LZ: Yes, there was a ranger station up there at Tunnel [Meadow]. That's where the district ranger stayed in the summer. And also at the Tunnel was the telephone operator for the mountain phones. It was usually the ranger's wife that did it.

RP: And they were at each cabin?

LZ: Yes. That's one of the things my husband did, as a ranger up there. One of his main jobs was keeping all the lines up. They had a good line system at that time, for many years, and we each had our own little ring. Ours there at Templeton was a short, a long, and a short. The Tunnel was four longs.

RP: On a typical day out on the range or the meadows out there, you'd get up pretty early in the morning?

LZ: Well, no, not in the summer, but when you're getting ready and taking the cattle in and bringing them out, you did. In fact, bringing them out, you brought the beef out first, and they had to be driven kind of slow or they'd lose all their weight. But we'd get up at two o'clock in the morning. I know a lot of times we'd get to coming out with the stock cattle, and it would be nine o'clock at night before we'd get pulled into camp down in the canyon. So they were long days. Taking them in and out. And gathering. When you gather in the fall, they're long, hard days.

RP: Did you ever lose any cows up there?

LZ: Well, they always would have to go back for a second drive to check out different ones. My dad could almost look at a herd and say which cow was missing. He just *really* knew his cattle. Or tell you which cow was which calf's mother. He'd know, after he'd kind of ridden through them. There'd always be some stragglers that were hidden around in the willows or somewhere that the cowboys had missed.

RP: So the cows would calve up there, too?

LZ: Sometimes. Now they calve in December and January, because the buying is different than it used to be. Ours always calved in the spring, early spring, and they'd be pretty good-sized by the time they were ready to start up. But there would be some that were born later up there.

RP: Recently, a lot has been made about antibiotics in meat and these implants. You didn't do any of that, did you?

LZ: No. About the only thing you vaccinated for in those days was black leg and hoof and mouth disease type of things. Most of the [cattle] was all raised here. Oh, they'd go and change bulls all the time, but they were always a good, healthy bull that the cattlemen would buy and bring in. But then they started bringing in cattle from all around, and then that started bringing in all kinds of different diseases. And then it gradually got to where they had to just vaccinate for—oh, every year there was something else added.

RP: I was going to ask if you were resupplied at all during the summer. You took everything, all your supplies up on that first trip?

LZ: Right, and then different people that might be coming up, they'd call and want to know if there was anything they could bring. Then in the latter years, the plane would bring us [supplies]. We had a strip just below the cabin there at Templeton. There was one guy from over [in the] Bakersfield area that used to fly into Tunnel a lot, and he fixed up a little camp just down by the runway where he'd come in for the weekend, just to get up there in the mountains and fish. And he'd call and bring us stuff, too. And then my dad would come out, I think around in August it was, to hay at Manzanar, to cut that wild hay and all, and then he'd bring back more supplies. So you never were too much out. And we butchered our own meat up there all the time. The best meat in the world. We furnished Cottonwood Lakes. They had a resort there all through the years. They bought their meat from my dad. We butchered and packed it over there.

RP: Did you have a spot, a little slaughterhouse, or just—

LZ: No, you'd just pull them up in the trees. And it was well taken care of. See, [my dad] was a butcher, and the nights, it cured your meat just beautiful up there. You covered it in the daytime, and it was shady, or built a screen thing, and in the shade it was always cool, and then real cold at night, cold enough that the meat kept real good.

RP: How was the fishing up there?

LZ: Golden trout. All golden trout. It used to be. It isn't now at all. It's just really fished out. Because in later years when I was in high school and college, why, the airplanes started coming in and bringing people, and they really just fished us almost dry there. Years and years ago, the cattlemen, a lot of them, planted fish. I think my dad as a young fellow planted. They'd carry the cans on a mule from one stream over to another or from one lake over to another. My husband and I had the Glacier Pack Train for years, and we packed in fish for the [Department of] Fish and Game into the lakes. And my husband also worked down in Lone Pine as a packer for Chrysler and Cook [pack outfitters], after he quit the Forest Service. And they packed fish in every year to Cottonwood [and] some of those Rock Creek Basin lakes. But they were regular cans that set right in the kayaks on each side of the mules. As you packed each mule, somebody had to be leading the other ones around to keep that water aerating. You'd take about five mule loads of fish up into these lakes here in the Glacier Basin.

RP: And those were from the Mt. Whitney hatchery?

LZ: From the fish hatcheries here, yes. They were the fingerling type. Then they started using the plane drops, which lost a lot of fish. They miss and a lot of it lands out on the shores or in the middle of the lake where the big fish are, and they just feed on them. When they packed them in, they'd let them off at the inlets or the outlets of the streams real easy and they had a fighting chance. We were up at these lakes one time when they were dropping them and it looked like an awful waste.

RP: One other thing I wanted to ask you about in regard to the cattle was, were you involved in any of the movie making in Lone Pine?

LZ: Up around our place, there were several shot there. Bill Boyd—

RP: Hopalong.

LZ: Hopalong Cassidy made several up there at our place. And *Cowboy and the Lady*, part of that with Gary Cooper was made right out our door. And John Wayne made several up there. He used to come in and sit. We had a great big screen porch around the house, and he would come in and sit on that screen porch and visit.

RP: Oh, really?

LZ: I never tell anybody because they don't believe you, but he was just a real friendly old stick. He'd rather be doing that than—they'd have to holler for him when they needed him. My dad worked with Mr. Spainhower [a Lone Pine rancher active in movie-making] with a lot of the movies. And he belonged to the Screen Actors Guild. They had to belong to it to work. And then my husband belonged to the wranglers that took care of all the stock, and they fixed the wagons. But my dad played little parts, cowboy parts in a lot of the different movies. And they always had a group of cowboys riding and everything, but you couldn't tell who was who, really. But all of those big movies, *Gunga Din*—

RP: They'd hire the same group of cowboys?

LZ: They all worked in them, all of those.

RP: He never had any speaking parts in the movies, that you know of?

LZ: I think a couple of them he had two or three words that he said as a guy off to the side or something. I know he came home saying, "Well, I was a big star today. I said, 'Go get your horse'," or something like that, just teasing about it because it was a joke, really. I mean, hours and hours of doing one thing. And the wranglers, they just had to sit and wait before something was changed and [they] moved the stock and the wagons. I don't know how they stand it.

RP: Those movies that were shot around your ranch at George's Creek, were you paid for the use of your property?

LZ: They reimbursed. Of course, they just used the meadow, really, and the corrals and that kind of thing. Like with *Cowboy and the Lady* they built a framework of a house. [Gary Cooper] was supposed to be going to get married and was building this house. Here was this house frame right out in the open, no trees or anything around it. And then when I saw it on the picture, I didn't recognize it because I was expecting to see that house sitting out there in the open, and here it was surrounded by trees. That's what happens in the movies, though. We learned a lot watching them.

RP: You can never watch them the same way again. So these movies that took place at George's Creek would have been around the 1930s, or somewhere in that era?

LZ: In the mid-30s. My dad loved doing that, working [in them]. And it was good money, which was good in those days for all of us. The cattle business isn't that booming, and for him it wasn't, because he wasn't that big ever.

RP: Let's get back to Manzanar. How much longer did you live there?

LZ: In '42 my folks had to move from there when the house burned down.

RP: What was the community like in those years, the late '30s and early '40s? Had most of the families moved out?

LZ: Yes, there wasn't anybody left there but us, and that was on George's Creek. Then they started building the Jap camp there. We were living there in the summer while my folks were in the mountains. They brought the Japs in the early part of 1942. I guess [later] that year is when [the house] burned down and they moved into Lone Pine. So they were there for a little while, while the Japs were there.

Scene from *How the West Was Won*, filmed in 1962 near Lone Pine, California, with the Sierra Nevada in the background. *Metro-Goldwyn-Mayer, Lone Pine Film Festival Archives, courtesy of the Beverly and Jim Rogers Museum of Lone Pine Film History*

RP: You say that [the farming community of] Manzanar was abandoned by that time. Were the houses still remaining?

LZ: Not too many, because they were all so old that they were gradually, I think, just torn down, and people [were] getting the lumber or the City cleaned [them] up.

RP: Do you remember the City coming in and uprooting trees at all?

LZ: No, not really.

RP: They just let the orchards go?

LZ: They just left them, and [many] just died.

RP: Your husband Jake worked in the early construction of the camp?

LZ: Yes, they were still constructing while the Japs were [coming] there. And I get really riled up when they tell about how bad it was and this and that. They had everything there. They could come and go up into the creeks and the lakes, and they just really skimmed the lakes dry of fish and stuff. My mother worked at Joseph's Market in Lone Pine at that time. She was the bookkeeper there. The Japs would go [into town] in busloads, and they weren't rationed. They could buy sheets and everything. We went in with our rations, you know, our little tokens and our ration books to buy, and they bought whatever they wanted.[7]

RP: I guess there was quite an outcry about them being in the town, and that was discontinued.

LZ: Just small groups used to come in and shop. And you know, they had beautiful gardens. There is nothing like a Japanese for raising gardens. And then they had a fair. It was open to the public, and we went in. And beautiful! I mean, their displays—I can see those displays yet of string beans. And they said they were out in the desert where nothing would grow, these stories tell, you know.
RP: So it was an open house for people in the valley?
LZ: Yes, you had to go through the gates to get to it. They had what they called the fairgrounds. Then they had entertainment. I can remember one Japanese girl just had a *beautiful* voice. I always wondered what happened, if she went on with that, because she had a beautiful voice.

NINE

Ritsuko Eder (b. 1917), Doris Semura (1912–2005), Dawn Kashitani (b. 1910)

On that day, the sand blew and it got into our eyes and oh, it made us weep

Introduction

When Japan attacked U.S. military installations in Hawaii on December 7, 1941, Ritsuko Eder, Doris Semura, and Dawn Kashitani were young American women of Japanese ancestry living in the Los Angeles area. In the early months of 1942, they were ordered to leave their homes, take only what they could carry, and board trains and buses for the journey to a dreary, hastily built barrack city in the desert that would be their home for months, perhaps years.

Three decades later, in 1973, the women traveled back to the Owens Valley and to Manzanar in separate, private pilgrimages. At the Eastern California Museum in nearby Independence, they met Catherine Piercy, who recorded these impromptu conversations.

Now, they are among the earliest public expressions of memories kept silent and locked away by a shame still fresh decades after the confinement. "We don't talk about that time," a mother admonished her young son in the early 1960s. But gradually, those who had lived at Manzanar did speak, as children and grandchildren—the Sansei, and Yonsei, or third and fourth generations—reached maturity and began asking the difficult questions about the years missing from family narratives.

The immigrant parents of these families, the Issei, first entered the United States in significant numbers in the 1890s. By then, fierce anti-Chinese sentiment across the nation, but focused in California and other western states, had forced a halt to the flood of immigration that brought nearly 300,000 Chinese laborers into the country between 1849 and 1865. Japanese immigrant workers, most from Japan's rural farm provinces, quickly filled the low-wage railroad and farm jobs once held by the Chinese. They soon demanded higher wages and gradually moved into more skilled work in farming, fishing, canning, and forestry. In 1900, with more than 18,000 Japanese living on the West Coast, the mayor of San Francisco sounded an alarm, declaring that Japanese ". . . are not the stuff of which American citizens can be made."[1] As the Japanese population nearly tripled in the next decade, anti-Oriental agitators, calling the "Japanese Invasion" the "Problem of the Hour," used a widespread, racist-inspired fear of the "Yellow Peril" to target the visible economic advancement of the Issei and Nisei.[2]

In 1920, 110,000 Japanese and their American-born offspring were living in the United States, nearly two-thirds of them in California. Earlier, the stateís white farmers, threatened by Japanese competition, had lobbied successfully for passage of the California Alien Land Laws of 1913 and 1920. Prevented from owning or leasing land, the alien Japanese suffered a further blow to their status in 1922, when the U.S. Supreme Court upheld their ineligibility for naturalization.

Despite the rash of restrictive laws, west coast Issei prospered; with property in their children's names, they operated farms, fishing boats, nurseries, and small service-oriented businesses. On the eve of Pearl Harbor, Nisei children were attending college in record numbers, preparing to enter the ranks of professionals as doctors, nurses, dentists, and teachers, and nearly three thousand Nisei men were serving in the U.S. armed forces.

The quiet worlds of Americans everywhere shattered in December 1941. Japanese Americans and their parents read with growing apprehension the increasingly ominous orders posted in their neighborhoods in the early weeks of 1942. Executive Order 9066, issued on February 19, warned that "any and all persons" could be removed from designated military areas. Presumably this included Italians and Germans, as well as Japanese, but there was little doubt that the 120,000 persons of Japanese ancestry living along the Pacific coast—two-thirds of them American-born—were its intended targets.

Within hours of Pearl Harbor, officials had rounded up the alien Japanese commercial fishermen—Ritsuko Eder's father among them—from Terminal Island, a predominantly Japanese enclave in Los Angeles Harbor. Singled out also as potentially disloyal were native-born Japanese known to be active in Japanese cultural or political activities—a group that included Dawn Kashitani's husband. Arrestees in both categories were taken to Department of Justice camps in Montana, New Mexico, or North Dakota and often held for months before being released to join families already in the relocation centers.

With construction barely under way at Manzanar, military officials pushed ahead with the well-publicized evacuation plans. Instigating the "Los Angeles voluntary

A convoy of two hundred or more private vehicles driven by their Japanese owners nears the end of a 250-mile journey from Los Angeles to Manzanar on March 23, 1942. It is seen here passing through Lone Pine. *Author's Collection*

movement," they called for the first mass departure of nearly 1,000 people from Military Area No. 1. The initial group of eighty-two, including Doris Semura's husband, took up the offer to go ahead of families and neighbors, assist with camp construction, and help set up kitchens, administration, sanitation facilities, and medical services. Two days later, on March 23, 1942, the largest group of 500 left soon after dawn from the Rose Bowl in Pasadena, California, in a convoy of military jeeps and more than two hundred private vehicles. Driven by their Japanese American owners, they were stuffed with household goods, appliances, tools, bedding, clothing, and flats of vegetable seedlings to be planted in the desert soil. Crawling up Highway 395, the caravan reportedly stretched for 6 miles. As it neared its destination, residents of Lone Pine emerged from homes and businesses and quietly lined the main street to catch a wary glimpse of their new neighbors.

The *Los Angeles Times* recorded the caravan's arrival at Manzanar: "In a good-humored, high-spirited mass migration, 1,000 [*sic*] alien and American-born Japanese glimpsed tonight for the first time their Owens Valley home from now until the land of their ancestors raises the white flag of surrender to victorious American arms."[3]

Ritsuko Eder—Interview

I was taken to Manzanar in March or April, in 1942. I was twenty-five, and I was married on the fifteenth of February of that year, so I had only been married a couple of months when we were relocated.

Catherine Piercy: How were you notified?
RE: I believe it was a Marine that came to the door and handed us an official notice that we had to evacuate within—I believe it was seventy-two [forty-eight] hours. This was in Terminal Island, where I lived at the time. Terminal Island consisted of a large group of Japanese people. [Most] of the male Japanese that lived on Terminal Island were actually taken without notice. My father was still in his nightclothes early one morning when he was taken. He was forcibly taken. And we had to send him all his clothes and whatever.
CP: Was that because he wasn't born in this country?
RE: Probably. I don't believe they took all the alien males, but Terminal Island was considered somehow to be a very vital location insofar as the war activities went.
CP: Did they give you a reason [for the evacuation order]?
RE: Just that it was an official order, and we were told that we would not be able to take any of our belongings, other than what we could hold in our hands. We couldn't take any furniture or anything large, so most people had to sell their furnishings. And people that owned businesses had to either ask a friend to take over or just abandon them
CP: You went in your own car?
RE: No, at that time we were just told to vacate Terminal Island, so each one of us had to find a place to stay. Many of us went to churches that provided places for groups to stay in. We were lucky enough to know someone that lived in Los Angeles, and they found a house to rent. My family consisted of several sisters, so since this house was very large, we all lived [there] until the other order came for us to be relocated.
CP: When did that come?
RE: That came in the latter part of March, I believe. I'm not too sure of all the dates. It must have been through the newspaper or something, but we all knew that we had to board the train in Los Angeles somewhere—Union Station.
CP: Then you came by train to Manzanar?
RE: Directly, and then [after a bus ride from Lone Pine Station], we walked into the camp area. Some of the barracks weren't completed. In fact, where we were sent, the windows hadn't been installed yet, and there were ten cots lined up and nothing in between—just ten cots on the floor, and we were each assigned a cot. Now, if there were six in one family, they had to share with some other family that had four.[4] But gradually the walls went up and we got more privacy.
CP: It was still cold in March.

RE: Oh yes, very cold. We were told ahead of time that we would be living in a part of the country that was not what we call developed, so we had all rushed out and bought boots and heavy clothing and things like that. We seldom used our hiking boots, but we weren't prepared for the wind and the dust. That was terrible. Sometimes we'd go to the mess hall for our meals and we'd have to wear scarves around our faces to keep the biting sand from our faces, and we'd have to protect our legs also.

CP: Was it hard on the older people to be relocated?

RE: Well, really, everyone accepted it as something we had to do. I mean, there was no sense to cause trouble. I personally felt that since it was so hard for most people to actually identify Japanese from Chinese or whatever, that it was up to us to cooperate. Because in many ways we would be protecting ourselves [being] isolated instead of just being free. I have many Filipino friends [who] were mistaken for Japanese, and they were treated very harshly until [the Caucasians] were told they were not of Japanese ancestry.

CP: You said your son was born at Manzanar?

RE: Yes, my first son was born in December of '42, in the Manzanar hospital. By the time my son was born, they had built a hospital, and I believe the doctor who attended me was an intern.

CP: Was he a Japanese doctor?

RE: Yes, there were many Japanese nurses, too, because in civilian life, many girls were already nurses, you see. After we left camp I had another child. We stayed at Manzanar a year, then we went on to Grand Junction, Colorado.

CP: To another center?

RE: No, no. See, at that time, if you could prove you could be self-sufficient and wouldn't be going on welfare, then you were allowed to go inland, but not [back] to the coast. My oldest sister had gone on ahead to Colorado, and her husband was working on the farms. He wrote and said that there were jobs that my husband could be employed in. So we left when my baby was four months old. And then when we were out [of camp] about two years, my husband's former employer got official permission for us to go back to Los Angeles. So we—my husband and I and my son—we returned to California, to Terminal Island, in fact. Well, we didn't live in Terminal Island, but my husband returned to his former place of work [there], in a fish cannery, while the war was still on. We lived in Long Beach several months, then the war was over.

Doris Semura—Interview

My husband was a volunteer, a skilled laborer, so he came to Manzanar March 21 or 22, 1942. We were living in Los Angeles and my son was six months old. The JACL [Japanese American Citizens League] were recruiting volunteers [to go ahead to

Doris Semura, 1943, in War Relocation Authority ID photo taken prior to leaving Manzanar. *Courtesy Doris Semura*

Manzanar]. They said if you volunteer, your wife and child would have preference [in housing]. So he volunteered without my consent and came home and told me. I said, "In time of where everything is so dark, why did you do that?" But he said, "Well, they wanted volunteers. If they don't have volunteers, nothing can be done. This is my duty to show them patriotism. I think I can be a big help to the United States." So we had a little fight in between, and I cried, and I said, "I don't like it." But he said, "Well, for my country I'm going to do it. Everything is going to be all right."

About two weeks later, I joined him because we were told to evacuate within forty-eight hours. So I put the canned foods and all kinds of things to do with camping, because that's all I could do is to take the belongings that you can hold. I had to [put] everything into storage, and some I gave away. And then about five o'clock in the morning I left from Union Station, and we rode on a train. We reached Lone Pine about five in the evening. After that we were loaded on a bus, and then we came to this Manzanar center.

Two days prior to that, I wired my husband that I was going in, so I expected him to be waiting for me. But he didn't know I was in. And then everybody was getting together as a family group and they were assigning them the apartments. I expected my husband to greet me, so I sat down and waited and waited. About 10:30 at night, I looked up and he looked at me, and he thought, a woman holding a child. He couldn't recognize me, and I couldn't recognize him either because he wasn't shaved and his face was all weather-beaten and all that. But through my son we recognized each other, and then, well, we were just real still, couldn't say a word. And I kind of grumbled at him.

So finally I got assigned with a single girl and a lady with a son, an eight-year old son, and myself—five in one apartment, in Block 3. Our beds were those bunk beds that [the] military use, so they assigned us two blankets each, army blankets, and they gave us a duffle bag for us to put some hay or straw for our bedding. We had to go about half a mile—in the nighttime we're shoveling those straws, and then we came back and we made it comfortable as we can, and that's how we slept. And in the morning it was about 50 degrees, because that was the beginning of April.

CP: And it was still cold.

DS: Yes. The hardest thing was using the bathroom, because [there was] no privacy. There was a makeshift building, and we'd all line up, about fifty behind you, and we'd have to go take a turn. And then the rooms were very cold and the roof wasn't in because it was just, you know, rough board. Later on they covered it with tar paper. So in the mornings sometimes when we'd get up, one side of our face was just windblown, with dust.

CP: What were the floors like?

DS: The floors were rough pine, too. And later on, they improved and they put some linoleum for us, those red or black ones. And so my husband was in Block 1—or 2, because he was one of the volunteers. About three months later they said, "Well, since the other blocks [are] open, if you want to join with your family or your friends, you may do so." So we applied and we got into Block 33, and we stayed there one year.

CP: To go back a little, what were your first impressions when you got off the train—of the area?

DS: Well, the way I felt was, I'm a second-generation and my son is just six months old, and we had no subversive activity or anything. And then the Bill of Rights and all that—they intern us. My mother and father always taught us honesty and justice and patriotism to your country where you are born, so I figured, well, if they put me out [of my home], why can't I take it with a smile and take it bravely. That's the attitude I had. So, with a smile I left, and when I entered I said, "This is it. I have to make the best of it." So as to the area and all, I wasn't thinking more than that. I was thinking in terms of my husband and my child's welfare more than anything else.
CP: What about the food? Was it good?
DS: In the beginning it was not, but after three months, yes. Then we had Japanese food more to our taste. Because even rice, the way they'd cook it was to steam [it], and the Japanese way is different. So all the time we were having half-cooked rice.
CP: What type of food did you have for the baby?
DS: Well, I carried in quite a [lot] of my own. I would get the milk from the kitchen. Oh, I had about a three or four months' supply of canned food. That was the main reason I hardly took anything for myself.
CP: That was a good idea. Did you mind the climate there?
DS: The climate, I didn't feel too bad about, except the wind and the dust and the big dust devils. Later on I used to tell my son, "Watch out, the devil wind could pick you up and make you into smithereens. When you see those, stay away, get away from them!"
CP: Did you get together in groups, socially?
DS: Well, I didn't associate much [at first] because my child's welfare was more important to me. I was a housewife, and I was isolated to one section. And later on, just before I started to leave out of the center, they were having all the social groups and church groups and all those things. We learned to knit and do all kinds of things, among ourselves. So we had some fun at the camp. We had nice times, too.
CP: How many years were you at Manzanar?
DS: One year. And then I noticed this camp life was easygoing, in a way, but I couldn't have any discipline because we eat at the mess hall, we bathe at the separate shower rooms—so my husband and I decided to get out of the place.
CP: How did you do that?
DS: Well, we had to have a clearance, so we had to sign lots of papers and all the questionnaires, and then we had our clearance from the FBI—or, I don't know, the agent. And then if we wanted to go out for relocation or for work, we were okay.
CP: When you left, you could leave if you went to another part of the United States?
DS: [We] had to stay [at least] 300 miles in the interior. So, we located to Idaho to a sugar beet farm. Lots of friends at the camp went to Idaho on the seasonal work, and then they returned and gave us a good impression about the people [who] were nice, so we went there to [be with] some of our old friends from camp. We stayed a year with a family there.

CP: A Japanese family?

DS: No, no, with a Caucasian family. And they treated us real nice, and I sure said, "Well, there isn't only devils in this world. There are really very nice people." And I said, "This is the real Yankee spirit." I have a very, very dear and sweet memory of that family. Then [my husband] was asked to go to work in Louisville, Kentucky, as a skilled laborer in carpentry—which he refused because his intention was he'd rather go to Hawaii [when the war was over]. I was from Hawaii. He's from Hawaii. Just before the war was over, some families who were clear, you know, their citizenship and those activities, I think went home to [Los Angeles] to straighten their properties and things. But not in our case. We just stayed in Idaho. We like it so much. We lived about four years there, then went back to Hawaii.

CP: On your way up here [to Independence], did you stop by at Manzanar?

DS: Yes, that's what we did, and we took the movie.

CP: How did you feel when you went back?

DS: Oh, the way I feel is—there's no trace of the camp, so I'm disappointed. They should keep at least a tower where they used to have the searchlights, and maybe one of the barracks, so they can display all that. It's a real thing, but if you tell it to the ordinary person, they won't understand because this was something very unusual.

Dawn Kashitani—Interview

The first time I came to Manzanar was April the 23rd, 1942. I was living in Redondo Beach, where my husband was pastor of a small Free Methodist Church. He was taken as one of the enemy aliens and was interned in Tujunga [at the Tuna Canyon temporary detention station]. [When the evacuation order came] I went to San Fernando, and with my father and mother and brothers, we were taken to Manzanar. I was in Manzanar two years, where my daughter Joanne was born, and I had one other child named Paul, a six-year-old boy.

CP: Your husband was not at Manzanar then?

DK: He went to a [Department of Justice Internment] camp in Santa Fe, New Mexico, and then came over to Manzanar to join me after about six months. So we were there about two years. Then we went to Pennsylvania, where he was an instructor at the university and he taught the soldiers and military men the Japanese language.

CP: What were your first impressions when you arrived at Manzanar?

DK: Manzanar was—I had never seen so many Japanese—black heads, slanted eyes, and sometimes crooked legs—all in one place before. And we had heard that it was going to be infested with big mosquitoes and fearful thoughts like that, but we didn't encounter any big mosquitoes. And we lived in our barracks. One thing I did

Dawn Kashitani, at age 91 with daughter Joanne, born at Manzanar, and son Paul. *Kashitani Collection*

Schoolchildren, Manzanar War Relocation Center, 1943. *Ansel Adams Photograph, Library of Congress LC302141*

not like especially was the latrines that were not private at all. It was just all open and the showers were all open. Of course, the ladies took with ladies and the men with men, but we weren't used to that in our old home, so that's what I didn't like too much.

CP: What was it like the day you arrived, do you remember?

DK: It was always dusty, and the wind was blowing. I believe that on that day, the sand blew and it got into our eyes and, oh, it made us weep. We thought of our old home. But as usual, we made the best of it. I think it worked out really well that some people, their talents were brought out, in gardening and making [furniture] and things. The Japanese have a special talent, I think, along that line, so it worked out well.

It's a chapter I don't like to think back to too much, but once in a while, I think about it, and I'm sure—I'm a firm believer there's a purpose, God has given us His purpose in life, and maybe that was just a little detour that He had to give us in order to work things out right for us. And so I don't begrudge anybody or anything.

There are always the happy memories, and it's a pleasure to come back this way again after over thirty years and to step once more on the ground [where] my daughter was born.

TEN

Nancy Connor Zischank (1907–2000)

I would give the Japanese an idea of what the country was like

Introduction

There was little in Nan Zischank's early life to suggest she would one day be a pioneer in the Eastern Sierra recreation and ski industry. Born into a wealthy and socially prominent family in Ohio, Nan lived as a young girl in Boston and attended finishing school on Cape Cod, where she learned the requisite skills—management of servants among them—for a life in East Coast society. In her long 1992 conversation with Richard Potashin, she skips over those early years entirely, to 1935. By then, her family had settled in southern California, and that year, she and her husband Max moved to an isolated winter cabin in the alpine scenery and deep snow of the Sierra Nevada eastern slopes. That, she makes clear, was when her life began in earnest. For the next sixty years, Nan was a colorful figure in the community of skiers, fishermen, and resort owners of the Mammoth recreation region. After retiring in Bishop, she lived in a small mobile home, where spectacular mountain views were a backdrop for the stories she told friends and visitors, in her familiar husky voice, of her history-making adventures in the Eastern Sierra.

The Zischanks' popular fishing lodge at Crowley Lake was typical of the rustic, family-owned resorts that hugged remote lakeshores and mountain streams in the West early in the 1900s. From those modest beginnings, the business of recreation mushroomed, and by century's end, sprawling ski developments and multi-use resorts had transformed unspoiled mountain slopes, desert valleys, and seashores into upscale playgrounds for urban dwellers. A few miles north of Max and Nan's place, Dave McCoy started rope-tow operations at Mammoth Mountain in 1941 and in

1955 installed the region's first chair-lift. In the next forty years, he expanded Mammoth into a multimillion dollar year-round enterprise, one of the West's largest, that caters now to skiers, rock climbers, mountain bike enthusiasts, fishermen, and backpackers. Fueled by the prosperity, longer vacations, and more reliable automobiles of post-World War II America, the growth of wilderness recreation owed its success to the swelling population of urban dwellers in need of refuge from the noise and crowding of cities and the artifice of suburban landscapes.

Wilderness, called the "cursed ground," of Adam and Eve's banishment from the Garden, is "as much a state of mind as a description of nature," wrote geographer Yi-Fu Tuan. Since ancient time, humans have assigned dual, seemingly contradictory images to the earth's uninhabited places—of refuge or contemplation, wandering or testing. Confronting the deep mountain ranges and endless deserts of the American West, explorers and pioneers could see only perilous barriers and threats to the permanence of settlement. The Hudson River School, meantime, embodied Romantic writers' and painters' far more benign visions of wild landscapes as places of quiet beauty and ascetic contemplation. By then, Thoreau, Audubon, and Muir were calling for their preservation, and the National Park and Forest Reserve systems had set aside the first large swaths of uninhabited land. More ambiguous contemporary perspectives borrow from all of the above: pristine wilderness as place of refuge and solitude, in need of protection and preservation. Yet wild areas beckon to greater numbers of contemporary adventurers to test their mettle against the natural world.[1]

For much of the twentieth century, the Eastern Sierra mountain region remained strikingly undeveloped and sparsely populated, existing largely as a vast watershed for the streams that flowed from it into the desert basins below. Those who braved the long trip across the desert were rewarded with solitude in deep wooded canyons, peace in alpine meadows, and a sense of "life which can only be compared to the bliss of angels."[2]

By 1920, with the Los Angeles Aqueduct open, Owens River water was the new premise for unrestricted growth in southern California, and the resulting suburban sprawl invaded the region's rural landscape of orange groves, cattle ranches, and small farms. The Owens Valley, meanwhile, its economy nearly moribund by 1935, was "selling itself to prospective vacationers" from the south. In 1940, one million people visited or traveled through the valley and left $5 million in its gas stations, stores, and lodging places. Residents of the Owens Valley appreciated the irony in this lucrative trade with Los Angeles city dwellers, who drove the long distance to ski the snow-fields and fish the pristine lakes and streams that supplied their water. "The lost product was bringing its own indirect return," noted historian Remi Nadeau.[3]

In 1942, Nan Zischank left her mountain lodge for a wartime job at Manzanar War Relocation Center. As the incarcerated people there were cleared to leave for jobs east of the exclusion zone beginning early in 1943, Nan drove them to waiting trains in Reno, Nevada. The long ride in her black van through magnificent Sierra scenery

Nan and Max Zischank, ca. 1943. *Nan Zischank Collection*

was an emergence into freedom, and for many, a departure from the exile to which they had been sent months and years before.

"The workings of conquest [in the West] tied . . . diverse groups into the same story," writes historian Patricia Limerick. "Happily or not, minorities and majorities occupied a common ground."[4] Valley residents watched the internees gradually depart; some were relieved, others indifferent, but, like Nan Zischank, nearly all would remain uncertain for years to come about their response to occupying a common ground with 10,000 people who looked like the wartime enemy.

Nan Zischank—Interview

Well, Max and I were married in 1931. We loved to fish, so we used to come up to the Sierras quite often. He worked for Standard Stations as an assistant manager, and so of course he could get gasoline a little cheaper. Even on a weekend we would take off just to do a little fishing. One day he came home and said, "Let's move to the mountains," and I said, "Suits me." So we gathered what we had together—we had a car that was paid for and we had ten dollars worth of groceries, a cat, and a dog—and we came on up to the mountains.

That was in 1935. That summer we stayed in a cabin up by Twin Lakes. Then in the fall we understood there was going to be an opening for someone to stay in all winter over at Tamarack Lodge as caretakers, so we applied for the job and got it. They gave us the big cabin called Fisherman's Lodge. There was one bedroom filled with wood—we had only a wood stove in those days. There was kind of a walk-in closet, only it was warm. And they put in all kinds of canned goods, and they wouldn't freeze in there.

We got twenty dollars a month and we thought we were doing real well because that was the bottom of the Depression. We worked all winter long, and of course the road wasn't even open from Highway 395 into Mammoth in those days. A storm [could] close everything. So our way of transportation was on skis. Ruth and Tex Cushion had the dog teams down at Old Mammoth, and about once a week we would put on our skis and ski down and stay all night. They had a tent house out in the back, and we would have dinner and listen to the little radio and hear what the news was. And then we would go back up the next day.

We had canned goods, and they had put in a few garbage cans full of rice and flour and sugar and beans and everything that was dry. So we had plenty to eat all winter long. We also had a half a beef—it was quite a chore to get a little hunk of beef. It hung out in the wood shed, and Max would say, "Well, let's go out and get a piece of meat to boil," or whatever we wanted to do with it. We would get out there and lay this half of a beef on a block, and the only thing we had to cut it with was a six-foot cross-cut saw. So we got all we needed to eat. It was really a delightful experience.

And we did [get] a battery radio. There was only a Kohler [generator] plant for electricity. So every now and then when the lights would get dim Max would have to go and start the plant and charge the batteries again. It would last for only so long, but it did supply the battery for our radio. That was the year the King [Edward VIII of Great Britain] abdicated and also the year of the big bands, all over the world. Well anyway, that is the way we spent the winter.

Then when spring came they decided to put in Highway 203 [from Highway 395 to Mammoth Lakes]. Morrison–Knudson was the contractor, and Max went to work for them and worked all summer. Then that fall when the highway was in he decided he wanted to work for the State [Division of] Highways. So we went up to [the headquarters at] Crestview and Max got on for the winter. Of course we had no place to live and they had no place for us to live either, so I went down to see my father who was quite wealthy, and he bought us a trailer that we put at Crestview. It was fifteen-and-a-half feet long and eight feet wide. They call them little travel trailers today. But we lived four years in that trailer with all of our possessions. It was quite an experience. Of course we had no inside toilet facilities, just a little outhouse. And we had water in a stand pipe out in back. All we had was a little Coleman stove, two- burner, and we had to heat our water on that.

And then in 1938 my father passed away and left us some money—seven thousand dollars. In those days seven thousand dollars was quite a bit of money. At that time, when we got the money, the Mono Tunnels were just being completed, so we heard that [the City of Los Angeles] wanted to auction off all the bunk houses [where the construction workers had lived] because they had quite a few. So we bid on one of the buildings, a hundred feet long and forty feet wide, and we got it for $160. Well, everybody got the same deal. Max had to cut it into four sections before he could move it. There was no electricity up there [at the construction camps] because they had turned everything off, so Max cut that building with three hand saws. He cut it into four sections and it took him quite a little while, of course.

But then we wanted a little piece of property. We couldn't get anything in Mammoth because we couldn't get clear title to anything. So someone said, "Why don't you go down to Long Valley? They are going to put in a lake down there pretty soon, and it might be a pretty good idea." So we went down there and we saw Harold Eaton—at the Eaton Ranch—and we asked if he would sell us an acre of ground, and he did. We had the building moved down onto that acre of ground. Across the street and up on the hill we had a spring that went with the sale of the property and that was our water.

So we opened up [the Long Valley Resort] on New Year's Day of 1941. And you know Pearl Harbor was December of that year—we had no more than opened up until along came the war. Max said, "I am not going to be a foot soldier. I work for the highway and I'm a mechanic." So he went down to L.A. and got into the Seabees [Navy Construction Battalion]. They are the mechanical end of the military. We had to close the resort of course—what little there was of it at the time. So we boarded up everything.

In the meantime, Bob Brown, who was head of the Chamber of Commerce in Bishop at that time, was a friend of Ruth and Tex Cushion and us too, and he said, "Look, I am going to be down at Manzanar. Ralph Merritt is going to be head of Manzanar, and I am going to be under him and I need some help, so would you like to come down and get a job?" So I said, "I certainly would." Ruth Cushion was my boss—she got the job first and I worked under her. We went down there and I said to Ruth, "I have to fill out these papers and it asks what has been your occupation." She said, "Well, you know real well how to drive one of these dog teams; you've done that a lot." She said, "That is what I put down." So that is what I did too.

Richard Potashin: Can you really drive the dog teams?
NZ: Oh yes, enough to know what I was doing. So I went to work at Manzanar just before Christmas in 1942, and I worked until 1945. When I first went to work, Ruth said, "Now, the internees have been down here [at Manzanar] long enough. And in the East, so many people have gone to war that they need help, in all walks of life. So the Japanese, the ones that have a clear record, will be allowed any place out of California [except western Washington and Oregon and southern Arizona]. They will be able to get a job that they think would be good." So it was put out throughout the country that the Japanese would work. And we had a billboard and the people would write in for workers and we would put their letter up on the billboard. Every day the Japanese would look over the letters and the jobs—Birdseye, you know, the frozen food place, they took a lot of them to begin with. And then they needed barbers and just all walks of life.

So when they would find a letter on a job they thought they would like, they would take it in to Ruth Cushion. She would start the process by sending [the application] to Washington. And they would check to find out if they had any record of

The Zischanks' Long Valley Resort at Crowley Lake, ca. 1950. *Nan Zischank Collection*

any kind. If the name was clear they would send it back to Manzanar with a ticket to the destination plus enough money to get there. Of course, they were not allowed to set foot in California without a police escort. And Ruth said [to me], "You are going to be the police escort."

The first people that went out, there were only [a few]. We rode the Inland Stage [Bus Line]—that was before Greyhound took it over. They would give us enough tickets to ride from Manzanar to Reno, and I wore a police badge. [Other] people on the bus wanted to sit, and if they gave up a seat for a Japanese they weren't very happy about it. So Ruth and all of them got together and decided it would be best if we would drive instead. The very first car that I drove was a wood-sided station wagon, one of those old Fords. And it finally got too small, and then they gave me a big Dodge—I called it the Black Mariah. It was like a van, and they put jump seats in it, and I could take eleven.

Now each and every one, when they went out, they were allowed one suitcase and [it] was put in a rack on top of the car. On the days that the wind would blow or there was bad weather, it wasn't easy to drive, believe me. But we would start out from Manzanar and we would stop at Lee Vining. The very first time that I stopped there, we went into old Bodie Mike's—Bodie Mike was never a citizen of the United States. That license was under his wife's name. Anyway, I stopped in and he looked at me—and he was a terrific swearer—oh, he swore terrible. He said, "You get them slant-eyed son-of-a-bitches out of here." I went back down and told Ruth and Ralph [Merritt]. And the next day they got in the car and went up there and had a little talk with Bodie Mike. So the next time I went through, he said, "Come in, come in."

RP: So you stopped there for lunch?

NZ: Well no, we brown-bagged it every day. But we did stop for the restrooms. It was only a very short stop. Then we would go on into Reno. I would get there and sometimes we had to wait quite a little while. It seems like the trains were always late in those days—sometimes as much as four and five hours late. So we would just have to sit around the station. It was up to me to see that they got on the Eastern trains and not the one that went back to San Francisco. So after I would get them on, at first I would turn around and get right back down to camp at three or four o'clock in the morning. But it got a little bit too much, so they decided I should stay all night in Reno. I had a per diem and everything worked out fine.

RP: How long of a trip was it?

NZ: Let's see, it's 167 miles from Long Valley, which is 33 miles north of Bishop—

RP: Plus the mileage to Manzanar.

NZ: So about 251 miles one way, I think I figured. Anyway, at the end of 1945, when the war was over and Max got back from overseas, I figured I had traveled 168,000 miles.

RP: How often did you go up there?

NZ: Every day up one way and back the next. And once in a while I would take two or three of them [as transfers] to Gila River or [other relocation centers]. Then I took three of them to the insane asylum in Los Angeles. I had to have a nurse go along and they sedated them first. They just couldn't take the camp.[5] But most of them had the idea that we are citizens and if that is what the government wants us to do then that is what we will have to do. Most of them were very, very placid about it. They have the patience of Job. We had five millionaires in camp.[6] All of them lost everything they had. They had to leave in such a hurry from Los Angeles that they left most of their belongings and possessions with Caucasian friends. Then when the bitterness became so terrible the Caucasians found out it was real easy to sell what they had and just walk off with it.

I had two or three kind of nice little trips that I would like to tell you about. You know we had fighting for us a Japanese division called the 442nd Division [Regimental Combat Team]. And the five-star general, his folks lived in Manzanar, so he got a pass from the Presidio and I met him.[7] I thought, "I wonder what he is going to look like." You, know, [I pictured] a great big moustache and a pompous-looking outfit. Well, I looked all around the train station in Reno and here stood this good-looking Japanese, all in uniform. I went over and asked him his name and he said, yes, that is who he was. So I said, "Do you want to stay in town." They like to gamble. And he said no, he would like to go home and see his folks as soon as possible. So we got in the car and on the way down, by way of conversation I said, "You fish, don't you?" And he said, "You know, when I was eleven years old my uncle brought me up to June Lake to fish." I said, "Would you like to see June Lake again?" He said, "If I could see June Lake I could go back and win this war all by myself." Well, it was in the fall and it was one of those times when the wind had not blown the leaves off of the trees, and it was a blaze of color. So I took off just below Lee Vining and went the loop, you know, and came around and showed him all the lakes. And then I showed him our little resort because that was before the freeway—we were on the old [Highway 395] road. He said, "May I come and see you after the war?" And I said, "I'd love it." He never showed up and I am sure he must have been killed or he would have come.

And then we had an orphanage in Manzanar and quite a few of the [babies]—the mothers were Caucasian and the fathers were Japanese, and the mothers were pregnant at the time the husbands had to leave. After the baby was born, everyone was so bitter about the Japanese, they would send the baby up to the father, because of the orphanage. And so the first one I picked up, I went to Mojave and this escort got off the train with this bundle in his arm, and he put it down on the bench and said, "Now here is the diapers and here is the food." Then he said, "Now I'm going to San Francisco and I'll see you," and away he flew. I looked at that and thought, what in the world have I got here. So I peeked under this blanket and guess what I saw. Here was a little six weeks-old baby with the cutest little Japanese face and blond curly hair. Well, there was an elderly woman who was waiting for the train and she was a grandmother. I said, "I don't know how to change diapers." Anyway, she said, "Look, I'll help you take care of it." And so she did, and I got on the bus and went into Manzanar with the baby.[8]

Then I brought in another baby from Reno. There again all they gave me was bottles. So I stopped in Gardnerville and went into a little restaurant where I used to get coffee once in a while, and I said, "Can you heat this bottle so I can feed this baby?" When it was warm enough I sat down in the front of the restaurant and I was feeding this baby the bottle, and in walked these two elderly women, and they looked at this darling little Japanese and one of them said to the other, "Look at it there, it only has eyes for its mama." And here I am a Caucasian far from looking like a Japanese, and this little baby was so sweet. Well, anyway, that is the end of those stories.

RP: Nan, did you live at the camp?

NZ: Oh yes, I lived with Ruth Cushion. [The War Relocation Authority housing] looked like the [auto] courts we have—all these apartments under one roof. And Ruth and I had an apartment, just one bedroom. It had a little kitchenette, and she had a bed out in the living room. We lived there but we ate at the [WRA] mess hall. We could do our own cooking if we wanted to, but we didn't. Then after the Japanese were allowed to travel on their own—this was just the last few months—I still needed a job.[9] Max wasn't back from overseas. So they put me in the office. I worked for Mr. Boczkiewcz—it was worse than your name or mine.

Another story was kind of cute. Ralph Merritt told the Japanese he was going to have a contest. Each block was to build an outside decoration—whatever they wanted. Ruth and I went with Ralph to each one of the places. Oh, there were so many. They took little branches and made trees, and oh, they were fantastic little scenery arrangements. But at this one cook shed they had built a little Fuji, you know, the volcano. At the foot of it was a little village. It was about six feet tall. When we got back, Ralph said, "I wonder where he got all the dirt for that mountain. I didn't see any excavation, did you?" So he went back up the next day and he said, "You know I'm a little curious as to where you got all the dirt for this beautiful volcano you built." The cook kind of hung his head and Ralph said, "Whatever you say is all right with me." "Well," the cook said, "I built a still underneath the shed and this is all the dirt I took out." So he gave Ralph a bottle of some *sake* and we all had a drink.

But you know, Manzanar was really and truly a small town all by itself. They had their own police force. They had their own fire department. But at the head of every department was a Caucasian. They had hairdressers—I always had my hair done there—and they had a Sears and a Montgomery Ward [catalog outlet]. And they could order materials, and there were tailors and dressmakers living in the camp. Everyone that I ever took out was always dressed in new clothes that they had made themselves. Every girl always had a corsage. They were made out of the silk that we use today to make flowers. There was only one time when I was in the bus that I was a little apprehensive. I started out and it occurred to me that it was the opening day of hunting season and it was a government car, and everyone knew there would be Japanese in it. I thought that somebody would take a pot shot at us. But we got all the way through with no problems.

RP: Were the Japanese nervous at all about leaving and going out into the world?

NZ: A little bit, yes. When we got out of camp, the first thing I would do was drive to the other side of the highway and stop and say, "Now you are going out among the Caucasians, and I would appreciate it and the camp would appreciate it, too, if you would not speak in your own language. When you get on the train and every place you go it would be wise if you would stick to the English language only." [Some] of them had never been on a train before. So I took time to make a drawing to show the seats and where the latrines were and what the dining room would be like. It was just one paper on both sides, and I would give those out to the ones that wanted one. And they were very, very appreciative. They had no idea what they were getting into. In fact, a lot of them had never really been in automobiles except down in L.A., and for me to do 45 mph, well, they were really flying. I couldn't go over 45 mph because there was a governor [a device to limit speed] on all of the government cars.

RP: On the trips going up with the Japanese, would it be kind of a social feeling? Would you talk a lot?

NZ: Not with me so much because they talked among themselves. They talked in English. No, if I would bring, say, one or two back in [to camp from work furloughs] then we would have little conversations on the way down. They were always interested to know about our resort and fishing. You see, Crowley Lake was filled in 1941. And so right after we built we knew there was going to be a lake there.

RP: Were they intrigued with the country and the drive up there?

NZ: Oh yes, and many of them kept oohing and aahing about the beauty. They really and truly appreciated the beauty of the ride, and they weren't afraid. They all told me when they got to Reno, they appreciated how I drove, most of them. And once in a great while—I was a heavy smoker in those days, I used to think it kept me awake—they would see what kind of cigarettes I smoked and they would buy me a pack or two of cigarettes. They are very, very courteous people, and their children are. A lot of our children could take a lesson from a lot of those children. They never made any noise and they were never any bother of any kind. And if they did have to stop at a restroom in-between where I wanted to stop, they would ask me. And I would stop. No, I had no problems with the people, not at all.

RP: Did you hear stories about the Japanese going out and going fishing up on the creek above Manzanar?

NZ: You know they had spotlights on the four corners and in between. They were manned by the MP's. But the Japanese, they all had fishing rods, of course, because they were fishermen, and they would crawl out when the spotlight was in the dark over the area they were crawling in and they would go out at night and fish and get back before dawn. Oh yes, they did. They never had any trouble with them in the mountains. Another thing, Manzanar was a pretty bleak-looking place. So they took trucks and loaded the ones that knew how to transplant a tree and they went up into the mountains and brought down trees. Manzanar was a beautiful little place. Really it was all due to the Japanese bringing the trees down out of the mountains and replanting them. And they were given grass seed, and they had beautiful lawns. It was really a lovely place to stay.

RP: They brought a lot of rocks down too and made their gardens?

NZ: Oh yes. Their gardens were just beautiful. Oh yes. And as I say, everybody worked that could. The government gave the ones that worked three dollars [$12–19] a month. Ruth and I had a maid, and she came every morning and made our bed and she would take any clothes and wash the underwear and wash the pants if possible, or clean them and press them and bring them back. And in the evening my clothes were always clean. The same way with Ruth. The Japanese loved doing that. Then quite often they would say, "When you go to Reno, would it be possible for you to buy . . ." a certain little something at the dime store that they would want. So I was more than happy to do that for them. Sometimes I would bring in something to make a cake with, and I would bring in enough from Reno to make two cakes. So we would ask the maid to make cakes, and she could have one if she made two.

RP: Now how much were you paid?

NZ: Let me see, my yearly deal was twelve hundred—twelve-fifty—how much is that a month?

RP: A little over 100 dollars a month.

NZ: That wasn't very much, but then I had a place to live and my food. And I had a six dollar-a-day per diem that I could hold over if I wanted to. I put every bit of it away, and at the end of three years I had quite a little stack of money. Oh, I would take a little bit of it. But I didn't need anything. I did get a suit from Utah Woolen Mills. A salesman came around and I said, "I want a suit, a skirt, and a pair of pants." You know, a regular men's suit. He made that for me, and that cost me eighty-five bucks. That was a lot of money, but then to get a three-piece suit that was all wool. I still have it. It never wore out. It was a beautiful suit.

RP: Nan, you said that you wore a badge. Did you wear a uniform too?

NZ: They didn't want me to wear a uniform. I did wear this suit. But no, they didn't want me in a uniform of any kind. And it was enough to wear a badge. Once in a while, when we got to Reno, we would be going over to the train station from where I parked and—we called these people armchair warriors. It might be an elderly fellow that didn't like the Japanese, and he would walk up to them and call them slant-eyed you-know-what. And I would walk over—I always kept it under the lapel on the jacket—and I would flash my badge and say, "Please leave." That is all it took, and we were never molested. That badge did it. Really, I didn't have to use it very much, but once in a while.

There were people who were bitter. And of course [the internees] had a face you couldn't mistake. That is why the government had to put them into camps. They figured if they left them on the streets of Los Angeles, they would have been killed right there. You know, we talk with people that live in the East, and they weren't afraid of the Japanese. They didn't have any bitterness towards them, but they did have bitterness towards the Nazis. And so you see out here we could care less what a Nazi was. The Japanese said they had no problems once they got back East. They stuck to themselves and did their work.

RP: So once you put them on the train, they were unescorted until they reached the East coast.
NZ: That's right, because they were out of California. [Western] Washington and Oregon, California [and part of Arizona] was the only soil they couldn't set foot in.
RP: The Pacific Coast.
NZ: The Pacific Coast. Anything further east of that they were allowed to travel by themselves. And another thing that people didn't realize, when they got their ticket to their destination, they also got a little packet of papers that they had to fill out—every month—I don't remember just how often. The papers said that they were still at the job they went to or else they had changed to another job and gave the address, and that was sent to [San Francisco]. So the WRA had this on everyone who left Manzanar or any of the other camps all during the war. They knew where everybody was. That was quite a job.
RP: How many internees did you personally take up to Reno to be sent east?
NZ: Well, now, I hadn't thought about that. That was in 1943, '44, and [part] of '45. That was [almost] two-and-a-half years, every other day. I would say I was taking an average of ten every time. That was a lot of people, yes.
RP: Were you taught any Japanese or encouraged to learn?
NZ: No, some of the school teachers that were Caucasian did learn the language, but I didn't have time, and I'm not a linguist. So no, I didn't make any friends, lasting

Leaving Manzanar War Relocation Center, 1944. *Ansel Adams Photograph, Library of Congress LC30214*

friends, with any of the Japanese. But there was this one Japanese whose wife was in Manzanar and she was pregnant, but he wanted to go and pick apples up in Washington or Oregon, and so he did. While he was up there, she had the baby. But she passed away, and the baby died. Well, Ruth said, "We are going to bring him back, but we really have no way to tell him. Maybe we can have the doctor tell him. So you are to bring him back." I thought, oh no. He came by train and I picked him up in Reno. He didn't know that his wife had passed away. He knew that there was trouble, and that they were asking him to come back to camp. But he thought that perhaps she was just ill or something and they needed him. I was not to tell him. So I rode all the way from Reno to Manzanar hearing about the little crib he made and all the things that he was bringing back for the baby, and when I got to Independence, I called in to camp to tell them that I was on my way. So then they had a doctor that met me at the gate and took over. But it was real sad.

Then after the war, one day at the resort, this Japanese walked in to the dining room and said, "I don't think you remember me." And he told me who he was, and it was this fellow. "I have since remarried," he said, "and I want you to meet my new wife." So I said, "Great, sit down and we will all have a cup of coffee together." So he told us that they had a new baby and everything was fine. I thought it was kind of nice to be remembered. And he said, "That was certainly a hard trip for you, I know." And it was.

RP: You mentioned that the Japanese were let out to go pick apples in Washington. Were they let out as farm laborers in California too?

NZ: No, not that I know of. They all worked in the fields around Manzanar, but they were all under supervision from the MPs. They loved to work, especially the gardeners. They were so proud of what they raised. They had [enough for] all of Manzanar and to send some to [other camps]. That is how big the fields were.[10] Do you know that this whole valley at one time was as fertile as Imperial [Valley] before they took the water away. So they gave water to Manzanar and they really brought all that land down there back to life.

RP: How about the orchards? They almost died out.

NZ: Yes, they brought them all back to life again, too.

RP: Quite a sight.

NZ: It was really. It was something to see those truck loads of Japanese leave the camp, and of course there were MPs to watch over them all day.[11] The food was sent out to them. They worked hard. A lot of people called me a Jap lover. I got one letter while I was in camp, that I was such a Jap lover, and I need never come back to Mammoth again. Not signed. But most of the people began to understand. I mean the idea of putting them into camp was really to protect them. And they were really grateful for being protected.

RP: Nan, what did you do after you left the camp?

NZ: We had the little resort at Crowley Lake, you know, that we had had to close. And let's see, it was the opening of fishing season, which is the first of May, and Max had gotten home in April [1945]. And so friends came up and helped him—old customers who were still friends. They knew that he had quite a job to get open again, and so they all stayed up there because we had four apartments with beds and everything, and they all helped Max open the resort. And then when I left Manzanar I just went right to work—I did all the cooking and I did all the meat cutting, and I took care of the apartments and the reservations and everything—but everything was all in order and ready to go.

RP: You left Manzanar what month and year?

NZ: Just before the first of May, 1945, just in time to open the fishing season. Crowley Lake had just been opened up. It became quite a notable spot. And then in the wintertime, of course, having lived at Mammoth and having to ski every place we went, we both skied, so we had a little rope tow across from the resort. And between cooking, I would go across the street and start the lift, and then I would help people do their skiing. We had a lot of fun on that lift. And then at noon—there weren't too many people in the country then—I would say, "Well, it's time to go have hamburgers." We would stash our skis in the snow, turn off the lift, and go eat hamburgers and go back to skiing again.

Last year one of our very first customers wrote and said, "Nan, I want to send you this. I don't know if you have one but I found it in an old pair of hunting pants." It was one of our first cards that Max and I had made to give out. On the front it had "Long Valley Resort, Nan and Max, Proprietors, 33 miles north of Bishop." Then on the back side it had rates: a cot to put your sleeping bag on, towels for a shower, three meals a day, home style—seven dollars a day. And we made money. Of course, I fed them the cheapest thing I could. That was the way we did our first two winters.

Then skiing became popular, of course. We had our own little rope tow, just a very short one. The one that Dave [McCoy] had, down on McGee Mountain, was half a mile long. It was called a shuttle lift. It had four hooks welded on the bottom and the other four hooks were welded on the top. My husband Max ran the lift. It was [powered by] an old Ford motor. He would put it into reverse, and he would take four people up the mountain and the four empty hooks would come down on the other side, and they would go back and forth, up and down all day long. But it was quite a lift. And that is, you know, the—

RP: Beginning of the skiing industry.

NZ: Yes. Once in a while we had maybe fifty people. And it was fifty cents a day.

RP: Can you tell me about Dave McCoy [founder of Mammoth Mountain ski area] in those years? What kind of a person was he?

NZ: He is without a doubt—his heart is bigger than his body. He lived in Big Pine, you know, and when he was a kid, he used to ski on bale stays. Then he got a job with DWP, and he lived up at Crowley Lake—South Landing. He was a hydrographer, and he had to go into the mountains every so often and measure the snow pack. And on the way up he always stopped at Ruth and Tex Cushion's, who had the dog teams. The first time he went up, he went on webs—snowshoes—and Tex said, "Dave, you know you are just wasting a lot of energy going on those things. Why don't you go up on skis? You could put skins on to go to the top, and at least you could coast down." He and Dave became very fast friends, and it was Tex who said, "Why don't we do something about skiing?" And it was up at Mammoth, because it got to the point where the snow gave out in the spring at Crowley Lake, you know, and there was so much more at Mammoth. And so that is how Dave got started at Mammoth. But everything that Dave has ever done has been not for himself, really, but for the country. I have known him since he was a teenager, almost—and of course, his wife and all of his children. She used to ski in and out of the hospital having children. We always used to laugh because here came another baby. But the kids all learned to ski before they could walk almost. Dave has been so philanthropic, and really, our country owes him a debt of gratitude. I know any of the old-timers will tell you the same thing. His money didn't go to his head. He is just a very wonderful person, I think.

RP: I wanted to ask you how long you had the Long Valley Resort.

NZ: Oh, we opened up in 1941, and we had to take it back three times. The first time was 1961. The man we thought we sold it to paid his down payment and just didn't pay any more, and we finally had to foreclose. And then two other people were going to do the same thing, and they didn't realize how much work there is in even a small place—although we worked eleven people all summer. We had a Union Station gasoline pump and five apartments and the dining room and cocktail lounge—we built that right after the war—and there was just a lot of work. But people would see you running it so efficiently and they would run it for the summer, and in the fall they would say, "You can have it. It's too much work."

RP: Is the resort the original building that you hauled over there to Long Valley—is it still up?

NZ: It's still as is. The last people that bought it, their names were Olson, and they really ran it successfully. But in 1969 we were hit by an avalanche—you heard about it. Really, if it hadn't been for the avalanche, we would have come out smelling like roses. But it broke every window in the building and filled it full of snow, and then we had to get an FHA loan to get it back to where we could get rid of it. After the avalanche, the Forest Service closed that old road six months out of the year. The minute the snow comes until the snow goes, they close that old road because of the new highway. The Olsons just couldn't make it on summer business only. So they sold the liquor license and they said, "We are going to make a home out of it." And that is what they have done. They have remodeled it so that they have two lovely homes.

Our building, of course, was a bunkhouse. It had a hallway down through the center. At one end there was one big room [the tunnel workers] used to gather in and chew the fat sort of. And then there were rooms on both sides of the hallway and they were ten-foot rooms. Each one had a window in it. So the boys all smoked and they all laid their cigarettes on the window sill. And when we got the building down to Long Valley, my job was to take all the window sills and sand them all down and take all the cigarette marks off of them. Anyway [the rooms] were easy to take apart, and Max made one, two, three apartments. When we got the building, we got all of the toilets and everything, all of the piping, and so he utilized what he could out of it.

All over Mammoth there are buildings from the [Mono Tunnel] camps, and of course the rest of them they just tore down. There were some that even the Hog Ranch got. Do you remember the Hog Ranch?

RP: No, you had better tell me about that one.

NZ: Oh, the kids always wanted to go see the pigs.

RP: This was up in Mammoth?

NZ: No, this was just south of Lee Vining. Big Litta had it. Big Bird had the house down in Bishop. It was a brothel and Big Litta and Big Bird would meet every so often in Lee Vining at Bodie Mike's and the fur would fly. When the workmen were there working at the tunnels, those girls were busy, busy girls. They were well taken care of, and the doctor saw that the girls were all clean and good, and it was quite a deal.

And Casa Diablo was another place I forgot to tell you about. It was a bar, and I used to make sandwiches down there. Oh yeah, I worked there a lot. This was when the tunnels were going strong. Max was bartender. This all happened before we got our resort, you know. They had slot machines in the country in that day and age. And so it was a bar and a dance floor, and they had dances there every Saturday night. And they had quite an orchestra—they were all Blacks. They lived up in Mammoth and oh, man, could they give you the music to dance by. It was really wonderful.

RP: How long was that bar at Casa Diablo? Do you recall when they dismantled it?

NZ: Well, when the tunnels were done. There wasn't anybody to stop in. [After that] we used to go up to Bodie Mike's just to drink. You know somehow or another we drank an awful lot but I can't remember ever getting beyond being able to drive or [into] fighting. We just didn't do those things. Somehow we controlled what we drank. Really, I don't know of a soul in the country that didn't drink. It was just a way of life.

RP: You mentioned that you got together socially with other people who lived nearby the resort?

NZ: Well, the first place was Tom's Place, and the next place was McGee Creek, then our place, and then you turned off to Mammoth and there was the tavern. Those were the only four places around. We had the old crank phones on the wall, you know—so many longs and shorts were your call. Well, we had one call, and when they would ring it, then everybody would go and get on their phone and then they would say, "Hey, tonight, potluck down at McGee Creek." "Okay." Later on, when more people moved into the country, we didn't go to each other's houses.

RP: The movies—movie crews came up to Mammoth—

NZ: Oh yes, and they used Tex's dogs all the time. You know, Tex called his place at Mammoth the Winter Patrol Station. People who had cabins up around the lakes wanted to be sure that the snow didn't cave in [the roofs] in the winter time. People would pay him to watch, and after every storm, if the snow was heavy, he would have to shovel it off, and in the spring when the snow would come down and hang from the eaves, he would have to cut the eaves, or the snow would tear the roof right apart.

Then every year there was a Sportsmen's Show in L.A. It always used to be down at—what was it—the Automobile Club down there, at Adams [Boulevard] and Figueroa [Street]. So we all went—Tex always took the dogs down, and he would take two teams. Max would take care of one, and Tex would take the other. Each year they had a platform, and at the back of it was a picture of a cabin so it looked like maybe it was up in the mountains, and they would put things that would make it look like the mountains. Every morning the Union Ice Company would come with their crusher, and they would blow ice in on this platform, and the dogs were all chained [there]. Tex and Max were turned in I don't know how many times for cruelty to dogs. Leaving them on that ice. The worst part of it was, if they had not had that ice, they would have died of the heat. People didn't realize that. Anyway, when they closed up the show every night, Tex would like to exercise the dogs, and so they would harness up the two teams and they would go down Adams, both of them yelling and whooping, and go down to the corner and come back. After the second night, people caught on to it and lined up on both sides of the road. They had a lot of fun doing that.

RP: Now you learned to ski from Tex Cushion?

NZ: I would say he had a little bit to do with it. But Hans Georg [an early Eastern Sierra skier] was the one that took me under his wing. You know the old Arlberg way of skiing is down, up, over, and down with your shoulder. He taught me the reverse shoulder, yelling at me all the time. I was the only one in the country who skied the reverse shoulder. And you know that Clarita Heath [1936 Olympian] and I are the only two gals that skied off Carson Peak?

RP: What was that like?

NZ: Well, I'll tell you—a guy was timing us and he would go "three, two, one, go," and when you stood at the crest to take off you couldn't see any part of the mountain until you looked way, way down. And as you took off, it was almost straight up and down. I don't know how I had the guts to do it now, when I look back on it, I really don't. But there were eleven of us altogether. It was an invitational race, and Augie Hess from Lee Vining and I were the only two from this county. I had won the Inyo-Mono Women's Division and he had won the Inyo-Mono Men's Division that year, and so we were invited. But of course, Clarita Heath, she was at the Olympics the year before —oh, she thought it was great. But then she was an experienced skier. There was also a German woman, and she had got to the top and she said, "I'm sorry but you gals can have this." So she walked down the whole thing. From the very top you look down on the Minarets—that's how high it is.

RP: Do you remember seeing Mono Lake at that time—when it was a big lake?

NZ: Oh my, yes. You know I often tell people I passed it every day going from Manzanar to Reno. And I would say it was the most fascinating sight because very

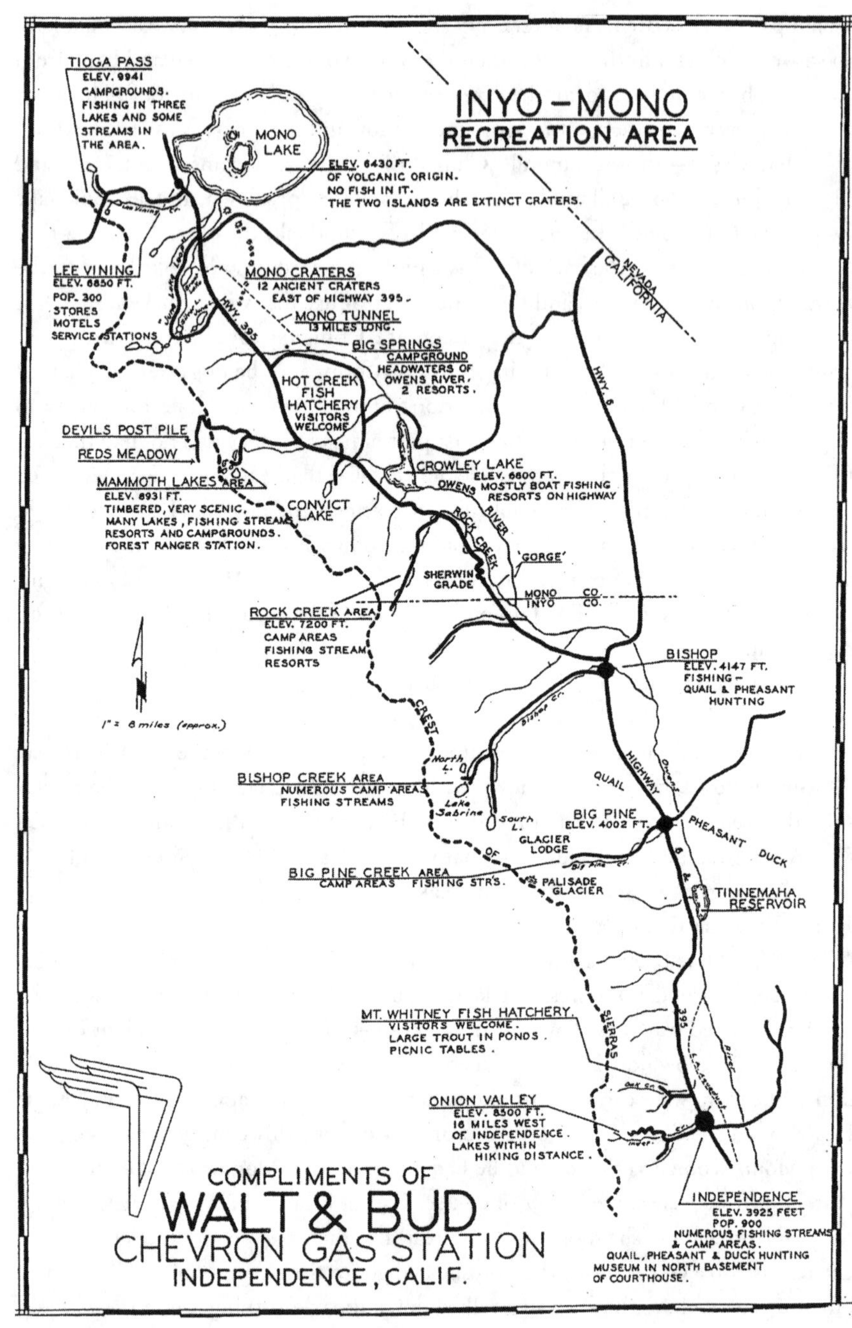

Eastern Sierra Recreation Area map, ca. 1950, by Independence artist Jack Fair. It was posted in the window of a gas station on Highway 395 popular with fishermen and campers. *Map by Jack Fair*

seldom was it two days alike. And of course in the winter there was lots of pogonip. Do you know what pogonip is?

RP: Yes. [Paiute for "ice fog," a dense fog of suspended ice particles]

NZ: There were many, many days of pogonip, and it was so beautiful. In fact the whole town [of Lee Vining] was covered in pogonip. Then sometimes it would snow and somehow or another the color of the sky changed the color of the water, and I would tell the Japanese a little bit and kind of give them an idea of what the country was like. They were really fascinated with it.

ELEVEN

Mary Kageyama Nomura (b. 1925)

I was able to continue singing in camp

Introduction

"Natural and built settings do not determine our lives or the course of history, but they do establish boundaries and supply possibilities"—provocative words to describe Manzanar, where federal policy established and maintained boundaries that seemed, temporarily at least, to deny possibility altogether.[1] Mary Nomura's recollections in this 1997 interview are exquisite in their suggestion that the bounded environment at Manzanar did offer possibilities. The people inside needed "cultural enrichment," she explained to internment scholar and oral historian Art Hansen, and so, encouraged by a dedicated Caucasian music teacher, she used her talents to bring it to them.

Mary Kageyama went to Manzanar in May 1942 a shy sixteen-year old with a velvet voice and gift for music: leaving in 1945, she had become the beloved "Songbird of Manzanar." Singing the popular swing tunes and romantic hits of the 1940s, she reminded her listeners of the America they too, were still part of, and starring in the elaborate musicals staged in the high school auditorium, she had audiences whistling and clapping for more.

Manzanar was "camp" to Mary Nomura and the other 11,062 people who lived there over three and a half years. Now a powerful symbolic allusion to "*the* central event of Japanese American history,"[2] it was then a term better suited to the 2,500 evacuee children, who more than sixty years later recall, almost without exception, a "good time" at Manzanar, with greater freedom from the confines of family and tradition. Far more demoralized were the older adults, the Issei, by the humiliation of confinement and the lost years of sacrifice for their children's future. Yet some, especially women, recall that in camp they experienced leisure for the first time in decades of hard work.

From the start, Manzanar eluded description. Initially designated an Assembly Center, it was the first of seventeen hurriedly set up—most in racetracks and fairgrounds—to house the "evacuated" people prior to their relocation to more permanent facilities. In March 1942, it opened as the Owens Valley Reception Center, under the Army-controlled Wartime Civilian Control Administration. A new civilian agency, the War Relocation Authority, assumed administration on June 1, 1942, and the camp was re-designated the more ambiguous Manzanar War Relocation Center.

The dilemma persists: what was Manzanar and what should it be called? The incarceration of parents and grandparents is a shadowed legacy for new generations of Japanese Americans. Many view the places of their common past as nothing less than concentration camps. They point out that President Franklin Roosevelt used the term, referring to the centers in early 1942. But as imagery born of history collides with linguistic correctness, veterans' organizations, other ethnic groups, Owens Valley residents, and some former internees take exception to a term now so darkly associated with the death camps of Nazi Europe.

Manzanar by any name imparted to its occupants a sharply defined imprint of place that remains little diminished after sixty years. Memories steeped in humiliation and loss are tempered by others, treasured for the simple attempts at normalcy they represented: dances, baseball games, high school graduation, friendships, and romance.

Mary's experience suggests, too, that Manzanar was a meeting place. In just under a square mile, 10,000 people were brought together from strawberry farms and fishing ports, rural towns and urban neighborhoods, often with little more in common than a shared ancestry. The crowded barracks, lack of privacy, and long mess hall lines produced shared indignities and frustration, and confinement exacerbated pre-evacuation political and cultural tensions that erupted in violent confrontation late in 1942.

Sweeter meetings took place as well: teen-agers formed clubs, musicians joined an orchestra, work parties built parks, and farmers together grew tons of vegetables to feed the camp. Five hundred forty-one babies were born in the camp hospital, and Mary met Shiro Nomura, who became her husband after they returned to Los Angeles in 1945.

Shikata ga nai, the residents of Manzanar said; "it cannot be helped." "We were making the best of a bad situation," they recall decades later. Shiro Nomura passed away in 2000, and Mary, vivacious and stylish at eighty-one, continues to sing. She returned recently to the stage of the former Manzanar High School auditorium with a lilting rendition of "Accentuate the Positive."

Mary Nomura—Interview

My father passed away when I was four. He was a carpenter, and he had a stroke just like my husband Shi. He could not do too much work, so he was at home doing

Mary Nomura, 2001. *Photo by Allan Nomura, Courtesy of Mary Nomura*

carpentry work. Then my mother was a teacher of Japanese music [and] dance. We didn't know much about her until my brother went back to Japan several years ago and delved back into her history, whoever might have known her. He found out that when she was just a little teenager, she used to cut school to go to a music school, to learn how to dance and sing. She was always interested in music. So from there she learned how to play the *shamisen*, the Japanese banjo, [and] the *shakuhachi*, which is a long, bamboo flute. She played the drums, she taught Japanese classical dancing [and] she taught classical Japanese opera-type singing.

Arthur Hansen: She was doing this all in Japan?
MN: She learned all this in Japan. She came over here at a very young age, before she was married, and she started music, in her home, I believe—I don't think she had a studio—and she started teaching all these things. My father came over illegally through Mexico—he was the true wetback. And I don't know what year they got married, my brother might know that.
AH: Sometime after 1900, probably?
MN: Oh yes.
AH: You're seventy-three, aren't you?
MN: I'll be seventy-two this year. But anyway, so she taught all this dancing and music. She never had the time to teach her children, so we just mimicked all the students while they were dancing and singing. We learned by just watching and listening. So music was always in our family somehow or other, [it] has always been a big mainstay.
AH: And where were you living when she had the home studio?
MN: In Venice.
AH: You later graduated from Venice High School, didn't you?
MN: No, I graduated in Manzanar.
AH: Oh, but you went to Venice High School before.
MN: Yes.
AH: Your family in Venice probably was a little bit unusual, in the sense that both your mother and your father were doing things that—Weren't most of the people in Venice celery farmers?
MN: They were farmers, yes. We never farmed. So we were a little bit different. By the time we were in Venice, when my mother was teaching her dancing and music, my father was already gone.
AH: In your mind, do you have visions of your mother doing musical things or only having her students do them?
MN: I only see her teaching, and I even remember some of the music that she was teaching the dance to. Of course, anytime there was a big program in Los Angeles, she took her students to perform. I don't know what she was charging her students, maybe fifty cents—everyone was so poor. And they all in turn had to buy their long, beautiful silk dresses and things, like kimonos. All I know is that she was a very gentle person, a very sweet, gentle person.

After my father died, shortly after, she married again, and from that she had another child. He is my half-brother. When she passed away in 1933—that was after the big [Long Beach] earthquake of 1933—we were supposed to have been taken to an orphanage because there were so many young ones—my brother was only sixteen, my sister was fifteen, and the rest of them all the way down to four years old.

The Japanese orphanage in Los Angeles came after us. My brother said, "No, you're not going to separate us," and he quit school, so did my sister, and they went to work and supported the rest of the family. [My half-brother] was taken to Japan with my stepfather. Oh, that was a bribery, that [was how] I was able to take singing lessons, because my stepfather was going to take my little sister and me to Japan with his son, take us all to Japan. And my brother said, "No, you can take your son but you cannot take my two sisters." So he said [to me], "If you stay, I'll send you to music school," singing school and dancing also. And so I said, "Okay, I'll stay." Because at that time, oh, to get to go to some other country? That would have been great. You know, we were living here in the Depression and just having a hard time, and so, thanks to my brother, I stayed here and didn't go to Japan and almost starve to death like most everyone did during the wartime.

[So] from when I was eight and my mother died, my brother somehow or other was able to put aside a dollar fifty a week to send me to singing lesson school in Santa Monica, and from there I was taking lessons till I was fifteen. Well, I was singing always since I was a little girl. I remember my mother teaching her old—we called them old, they must have been thirty years old—students how to sing the Japanese opera. By mimicking their opera, I sang. There is a picture of me performing when I was four years old. I was able to do this program at a big show in L.A. People threw money on the stage; they were crying and everything because here was this little four-year-old girl singing opera. Then in grammar school we used to sing at little talent shows and we'd get paid off in little candies and stuff.

AH: This wasn't at the Japanese school, this was at the public school?

MN: The public school, yes. I was about eleven, I think.

AH: And you were singing American ballads and stuff, popular songs?

MN: Yes, and then when the JACL [Japanese American Citizens League] used to put on talent shows, they asked me to sing, and from there we found out about the Nisei Week shows [every August] in Los Angeles at the Yamato Hall. My brother took me for an audition and we tried out. Even he sang, my sister sang—we had a trio. And I was, what, thirteen? I think I was thirteen, and I would sing.

AH: One of the stories that gets told about you and Shi was that Shi had heard you singing at Yamato Hall.

MN: Yes. The war broke out in '41, so it was August 1941, I believe, and he wrote in his little memoirs that that's when he first heard me sing. And he was kind of smitten with my voice, I guess, when I was just a little fifteen-year-old singing these big people's songs.

AH: What songs were you singing at Yamato Hall when you won that contest?

MN: I sang "Liebestraum" by Franz Liszt, in Japanese and English, and, oh, what else did I sing? Then I closed the show with "God Bless America"—I remember that.

AH: Did you have Issei and Nisei both in the audience?

MN: I think mostly Niseis were there, people in their eighteens and twenties going to the shows.

AH: And were most of the songs that others were singing at that time—
MN: Oh, all pop music, westerns.
AH: A lot of the groups who were at Manzanar were from Los Angeles County, and a lot of them when they went to Manzanar resided in the same blocks. Like we were earlier talking that people from Terminal Island were largely in Blocks 9 and 10. Where did the Venice people go in Manzanar, what blocks?
MN: I believe they were in 24 or 25, way up on top.
AH: Was that your block?
MN: No, we were in 13 because we were going to school, so we had to be near a school. But then after a while when my sister got a job at the hospital, we were able to move up to 29, which is next to the hospital, and so we lived in 29 most of the time there.
AH: Now, some of the people who came, they also reconstituted their organizations, like their sports teams. Did you bring a group or something that used to sing together before the war and then sang again at Manzanar?
MN: No, I didn't do that. And any kind of music thing that was formed while we were at Manzanar, it was formed by word-of-mouth or by the newsletter that said this is happening, a music group is going to start here, a band, a thespian group, or a Japanese dancing group. They were recruiting people for different things then, for people to keep their sanity going in that camp.
AH: Now, why don't you try to explain your own personal involvement in music at Manzanar—you've become identified with your moniker there of "Songbird of Manzanar." But if you could also talk about music and the role that it played in Manzanar—your experience, and then the experience of the entire 10,000 people that are there with respect to the different types of music, because you would have been sensitive to that going on.
MN: Well, thanks to Louis Frizzell, who was the music teacher in Manzanar—he did the orchestra, the choirs, and the a capellas and the drama—we were able to put on these big shows. You know, people in that camp were hungry for doing something like going to see a good play, going to see music or a choral group. Even if it was a high school group, they all attended those things. Somehow or other they found out that this was happening. I guess it would be in the *Free Press* newspaper and by word of mouth from the children going to school. If there was something going on, like a movie we've never seen before, or a play or classical music or orchestra, we all went because we all wanted to have something to go to for—what do you call that?
AH: Cultural enrichment.
MN: Yes, that's what it is, cultural enrichment. They had to because I mean we were within barbed wire and couldn't go anywhere, do anything, except survive day-by-day. But when something like that came up, we all made it a point to either as a group, with a bunch of girlfriends, or with dates or with a club or whatever, we all tried to make those functions.
AH: And what were the functions consisting of? I know there were different groups there, like the Jive Bombers, and there were the Sierra Singers and a number

of things—and those are the more Americanized music, but I also read about huge crowds that would go to these talent shows pretty much run by the Issei and things. Did you go to any of those, too?

MN: You know, I'm ashamed to say I didn't get to go to any of those Japanese cultural type of things, but I know it was going on. I found out later they had beautiful productions, and, like you say, they were run by the Isseis. And there were all these young people [whose] parents wanted them to keep up with the cultural thing. I don't know how they managed to put on these beautiful things with their silk gowns. I guess some of them were even made out of whatever material they could buy from Montgomery Ward and Sears, and they were able to put on these shows.

AH: Then there was a cleavage in the camp between the more Japanese cultural arts and things and then the Americanized ones. And you participated exclusively in the Americanized ones.

MN: Yes, because I—we didn't even speak Japanese—basic words, maybe, but not to be able to understand a conversation or keep up a conversation. Since we lost our parents, we spoke nothing but English in our family. It's only after we came out of camp that I learned how to speak Japanese because I lived with Shi's father and mother.

AH: Can you recall your first involvement in some musical things? You were only fifteen when you went to [Manzanar]?

MN: I was sixteen. Having sung for these JACL groups in Los Angeles and Santa Monica—and I even went to army camps to entertain—when I went into camp I guess people knew that I was able to sing, and so they would ask me. The very first program that they had in Manzanar was for some kind of meeting, and I was asked to entertain. The high school had the a capella choir, and from there on, every time we had some kind of a program, I was the soloist.

AH: It wasn't until 1944 or so that the auditorium that's still standing at Manzanar was built, and you probably ended up singing in that auditorium before you left camp, didn't you?

MN: Yes.

AH: Where would you do the singing before?

MN: It would either be in the open-air place—I don't remember singing there but I do remember singing in the recreation halls, which was just one regular-sized barrack [in each block] set aside where they had a piano and you could dance, and small parties were held in there. Or if there was a big dance or something, then it would be held at the mess hall, and that would be the double barrack. Those were the kinds of places that I used to sing in.

AH: You became part of a group, too, didn't you, like the Modernaires or something?

MN: The Modernaires was a social club, a sports club. We used to play baseball and then we used to have dances and things like that. And we still get together after all these years. I just got together with a bunch of them last October in Las Vegas when we had our high school reunion.

The Manzanar High School Commencement, 1944. Ceremonies took place in the high school auditorium/gymnasium that now houses the Manzanar National Historic Site Interpretive Center. *Photograph courtesy of Archie Miyatake, from the Collection of Toyo Miyatake Manzanar Images*

AH: And did some of them sing?

MN: No.

AH: When you were at camp then, did you get a chance to practice somewhere?

MN: Mr. Frizzell, the teacher, would have me practice with him. He would go out in the city and buy sheet music for me and pick out songs for me to sing at these different functions that came up. Thanks to him, I was able to continue singing in camp.

AH: What did you know about his background, what was it in terms of music that he was able to do all this stuff?

MN: All I know is that he was going to UCLA, and I don't know if his major was music or what, but he found out that they needed a music teacher in the camp and so he volunteered and went, and then he became head of the music department there.

AH: Was he pretty young then?

MN: Very young. He was about a year older than Shi.

AH: Like twenty-seven or something?

MN: Not even that old. See, he was quite a prolific songwriter, and he wrote plays and he put on these big [productions], and he was the director. Oh, he was quite a man! And he wrote all different kinds of things. He even wrote a Christmas cantata, with me being the part of Mary, and I just really appreciated that.

AH: Was he hired by the school system? I mean, did he teach in the school, or did he do extracurricular things, or both?
MN: No, only taught music. He was our music teacher. Let's see, he must have taught harmony, I didn't learn that. Music appreciation someone else was teaching—I took all that. But the singing part, the a cappella choir and [orchestra] and the little groups that he used to make up, he was the teacher of that.
AH: And was music popular in part because of [him]?
MN: Oh, yes. I mean, if someone wasn't as likeable as he was, I don't think it would have taken off and been as successful as it was.
AH: I know he later became an actor.
MN: A character actor, yes.
AH: And was in many, many Hollywood movies, including *The Summer of '42*. I remember seeing him playing a druggist, and there were some hilarious scenes. He must have been in as many pictures as almost anybody of his generation, in terms of character parts. How did he ever get into movies after Manzanar?
MN: I don't know, but he always said after he came out [of camp], "Do you know, if I didn't go to Manzanar I could have been the next Gregory Peck!" He used to make us laugh. But he was such a wonderful person as a friend. And when he passed away, he was in his apartment and no one knew he was already gone. He had cancer, and he didn't tell [anyone] he was ill. So Mr. Frizzell's aunts and uncles went after the funeral to clean out his place [and] threw away all his manuscripts and music and everything that he composed in camp.
AH: They threw the stuff away?
MN: Because they figured it was all junk.
AH: Oh, that's so sad! And there was a voluminous amount of it?
MN: Oh, yes, he always wrote music and he always had plays written. He was an artist also, he painted. But we do have the original music that he wrote of the Manzanar song that I used to sing all the time, but that's all we could save.
AH: So he was a really important person, not only to you but to the camp as well.
MN: Oh yes, very much so.
AH: Now if you go to the Eastern California Museum, they have a record there, a 45 record, and it was made apparently in camp by you—
MN: No, the 45 was made [later] in Pasadena. I am singing a song that Shi had composed. After I came out of camp, Shi used to send me poetry. See, I got out in January [1945]. He didn't come out until March, I believe. In the meantime, he had sent me the poetry, and I would put it to music. Then I took it to those dinky little studios where you could record it with no background music, and I sent it back to him in Manzanar. But the 78 that's there was recorded in Manzanar with Louis Frizzell playing the piano. He brought in all the equipment from outside to record music in Manzanar, and that's when I recorded a couple of songs, one on each side, and that's the one that's in the museum now, for posterity, I guess.
AH: Okay, and what's the song on the 78?

MN: It's one of those Bing Crosby songs, "Day After Forever," and, oh golly, I've forgotten what was on the other side.

AH: And what was the signature song of Manzanar that you were referring to earlier?

MN: It's called "When I Can"—the last words are "when I can." But it should be called "The Manzanar Song" because it's all about life in there.

AH: And did Louis Frizzell write that one?

MN: He wrote "When I Can."

AH: Now at the time, this was in the 1940s that you're coming of age—what models of singers with bands and things did you identify with?

MN: I should say it was Judy Garland. I always liked her singing. She was young and I guess she would be about my age anyway. Right now it's Ella Fitzgerald that I like, but in those days I wasn't hearing her. But Judy Garland I was listening to. And Deanna Durbin was all classical, so I wasn't interested in that, but she had a gorgeous voice. [And] Helen O'Connell—But I really did identify more with Judy Garland, the kind of songs she sang and the range of her voice and all that.

AH: In the Owens Valley, there started to be some interaction between the people living in the surrounding communities and camp. There were these affairs they had where people came out, and sometimes Mr. Merritt, [the camp director], even went out to different service clubs and things. Were you ever involved in singing to groups outside of the camp or singing before visitors from the outside?

MN: Not going out, but we did have a program where others were invited to come and hear Louis Frizzell's Christmas—no, it was not Christmas, it was more patriotic. Music that Paul Robeson sang. Oh golly, I can't remember the title, but it's a story about the Constitution from the beginning to the Machine Age. It's a pageant, all singing, and that was introduced to the people of Inyo County to come and listen to. And they wanted to take this group to other camps to play, but we could never get the clearance to go to the other camps.

AH: So you sang it just in Manzanar?

MN: Only in Manzanar.

AH: You probably sang before bigger crowds in Manzanar than you have ever since. In the auditorium you had probably several thousand people that you could have sung in front of at the time.

MN: (laughter) Oh, I guess. Well, I don't think a lot of the Isseis and Kibeis [US–born Japanese educated in Japan] came to some of these things. They were more geared to the Niseis and to the younger kids.

AH: When you see people that were at Manzanar from your generation, is one of the things that always comes up the fact that you used to sing? In the [Jerry] Stanley book [*I Am An American*] there is a picture of you singing, and it says "Mary Kageyama, the Songbird of Manzanar." Is that your identity in people's minds?

MN: I'm afraid so. Because I never was an athlete or never was a real popular girl with the boys or anything like that, just because I used to sing.

AH: You actually provided the entertainment rather than being able to go out and dance—

MN: That's right. I was like a stick, I couldn't dance worth a darn, and anytime I was asked for a date it's because I was singing. I was, gee, next to a wallflower. (laughter) But thanks to Shi—Every year his club [the ManzaKnights] had this big dance called the Turkey Trot, and I had no one to go with because my then boyfriend had gone back East, relocated. You know, in a place like Manzanar everybody knew what everyone was doing or what happened, so they knew that I didn't have a boyfriend at that time, so that's when Shi thought I should have an escort. And there was no one in his club who was tall enough or who wasn't already spoken for, so he volunteered.

AH: Well, he was a nice volunteer since he was such a good-looking man, too.

MN: Oh yes, he was quite a catch. (laughter)

H: Now since you sang before the war and you sang a lot during the war at Manzanar, and you were even experimenting with making records, was there some thought at all that you might—Was the economic situation such after the war that it was impossible for you to consider a musical career?

MN: Well, when I was in high school my goal was to someday become a singer on the radio. Actually, at a show in 1947 or '48, when I was already married, a young man who was a singer approached me. He said, "Would you like to cut a record with me and make a record of some nice songs?" I just listened to him, and Shi, standing by me, said, "I wish you wouldn't." Shi was very possessive, and he felt that if I went into that then I was going to take off. And to this day I have a girlfriend who says, "You know, darn that Shi, if it wasn't for him being so possessive, maybe you might have made something of yourself in the music world." And I say, "Well, no, I'm quite satisfied having raised my five kids." But I always did just like to sing. After that, after having gotten married, I didn't have the aspiration to become a singer of any kind.

AH: Well, you didn't stop singing, though. Even though you define yourself as a mother and a wife, do you still maybe get a chance to exercise your vocation, the sense of calling that you have as a musical person?

MN: It's only for my love for singing that I sing. If someone asks me to sing next year for some kind of event, I would really have to think real hard. But I'll practice; that's what keeps me going. If someone wants me to sing someplace, I'll try.

AH: After the war, when you and Shi were trying to get started as a young couple—having five children and raising them and everything—at some point you moved out, as a lot of Japanese Americans did in the 1950s, into the suburbs. You're still here in Garden Grove. What called you and your husband out to this area to open up a fish market—and I assume you must have done some work in the market, too?

MN: Every day.

AH: Can you tell us about that?

MN: Well, by the time I left [camp] in January '45, we were more or less promised to each other. April Fool's Day was Easter Sunday in 1945, and we got engaged, and we got married in June, so it was quite a whirlwind courtship. When we were engaged, he went on the bus [doing] gardening and used the customers' tools and whatever to do their yards. After that he was able to borrow $500 and he bought himself an old car, and from there he got together with some good friends and they started a partnership in a furniture business. [They] were the very first discounters. He had furniture in this big old building, and if you got a card from his company, you were able to go to this big store—I think it was called [Three Crown] Furniture Company—and you were able to buy something at a big discount. After that, he demonstrated and sold Pfaff sewing machines. Then, he started to work for All-American Markets—they're gone now. We moved from Pasadena to different places, and then we ended up in Norwalk. While he was working in the All-American Market in Downey, the one in Orange County opened up and so he started to work there. So we finally decided we'd look for a house over here, and we found this place and now we've been here for thirty-nine years.

AH: Was it difficult for Japanese people to get homes in Garden Grove at that time?

MN: Oh yes. In Garden Grove, yes. But when we were going to buy a place in Norwalk, there was a Jewish man and an Italian man, they came to the house and said, "We don't want you in our neighborhood." And we just didn't pay any attention to them, we bought the house. We became friends. One was our next-door neighbor, and one two doors away became my kids' good friends. And so we bought this home in Garden Grove in 1958. In 1959 [Shi] decided he wanted to start his own business, and so he borrowed money from his father and bought this little old place and started a fish market, and we had that place for twenty-two years. It was right by our house—I was able to walk.

AH: Who were your customers in the early years when you first opened up?

MN: Mostly Japanese, Caucasians, and then we started putting in groceries from the Philippines, Korea, Vietnam, China, and so we had all those different ethnic groups coming in. We were the only Oriental market there then.

AH: Your store was open when the first big wave of Southeast Asians came into Garden Grove [in the 1970s].

MN: Oh, yes.

AH: Did that change the nature of your business? Did you make a lot more money?

MN: I think so. We made more money at that time. Eventually, after twenty-two years, the influence in the whole area became Korean. They were all coming out of Los Angeles and settling here, some in Westminster, some in Anaheim, but mostly Garden Grove. Right before we closed our store, because of the influx of the Korean trade, the Japanese would not come to our store. The said they felt uncomfortable. They had that hardheaded animosity towards the Koreans at that time—some were very prejudiced.

AH: What happened to your store? You're not running it anymore, but did you sell the store and somebody took it over?

MN: We could have sold it with the name. The name was quite famous from all over, but Shi said, in all honesty he could not sell the store with his name. He knew it was going to go down because of the area changing, so we just sold the building and donated whatever was left after our big sale to all the different churches.

AH: And when was that, Mary?

MN: Nineteen eighty.

AH: Now [before that] there were the early years when you probably had no contact with Manzanar, when you were just trying to start your family. But what originally got you back in touch with that part of your past—with your common past, really—you and Shi?

MN: I think it was in '70 or '71. My daughter was in high school, and on the way [back] from a trip to Sacramento we stopped in at the [Eastern California] museum [in Independence] because we heard that there were a few things there from the camp that the people who lived in the area donated to the museum because of their ties with Manzanar—the furniture and whatever, artwork and all that.

AH: Had you ever been back to the camp since you left?

MN: Oh, we went to visit the camp, yes, with the children, but we never went to the museum. On the way to Tahoe we'd stop in and walk around with the kids and show them.

AH: Was that a pretty haunting experience for you?

MN: It was a nostalgic trip for us. We looked at it more fondly for the children, saying that this is where we met and this is what we did and this is where we stayed—not too much negative things to talk to the children about.

AH: This trip when you stopped at the museum—

MN: Yes, we met Henry Raub, who was the director at the time. The museum was closed already. We looked in, we were just peering in to see what we could see, and Mr. Raub was still in there and he invited us in and let us see the articles and the artifacts, and then we started to talk, and he said, "Well, come for dinner." So we had dinner with him, and from then on he just got Shi interested in bringing whatever was in the house from the Manzanar days to put into the museum. And so it was from there that Shi would [ask] relatives and friends for any artifacts that they might have in their garages stored away. [They] would call us and say, "Well, I have this and I have that," and we'd go get it. I don't care where it was, Shi would go get it. So, thanks to their generosity, we were able to put some of those things into the museum.

AH: Did it become a passion for him?

MN: Oh, it was a great passion for him.

AH: Did you share his enthusiasm for the museum project and collecting materials?

MN: Oh yes, I went with him everywhere. And then we still had the market, but we had good workers—mostly relatives—and we could leave the store for several days and go off to Manzanar to walk around the place and collect things and take pictures and write down things and then go to the museum and spend time there. We were still making money, so we were able to do things like this. We couldn't have waited till after we retired, because the interest for him would have been gone by that time.

AH: And Henry Raub was enthusiastic about developing this collection too, right?

MN: Yes, very much so. He is the one that got Shi interested. It never would have gotten off the ground if it wasn't for Henry Raub.

AH: What were some of the results and ramifications of having the exhibit up there? Did it put you back in touch with people? Or did some people come through, [then] get in touch with you? It was a visible sort of thing—the Eastern California Museum is a nice museum to stop at and it's on an artery that runs right through the Owens Valley.

MN: Shi wanted to perpetuate the memory of whatever happened. He wanted people to know what happened—good and bad. And he had this little thing for people to sign as they came [into the museum] saying if they were in camp, what camp they were in, were they in any club affiliations and things like that. And from that he would make a file and he would send out Christmas cards or whatever to keep in touch with all these people. He wanted someday to be able to be one-on-one with them, but he never did get that far. He just wanted to make it more personal.

AH: As opposed to locating memories and memorabilia from people who had been at Manzanar, what other kinds of artifacts and stuff did he locate in the Owens Valley?

MN: He found things that were around the stone pillars [by] the grave marker in the back [of the camp]. A person who had that on his property told Shi he had it, but it's part of his property. So we went to see it and took pictures of it. And then another person said, "My house used to be a barrack," and so we'd go over there and take pictures of it.

AH: So sometimes he didn't take it, he took photos of it.

MN: Yes. And then one lady had a thing by her gate with someone's address—barrack number and their name—on it, as a step-way into their property. She said, "If you want it you may have it. Take it to the museum." But Shi never did take it because it was part of their house. So he just took pictures of it and took it to the museum.

AH: So that's the portion of the exhibit where it says "What it was at one time and what it is now" side-by-side—he would write the captions for that?

MN: Yes.

AH: One thing I was surprised to find out is that you and Shi actually bought property [in the Owens Valley] and ran some kind of store. How did that come about?

MN: We bought property there in Independence. It's a mobile home property, and to this day we still own it and still pay taxes on it.

AH: Where is that lot, exactly, in relationship to the museum?

MN: It's about two or three blocks south of the museum and on the very end of Independence. It's a very nice location, a beautiful place to build a home. You've got the majestic mountains there. That was both of our ideas, to buy a nice mobile home—we even looked at mobile homes—and put it on the lot.

AH: What would you have had in the way of a community of friendship up there, aside from Mr. Raub, if you were retired people up there?

MN: We made quite a few friends up there, and every time we went to Manzanar, did something for the project there, we would take things for all our friends that we'd meet up there. One of the ladies we made friends with used to work at Manzanar. Anna Kelley. She was a feisty old gal.

AH: She ran a Red Cross station [during the camp construction].

MN: Right. She brought in a lot of things that she had collected during the time she was in Manzanar. When her husband passed away we went up there to the funeral.

AH: So you got to meet some of the locals up there and got to be friends with them.

MN: Yes, and so I knew that if we ever moved up there we wouldn't be the only ones just with each other, we had friends there.

AH: Now, did you once own a small store?

MN: Yes, in Lone Pine, [at] the old Lone Pine Hotel. Each one of those little rooms became little stores. So we had this little gift shop. We called it Shi's Oriental Bazaar, and Mr. Raub was quite a sign painter. He made a beautiful sign and made a little Japanese *torii* thing. We sold things like tea and cookies and crackers, plus all the Oriental giftware that would appeal, fans and all those things.

AH: Did you live there for a while, Mary, up in the Owens Valley, and stay there or in a mobile home or anything?

MN: No, we used to stay at the Winnedumah Hotel every time we went, and then later, we started staying at the Willow [Motel] in Lone Pine.[3]

AH: Now, the store was only open on weekends?

MN: Yes, because there was no one to run it during the weekdays. Mr. Raub would go there and run the store on Fridays and Saturdays.

AH: And what kind of success did you have with the store?

MN: Made rent and made friends. And people would go in and say, "I want this, I want that," and Mr. Raub would phone us or write and then we'd take it up there the next time we went. We couldn't just go up there [anytime] because we still had the fish market.

AH: What ended the venture?

MN: It was just getting too hard for Mr. Raub. He was in his [seventies] when he was doing it for us. [We had it] three or four years. We had the fish market and we had the Manzanar project, and then we had that little store. [Shi] thought [of] eventually making it into a larger store and selling more perishable things. He was thinking of living up there, making runs into Los Angeles to pick up fresh fish and whatever, fresh vegetables that you can't buy up there. He thought he would draw from Bishop, and then Ridgecrest isn't too far from Lone Pine. There were a lot of Oriental ladies there at China Lake [Naval Weapons Test Station] that were married to the Caucasian service people. He had this long-range plan.

AH: Okay, that was a somewhat ambitious kind of thing, that when the store closed here you would sell this house in Garden Grove, relocate up to—excuse the word—move up to the Owens Valley, and then live on that property you had. What finally did that plan in?
MN: Me.
AH: Oh, you?
MN: I didn't want to go there and live so far away from our grandchildren, who were starting to come. By the time we started that venture in Lone Pine, I already had one grandchild, and then shortly after that, I had another, and then boom, eleven of them. But I said I wasn't about to live that far away from my grandchildren, so that quashed that.
AH: Now, by 1989, Shi had already experienced some health problems?
MN: Yes, 1989 is when he had a stroke, and from there his mind was slowly fading, and we had no idea, we thought he was hard of hearing. We found he was not socializing with the family anymore. He would go into his room and start doodling or whatever because he wasn't understanding what people were saying. He didn't know what the words meant. He was not able to speak what he wanted to say. People would ask him something and he would say something contrary to what I'd think he should be saying because he wasn't thinking, and it would hurt my feelings. He couldn't remember my name even. He had to ask me, "What's your name?"
AH: How old was he in 1989?
MN: He was seventy.
AH: While this was happening, was he still continuing to go to Manzanar?
MN: Yes, he was going up to Manzanar for the pilgrimage, but then the last time he took things up there he was displaying things beautifully like he always had been, but when the pilgrimage group came he would hide behind all the displays [or] in the back room were everything was stored. From then on he was hiding when people came to talk to him. I didn't realize that his memory was going so fast.
AH: Do you remember the last time you went to Manzanar?
MN: At the pilgrimage, it must have been '90 or '91, but he wasn't happy at all there because it was just too bewildering for him.
AH: He didn't recognize anything?
MN: No. When we went into the museum and people said, "Hi, Shi, how are you?" he wouldn't say hello or anything because he didn't know who they were.
AH: Shi's philosophy towards Manzanar was something that people—those who may have said that this was really a prison, a jail, or something—raised questions about, that it seems to be romanticized, not only through your relationship but the whole business of the museum exhibit and everything. And some people say, "A lot of this museum exhibit is nostalgia and reminiscence, but what does Shi really feel about this whole evacuation business?" You people were able to go and stay up in the Owens Valley and to make friends there, and some people probably wouldn't have

been able to do that. Did Shi ever feel that some people went too far in painting the experience in dark colors?

MN: Well, he always said to people that Manzanar and the whole evacuation process was wrong, but the only good thing is that "I met my wife there," and he always left it that way. But he thought that putting the collection over at the Independence museum was something for people to see now and in the future, that things like this that did happen shouldn't happen again. He wanted to make sure that people know this is not made-up stuff. Like this man in Bishop who says all that stuff that Shi put up there is all lies and all touched up and they're fake. I'm so proud of how he started that and kept it going. The Manzanar story itself, he felt that it belongs right there by Manzanar, in Independence, not at the big museum in Los Angeles. It was really hard for him, running a business at the same time, but being what kind of person he was, he did both very well. The market was a business. He made good friends and everything there, but really his love was for putting that museum thing together, and that's what he really was dedicated to.

AH: How do *you* put Manzanar into a sort of perspective?

MN: I felt that some of those people just all had tunnel vision. All they wanted to talk about was the injustice and the darkness. But Shi and I always felt, you know, it happened, it happened, and just make the most of it. But I can't say it was a beautiful place or a beautiful experience or a beautiful thing done to us. Manzanar is a big thing for me, a main thing with me. And my children, too. They know what Manzanar meant to the Japanese and to just their mother and father. It's something that will be part of me for as long as I live.

TWELVE

Keith Bright (b. 1915)

I enjoy being involved

Introduction

"All politics is local," former Speaker of the House "Tip" O'Neill famously said. That ideal, of a self-governing small town, the "purest form of politics," drew Keith Bright into Inyo County issues soon after he moved with his family to the Owens Valley in 1968.[1] He recalled that time, with his wife Jane participating, in conversations with interviewer Richard Potashin in 1998 and 2001 at the Bright home near Independence.

Keith is a tall man, his stature matched by the gregarious personality, outsize sense of humor, and sharp intellect that served him well as he began negotiating the workings of Inyo County government. Before that, success in the oil business had taken him to the far corners of the globe—and gained him access to the inner offices of Washington's political elite. When the Brights and their children left southern California to try cattle ranching in the Owens Valley, they settled on a historic 160-acre spread just outside Independence, one of the few ranches in the valley still in private ownership.

Nationwide, 1968 was a tumultuous and tragic year, a time of social and cultural ferment. Among its legacies, an unprecedented grassroots activism found expression in the national environmental movement. Loosely organized local groups and individuals—college-educated young adults in western states, for the most part—joined with the Sierra Club and other established organizations in challenging long-held assumptions and policies related to resource use and their effects on natural environments. As the movement found a place in national political power structures, its members lobbied successfully for hundreds of federal, state, and local regulatory laws. Among them, the 1971 California Environmental Quality Act (CEQA) for the first time required an Environmental Impact Report for publicly funded projects. The following year, Inyo County, backed by local environmental groups, cited the CEQA when it took the City of Los Angeles to court over increases in groundwater pumping in the Owens Valley.

"Environmentalism," applied to court cases locally and nationwide, pressed for more responsible governmental and corporate stewardship of the earth's resources. But in places such as the Owens Valley, its meaning expanded to encompass the debate over local control of resource use and protection of communities' immediate environments.[2] There, the gauntlet of local self-determination had been thrown down with the 1972 lawsuit, and it was into that arena of litigation that Keith Bright stepped as an Inyo County Supervisor in 1986.

An experienced political mediator, he helped steer Inyo County and the City of Los Angeles through years of intricate negotiation and legal wrangling as they worked toward adoption of a long-range groundwater management plan for the Owens Valley. That joint effort would have been unthinkable even thirty years earlier, when the right of Los Angeles to the valley's water was unimpeachable, backed by California water law—and Theodore Roosevelt's enduring 1906 pronouncement that municipal use of the water constituted "the greatest good for the greatest number of people." A measure of the shift in national priorities, the pleas of Owens Valley farmers to the President a century ago went unheeded, whereas contemporary advocates for the environmental health of the valley have successfully taken advantage of a legal system fully attentive to those issues.

Keith remains engaged in civic debate, urging reasonable solutions to the valley's vexing dilemmas. He typifies a sensibility of the true patriot, that "citizenship is virtually co-extensive with being involved with one's neighbors for the good of the community."[3] The 1992 legislation designating the former relocation center at Manzanar a National Historic Site called also for an eleven-member advisory commission to meet and consult with National Park Service officials on "matters relating to the development, management, and interpretation of the site." It was to include representatives from the Native American community in the Owens Valley, local residents, former interned residents of Manzanar, and the general public. Keith Bright was an immediate and logical choice.

The Bright ranch is hidden among old growth oak and cottonwood trees far up the willow-lined canyon where Oak Creek flows out of the Sierras near Independence. It is another of those places like Manzanar where the landscape evokes an accumulation of pasts. Paiutes camped and hunted along the creek, and in 1895, a white homesteader from Wyoming, reportedly a fugitive, claimed the 160 acres. As the Parker Ranch between 1912 and 1958, the homestead grew from a small shack to two ranch homes and several outbuildings. Cabins built later were rented out to fishermen.

Keith Bright, ca. 1990. *Keith Bright Collection*

The Parkers also mined ore in the hills above the ranch and planted a large apple orchard. For a time, George Parker was the first ranger for the newly designated Inyo National Forest and worked out of the ranger station located nearby. Today, deer roam the property, and the weathered sheds and barns, ranch homes and guest cabins stand amid Keith's collection of old farm equipment, Jane Bright's colorful gardens and fruit trees, and the pickups and SUVs of a new century.

Keith Bright—Interview

I started working in the oil business when I was nineteen years old. I was born in 1915 in Lemoore, California, where my dad worked in the oil fields as a cable tool driller. I finished high school and junior college in Taft, California, then went to USC [University of Southern California] and studied petroleum engineering. I worked for the General Petroleum Corporation and Baroid in California before I went into business for myself.

Richard Potashin: What did you do in your business?
KB: I was in various phases of the oil business, some of it in production and drilling. We also developed a couple of little gas fields, and an oil field. Three of us formed KEN Corporation, a company that manufactured and sold oil-based drilling fluids.
RP: Can you tell me what brought you up here to the Owens Valley?
KB: What brought me up here was that we were drilling out in a place called Devil's Den in western Kern County. This happened in the 1950s. It was hot and it was dry and it was miserable, and I think we drilled a dry hole. There was a fellow who used to ride horseback up and down the state visiting his friends, and he happened to stop in there. I told him I was looking for a place, and it had to have water and a stream running though it. It had to be completely surrounded by Forest Service [land] and had to be within 250 miles of Los Angeles. He said, "I think I know the place. The Parker Ranch [over in the Owens Valley] is up for sale." A short time later we came up here and took a look at it and we took an option on the place. But then I took off for Texas or someplace on business and the place was sold. In 1963, we finally made a deal with a fellow named Vern Cyr [who owned it then] and we bought the place. We paid twice as much and got half as much as we should have gotten if we had dealt with the Parkers.
RP: When you took the ranch over, did you get into the cattle business right away?
KB: There was a little time interval before we got in the cow business. We bought Harry Miller's DWP [grazing] lease and his cattle, just east of the [Fort Independence] reservation, down towards the aqueduct. There were forty or fifty head—I don't really remember what he had, but it wasn't a whole lot. We bought more cattle, and we had a BLM [grazing] permit and Forest Service permit up here running from Thibaut Creek almost to Shepherd Creek.
Jane Bright: We bought it in 1963, but we didn't actually move here until the later part of 1968. So in those years, we had people who stayed here and cared for it, and we were running cattle at that time.
RP: When you first got into raising cows, Keith, what was the state of the industry here in the valley?
KB: There were different people in it. The ownerships have changed, but the size of ranches has not changed, because of the limits of the DWP leases. There have been some ranches sold, like Lacey sold at Olancha, and then leased it back. We maybe have the same number of head of cattle running in the valley as we always had, at least through my experience. Except when we had seven years of drought, [then] everybody reduced the size of their herds, and that's why we got out of it. We were in it about two or three years into the drought. We couldn't feed them. This country up here wasn't any good at all, it was so dry, and you couldn't stand there and buy expensive hay to

carry a bunch of old cows. The City leases we had didn't have sufficient water to irrigate them, and so that's when we decided enough was enough and we got out of it.
RP: In regards to your leases with the City, did you have a smooth relationship with them?
KB: Oh yes, the City generally treated the lessees very well. In fact, back then they were better to work with than they are now, as far as the lessees go. If you needed fence post and wires to fence the perimeter, they'd give it to you. I never had any problems with them at all in that way. But we've had all kinds of relationships with the DWP over the years.

A group of us wanted to start a college here in about 1970 or so. We wanted some land and went to the DWP. A fellow named Bob Phillips was the head of the DWP then. At that time their attitude was very strong in the opinion that they didn't want any more people in the Owens Valley. People cause problems for them, so we didn't get along very well in that way. Bob Phillips has been a good friend of mine since then, and I appreciate it because we always knew where he was coming from. You knew his job was to continue getting water for the City of Los Angeles. He was very pointed about that.
JB: I've seen a big change since we first moved here between what the DWP was like then, and what it's like now.
KB: What happened, very simply, when the Mono Lake [controversy] developed, and the environmental laws that came out of that, the DWP was very slow in reacting to them. [Inyo] County brought a lawsuit against them in 1971 or 1972. Under the environmental laws their [groundwater] pumping activity was found to be detrimental to the valley environment, and [the county] won that case. Slowly the DWP has replaced old ways by new attitudes, and they are now much easier to work with in total than they were.

A lot of things have been happening to them—I don't have much to do with them anymore, but nobody thought we'd ever get a water agreement. That [Long Term Water Agreement] was very good for Inyo County and very good for the DWP. It isn't perfect for either one of them, each side had to give something, and that's what you get in negotiations. Of course, they have Owens Lake [dust mitigation] down here now, and that's a problem to them.
RP: Was the dust issue much of a problem when you first came to the area in 1963?
KB: The dust issue is one that's been there for a long time. If you could talk to the old-timers, you'll find out that before the DWP got here, they had dust around the edges of Owens Lake because the farmers here were taking water out of [Owens] River. The lake was drying up then, and DWP just finished the job. In my opinion, if the DWP hadn't come in here and bought up the valley, we would now be looking at something similar to San Fernando Valley, when they had the small ranchettes. Everyone had a well or was taking water [from the river] through the canal system. The lake would have dried up anyway. If you had put ten thousand [more] people

scattered up and down the valley—which is not out of the question—and have them using water, I think the lake would be dry by now, anyway.

RP: A result of agricultural diversion?

KB: Sure. They would have had lawns, and a little alfalfa—they'd have a horse and they would have this and that. Now what do we have? At least we have open spaces that the public can enjoy. When we had our [City] lease we could only keep 25 percent of it fenced—just a small percentage that you can actually keep the public out of.

RP: That was a DWP condition?

KB: Yes, for leases.

RP: Keith, on your leases with the BLM and the Forest Service, did you see any changes in their policies in regards to grazing in those early years?

KB: You never knew exactly where they were going to come from. Their policies were not written for desert activities. I'll give you an example. One year I didn't put any cattle up here [on the Forest Service grazing land], and one of their people got hold of me and said, "You have to put cattle up there or else you have to take a non-use permit." I got in touch with the ranger in Lone Pine, and I told him I wanted him to come up and show me where the feed was. He came up, and we went over to the North Fork [of Oak Creek]. He got out and looked around and said, "You haven't got any feed. You can't put cattle up here." The range manager had told me that I had to put cattle up there, and he didn't know what he was talking about.

So many times the Forest Service or BLM will put people out here that have never had any experience, and they will tell you how to run something. They don't know what they are doing, but they have the authority and a regulation book behind them. But you are in the business, and in this instance I didn't want to put cattle up where they were going to lose weight, because weight is money. They don't know that. Then you'll run into some like the ranger who came up here with me, and he knew all about the cattle business and he understood.

One of the things about the Forest Service and the BLM—there's an arbitrary line that runs past the [Mt. Whitney] Fish Hatchery and goes south. We're on Forest Service land, below that is BLM. You had permits that said you could run so many cattle on the BLM land for a certain length of time, and then they had to be up on the U.S. Forest Service [land]. There's no fence in between.

You would put cattle up on the BLM land, and the regulations could not take into account what kind of a year you had, when the grass was ready. They'd say you have to be there on a certain date, but the date might be way too early because you could still have a lot of cold weather and there wasn't any feed, but you had to be up here. The other thing, when the feed would get bad down there [on the BLM land] and the cattle would start moving up and going onto the Forest Service land, you'd think you'd done something really wrong. They would call up and say you have to move your cattle down. There were no considerations to the fact that the cattle have to go where the feed is. Every year would be just a little bit different. That made it very difficult, so what we did was not say anything and not pay too much attention. Yes, you'd go move [the cattle] down, but the next day they'd be back up. Hopefully that guy would be someplace else, because it didn't make any sense.

RP: Were you active with the Inyo Cattlemen's Association?

KB: I was a member.

RP: We were talking about the close relation between the City and the cattlemen. How strong a voice did cattlemen have in county politics?

KB: Remember this was a cow county—an agricultural county—so naturally many of the people who were former supervisors in the county were in the agricultural business and had a lot to say about it. I think [their influence] gradually diminished down through the years as tourism and other things took over. When I was on the [Board of Supervisors] I think I was the only cattleman. Previous to that there would be two or three guys that were in the agricultural end of it.

RP: Keith, I wanted to talk about your stint as Inyo County Supervisor. Did you have any previous political experience? What made you decide to jump into that ring?

KB: My previous political experience had been that Jane and I had been very active in the Republican Party. In the process we became acquainted with quite a few elected officials and so forth. I forget what date it was in 1970, but our congressman Bill Ketchum died, and the way they replace congressmen when it's too far away from an election, the various Republican central committees will meet and candidates will throw their name in the hat, and they vote to see who the next congressman will be. Bill Thomas was an assemblyman, and he threw his name in the hat—there were six or seven others, including me. I won't go into the details, but it was finally decided that Thomas had it.

What was interesting about it, we had to travel around the district and give speeches. It was a regular campaign, and we didn't know all the ins and outs of the political system when it came to voting, and how the State Central Committee got involved. You learn a lot about politics in a hurry.

RP: When was your first run at County Supervisor?

KB: I was appointed when Johnny Johnson passed on. He was the supervisor in the [Fourth] District. A number of people applied for the job, I threw my hat in the ring, and I was chosen. I finished his term for two years, and then I was reelected for four years.

RP: What year was that?

KB: It was 1986. I'd been quite active in the background in politics in the county anyway. I knew them all pretty well. I was very active in the Independent Oil Producers group and made many trips to Washington D.C. for [them]. We'd each be assigned so many congressmen and senators to see, about whatever situation was facing the oil producers. I never stayed just on that subject. If the county had a problem, I'd bring that up, too. So gradually I'd be involved.

RP: So you built a good system of contacts.

KB: That's right, I got to know all of them—[Senators] Hayakawa, Dole, the whole bunch of them.
RP: How did you end up getting on the negotiating team for the [Long Term Water Agreement]?
KB: When I first went on the Board of Supervisors, I'd go down to the meetings [in L.A.]. Even though I wasn't on the negotiating team, I'd go anyway because in my mind it was so important to the county that I wanted to hear what went on in the negotiations. Finally I was put on the team because I had all this background.
RP: What was your position, then, on the negotiations?
KB: [Inyo] County wanted to push the water ordinance that we had.[4] It went to court down in San Bernardino, and the court said the county didn't have the authority to do these things. It was apparent to me that, yes, we could have fought it in court, but we didn't have the money to fight it clear to the Supreme Court. The DWP was pretty well-heeled then. It appeared to me that it would be in the courts from now on. The better policy would be to sit down with them and work out a deal. We had forced [the DWP] to write an [Environmental Impact Report], and it came back and the court said it wasn't acceptable. Then we forced them to write the next one, and that wasn't acceptable. And then with the third one, it was decided that it would be better to stop fighting with one another and sit down and try to work out an agreement. That should have happened a long time before, but the DWP was in the process of changing, too.
RP: That was the transition we were discussing.
KB: Yes. I think one of the moving forces on their side was Jim Wickser [Assistant General Manager-Water, for the DWP]. I think he should get a lot of credit for the fact that he stood up for getting an agreement between the City and the county. There were others on the [Los Angeles] water commission who could see the handwriting on the wall, too. This was a no-win deal for them. It was a no-win deal for the county if we kept it in the courts, so we kept pounding it out and meeting and meeting, one right after another, trying to get an agreement.

Of course, the Department of Fish and Game got involved, and so did the Sierra Club. How many trips did we make back and forth to Sacramento. We'd sit down in a meeting with Fish and Game representatives, the DWP, and the county and others. There would be half a dozen lawyers around a big table, and we'd pound out what we thought was an agreement. We'd go back the next month, and [some of those groups] would act like they'd never heard about it. It was a very discouraging experience for me to see how bureaucracy could perpetuate itself.
RP: In your negotiations, can you recall what the biggest sticking points or confrontations were over? Was it setting [groundwater] pumping levels, or the Lower Owens River Project, or what?
KB: Every one of them was a problem at the time. The pumping levels, how many wells could [the DWP] drill, replacement wells—and there were a lot of side issues that came up—whether the county would have authority to tell DWP to shut their

wells in if the water tables dropped to a certain point. That was a real bone of contention, but [DWP] went along with it because if the county wanted to protect the environment, it had to be the one to say shut that well in because it's damaging the environment. We were real lucky in getting Greg James as head of the [Inyo County] water department, and forming it at that time.

RP: When did the water department first begin here?

KB: We had water commissioners back in—I was on the [Inyo County] Water Advisory Committee in [the 1970s] I think it was, and at that time we were concerned about pumping and the DWP activity, but we didn't have any authority. It wasn't until after the [1972] lawsuit—and we won that—that any authority was vested in the county. I kid these guys who are on the water commission now. I tell them I'm still on because I was never fired.

RP: Were there any other parts of the agreement that you felt were tough to come by in terms of negotiations?

KB: The Lower Owens River Project. It was a big argument, and still is, about how much water you have to put down the Lower Owens River. They fought over the location for a pump-back station [at the outlet to Owens Lake to put the river water back into the aqueduct] and how much money the county would have to pay, and what the DWP would have to pay. I think the county's share was $3.75 million. At that time there was a lot of interest from other agencies. In fact, the Department of Fish and Game said they would come up with something like $1 million that would count against the county's share. And since then, our congressman, Jerry Lewis, was able to get $3 million in federal funding to take care of the county's share of the Lower Owens River Project, including the pump-back station. The federal government and the state had an obligation, too—mainly the state, because they are the ones who allowed DWP to dry up the river. The bottom of that river belongs to the State of California, it doesn't belong to the DWP, and the State has an obligation, too, to see that it's reestablished.

It's an easy sell to get those people and groups who are environmentally oriented to see the value of having that 60 miles of river [from Aberdeen to Owens Lake] reestablished with ponds and so forth. Anybody who is blind to that has a problem. In fact, we have talked to Lewis again, and he is trying to get more federal money for the project and the pump-back station.

JB: One of the problems all along has been that the vast majority of the voting population [in the state] is in the south, in Los Angeles, and they are the ones who are the recipients of the water. That was one of the things that took so long—to even get a consideration of doing anything at all about the water situation in Inyo County. The majority of the state legislators are from Los Angeles.

RP: I was curious to know what was the mood of county residents at the time of the ground water pumping and the lawsuits. Was there a lot of anger out in the communities?

KB: A lot of the people wanted DWP to go away, just go away. That wasn't going to happen then, and it's not going to happen now. They resented the DWP. I think the best way to point out the attitudes of the people—and it still exists—is the town water systems. When we got the water agreement in, the DWP said, we aren't going to be the water company for the towns. That's it. So we framed how the DWP would fix up the systems and so on, furnish tanks and a well for Lone Pine. A lot of people now will say, I don't want to have county or local control over the water, I want DWP to run it. Those same people will say how much they hate the DWP, but they'll turn right around and say I want DWP to run the water system. It's kind of a love/hate deal. They want them out of here, but they want all the open space to remain.

The DWP deserves a lot of criticism for some things, but they don't get praise for some of the things they do. For instance, [at] that Lone Pine sports center [they] spent I don't know how much money on leveling and helping out with the piping. I'd say several hundred thousand dollars. When it was over, we had a get together with the public, people got up and talked, and I didn't hear anyone praising the DWP's efforts. I did. I think when anyone does something good, they should get credit for it.

RP: In the negotiations over the water agreement, is there a particular story that sticks out in your mind as being rather humorous or interesting?

KB: Yes, I can pick out one thing. We signed the agreement down there [in Los Angeles] with the City Council, and Mayor Bradley was there. I signed it, and Bob Campbell signed it for the Board of Supervisors. I was sitting next to Bradley, and when they took the picture, it came out in the *Los Angeles Times* and it looked like we were holding hands. I got to know Bradley pretty well. I didn't like his politics, but I liked him. He was a reasonable sort of guy. He and I laughed over that afterward. It looks just like we are holding hands.

Those were some interesting sidelights. Of course you develop a relationship and a friendship, even though you are on opposing sides with some people. [Jim] Wickser and I have been at each other's throats down through the years. If anyone saw us, we had derogatory remarks, but we really like each other.

RP: Keith, were you in on any of the Desert Bill issues that came up?

KB: Yes, I was very active on the Desert Bill with Jane. I made a trip to Washington D.C. before the Senate opposing it. I don't know how many trips I made around the country opposing it.[5]

RP: As a county supervisor?

KB: As a supervisor, and as an individual. I still don't like it. It denies people my age, and people with families, the right—they can't go out in the desert and carry all the water they need to enjoy the desert. The abandonment of roads, the lack of delineating where the boundaries are—you can be out there and you don't know if you are in the wilderness area or outside of it. I was against the expansion of Death Valley [National Park]. I think they bit off more than they can chew. Before they ever expanded it [the National Park Service] said they didn't have enough people [to oversee it].

You get down to something very basic in this county, very basic. This county is supported, in the majority, or by about 60 percent [of the taxes paid], by natural resources. The export of water—under the formula of the state constitution, DWP pays quite a few million dollars [in taxes]. And you take the Coso Geothermal Project and other activities. I see nothing on the horizon that will change that. They keep talking about tourism. Tourism is not going to take the place of what these natural resources provide. I think tying the mineral resources up into the wilderness area did this county a great disservice. The people in this county should have just as good services as people in any other county. Without the revenues coming from the natural resources, they wouldn't exist. If Coso Geothermal hadn't come in when it did, you wouldn't have a library because there wasn't any other place to turn to for money.[6]

You look at about 98 percent or so of this county being owned by the federal government, the state, or DWP, with the federal government being the major owners. It only pays about half a million dollars a year in lieu of taxes. That's a drop in the bucket when you try and run a county on it. My feeling is, down the road—where are they going to get the money to run the county? When you get into doing anything now with all the environmental laws and everything else, it discourages people. Look at the [Owens] lake project down there.

RP: The soda ash facility?

KB: Yes, there would have been 100 to 150 people hired. They would have made a $100 million investment, and the county gets some percent of that for taxes. That would have gone a long way to help.[7]

RP: Are there other significant achievements that you can recall during your six years as a supervisor?

KB: I was involved in lots of things during that time. We needed a new jail, we couldn't stay in the old jail, and I got involved in that. I got involved in Juvenile Hall. We were exporting kids to other counties because we didn't have any place to keep them. We were fortunate that the county was in good enough shape so we could borrow the money to build things. There was the need for a fiber optic line. I was able to help, because I had connections in some places. You see, it's not that you are so smart, it's that you happen to be along at the right time, and your past history has connections to help you out. I did a lot of things, and I had a lot of fun, and I enjoy being involved. You make some mistakes—so what. You get in some problems, like the recall that we had.

RP: Was that over the water agreement?

KB: It was all about water. There was a lot of false information out about the water agreement and our negotiations. It was based on the fact that I believed in the water agreement, and these other people wanted to go back to court—and they wanted [my] job. They wanted to run the county, and that's why they recalled three of us [supervisors]. But they failed. Anyway, it was an experience. Everybody should go through a recall once in their lifetime. (laughter)

RP: I'd like to talk a little about Manzanar and the National Historic Site. Can you tell us about your initial involvement with Manzanar?

KB: The first meeting I [went to] was when the state was going to get involved with Manzanar [in the 1970s]. I guess people know that the [State Department of Parks and Recreation] once thought of taking it over as a state park. We had a meeting down in Independence, and Johnny Johnson, the [fourth district] supervisor at that time, and I went to the meeting. We asked questions—they were going to call it a concentration camp, and we took exception to that. After the meeting, Johnny Johnson asked the [state] people who were there, "We didn't see one of you taking notes, and you didn't have a recording device, so what was the use of the meeting?" Well, the state took off. That was the end. They put that rock down there [at the entrance], where they called it a concentration camp.[8]

There was a break for several years, then Congress, I think it was in the late 1970s, [was naming] different areas in the Pacific Theater of World War II that they wanted to memorialize. Manzanar was one of them, and that started the ball rolling, and the federal government got involved. I was put on the Manzanar Advisory Committee in 1993, and I've been on it ever since.

RP: How much opposition was there to the wording of that plaque from the local people?

KB: There was a lot at first when they put it in, and then when the federal government started to get involved, there was more opposition to [using that term]. When I got on the advisory board, I had a lot of calls about it. It still crops up to me once in a while. People wondering why do they call it a concentration camp. Some of the veterans—in fact one of them lived in Bishop, and he was a prisoner of war with the Japanese. He was adamant, and you know there are others out there who are adamant. One Japanese gentleman told me to look it up in the dictionary. What the dictionary says might fit, but after World War II, we found out truly what concentration camps were like.

RP: Who was it that contacted you to be on the Manzanar Advisory Committee?

KB: I had been involved with Manzanar [before], and was recommended [to the National Park Service] based on that. There were several of us [who started] at the same time.

RP: Can you tell us some of your involvement before that with getting Congress to legislate a bill establishing the National Historic Site?

KB: One of the main issues was the auditorium. [Inyo] county had their heavy equipment shop in the auditorium. You couldn't have a Manzanar National Historic Site as long as the auditorium was [occupied] by the county. I went to our road department, our public works man, and I asked him how much money would it take to build a new heavy equipment shop; that's what the county had to base [the request] on. We came up with a number of $1.1 million. I got hold of Jerry Lewis, our Congressman, and he put it into the bill for the [establishment of the historic site]. The House passed it. When it came before the Senate, they pulled [that appropriation]. We had to do something, so I got hold of Senator Ted Stevens, who I happened to know well. He was on the Conference Committee, and I told him the story, and he brought it into the committee and put the $1.1 million back in. The Conference Committee okayed it, and it passed both houses. We got our $1.1 million.

Then we waited I don't know how many years before the Park Service gave us the money. They had the money but didn't give it to the county. It just sat there. I didn't like that one bit. It was 3 percent inflation, and you could just say we're losing that much every year. If we were going to build a new equipment establishment, we needed to have the money right away to get started so we'd have enough. Anyway, it finally loosened up and they built the new heavy equipment shop down in Independence, sometime in 1996.

RP: Early on, when you worked on the advisory committee, what did you work on with the other people?

KB: Nothing was happening, it just drifted along. On a number of occasions I called Jerry Lewis, our congressman. I know in one conversation I told him that it was a disgrace to call it a national historic site with the facilities that were there. I said that it doesn't look good to have a sign posted by the federal government saying "Manzanar National Historic Site" and not do anything. You either get in or get out. That was my feeling. [Committee chairperson] Rose Ochi was working hard on it from her side, and there were a lot of others involved, so that had some effect on getting some money down the road to get the thing off and moving. I felt very strongly that if we were advertising it, get it fixed so the public can see it.

RP: Did you have to go to Washington at all to lobby?

KB: No, I'd quit going to Washington by then. Lewis would come out here and I don't know how many meetings we had out here—some on other subjects, but Manzanar would come up in the conversation.

RP: From your point of view were there some strong economic arguments to be made for establishing the site, in terms of bringing more tourism and visitation?

KB: Well, yes, that's always been a strong argument as far as the county is concerned. This county counts on a source of its revenue from tourism. However, remember, the main source of revenue in this county is not tourism, it's natural resources. Since we only have about one and a half percent of the land in Inyo County in private hands, there are not many places to establish industry that will have a large tax base.

RP: Right. Did you detect any sentiments from the local people about having more federal involvement in the county?

KB: That never came out as a real major issue. Remember, the land they were going to get was DWP land.

RP: What issues did emerge, from your perception?

KB: Well, first of all, [the camp] was started roughly sixty years ago and a lot of the people who were involved with Manzanar when it was in effect had lived here locally, and they have either died or moved. There were numbers of them that I knew. Some of the resentment I heard, that they couldn't get butter, and couldn't get this and that, and the Japanese were fed better—you are always going to have comments like that, and you let them pass on.

Then [later] there was [the feeling] that we don't need [the historic site] here, and why should we have something for the Japanese. Some of them wanted to know if they were going to do the same thing in other places where Americans were held in prison camps. That would just crop up with one or two guys. The main thing was in calling it a concentration camp. That was the main thrust by the people who would call me. I appeared before the American Legion in Independence on three occasions and discussed this with them. The last meeting I went to—it was a very nice meeting—and one of the high-up officials from the American Legion was visiting the various posts. He'd been a colonel in the U.S. Army, and he was Japanese. No questions about Manzanar came up at that meeting. It was very interesting.

RP: He was a Japanese American.

KB: Yes. He'd been in the Army, I gathered, as a career.

RP: Keith, did you have to do much lobbying of local officials and other people when the national historic site legislation was enacted?

KB: The thing about it was that Congress had already committed itself that Manzanar would be one of the sites to memorialize the Pacific Theater. Manzanar was here, and it was convenient to Los Angeles, and it was on the main highway. And it was going to happen, so what was there to argue about? That's what I would discuss with the American Legion. I told them they were a little late, they should have been fighting [the national historic site designation] before it went to legislation. They have lobbyists in Washington. Somebody was asleep at the switch, because after it becomes a law, you aren't going to change it.

RP: What about the issue—and I recall this coming up during discussions about Manzanar—the concern about the whole story of Manzanar being represented rather than just the narrow focus of a relocation camp?

KB: That's right, and I supported it. I think the Indians and the pioneers certainly should get recognition that they occupied that site, and they ought to get recognition like the Japanese. I think it was a real good move when we expanded the [historic site] acreage out to eight hundred and some [814] acres.

RP: The advisory committee issued a formal recommendation for that?

KB: That's what we did. Then it had to go to Congress. The main fight, or concern, was to get the DWP to [go along with it].

RP: Were you involved with any of the negotiations on the land swap [with the DWP and the BLM]?

KB: No, Bob Gracey was on the Board of Supervisors then, and he handled that part of it.

RP: When you were discussing things as a member of the advisory committee about how you wanted to see the site portrayed—the whole historical story—how was your relationship with other people on the board? Did you have some serious disagreements?

KB: You put forth your concerns, and there were never any real arguments about it. The Japanese American people I work with, I really like them. I have not met a lot of Japanese out in society. When you live in Independence, we don't have [many]. I admire them. I've talked to some of my Japanese friends down there at the commission, and one of them tells me how he used to shoot marbles at the guard towers. They were just being kids. Some of the photographs—and especially one that really influenced me about life there [in the camp], was the graduation. There is a film about the [high school] graduation from Manzanar. I look at those laughing kids marching down the aisle with their gowns on. They weren't depressed or down in the dumps, they were having fun. Numbers of my local friends worked down there, and they told me about the Japanese going fishing back in the mountains. They went through the fence and went fishing. The first few months that wasn't so, but I think the authorities found out the Japanese weren't a great menace, and they must have relaxed the rules. That said a lot. Again I come back to the industriousness of the [internees] and what they did to that area to convert it into a garden. All you have to do is look at the old photographs where they turned that desert into a show place in the short few years they were there.

RP: Did you see your attitudes toward the Japanese people change over the years from before you were involved on the committee up to now?

KB: Early on, before I even got involved in Manzanar, I'd look at pictures, and then at the desert, and I'd see what they'd done. I could understand that they must have a strong work ethic and an eye for beauty. I didn't like what the [Japanese] Imperial government did. But as individuals, I looked at them as fellow Americans. That attitude, as I worked with them on committee, became cemented in place. That's why at every meeting for the last three or four years, I've stood up and said I think it's time we [restore] or establish Japanese gardens to show the people: here you have a desert, and here's a Japanese garden. This is an example of what the Japanese did here in this particular spot. It's all the monkey business you have to go through to get something like that done.

RP: Before you got involved with Manzanar, did you have an attitude towards the justice or injustice of the relocation?

KB: You have to remember one thing: it was war, absolute war. People who weren't around at that time [don't know]—and a good part of our population now wasn't even born. We were challenged, our way of life was challenged. We did not know if the Japanese were going to make a landing. Our Pacific fleet had been destroyed and America was in terrible shape with defense. After the attack on Pearl Harbor, there were strong feelings against the Japanese. People didn't know the Japanese as well as they do now. In fact, at one of those meetings, I met a Japanese lady who had been to Manzanar, and she said that Manzanar wasn't all bad. I asked her what she meant, and she told me that before the war the Japanese had lived in their own communities and sort of isolated themselves from the mainstream of American life. After Manzanar, because they went in the Army, and [dispersed]—people didn't know it, but if [the internees] could get a job or have someone in [the East] or Midwest vouch for them, they could leave and go back there. We had a lady [here in Bishop] who I knew very well that hauled them to Reno and put them on trains to go. They spread throughout the United States. I thought that was a very important comment.

It was too bad that we moved them, the ones who were American citizens, to the camps. It was a shame we had to do this. Our government should have taken care of [their property] and preserved all the holdings—whether it was homes, businesses or whatever it was—of the Japanese and held them so they were not going to lose money or suffer any great losses. That was an obligation of the government and they didn't do it.

RP: The Manzanar Committee that began making the annual pilgrimages to the site in 1969, they were pretty instrumental in lobbying for state recognition, and even for federal recognition. Have you gone to any of those pilgrimages?

KB: I think I've missed one.

RP: Keith, after the historic site was established, there was a very small staff of one, Ross Hopkins, the first superintendent. Did you have conversations with him about how difficult it was for him to do everything?

KB: Well, I had a lot of conversations with Ross. Ross was a very dedicated [National] Park Service man. The park, I believe, would not be as far along as it is if Ross hadn't been there. He was instrumental in getting things moving. He tried everything to get people off the dime and get things done. The Park Service hierarchy—that's where he was having problems.

RP: And there were some funding shortages.

KB: Oh, funding shortages—and a lot of double talk going on.

RP: Ross went through some pretty tough times, getting a lot of strongly worded letters from locals and from veterans—even some death threats during that time.

KB: You've always got those people out there, I don't care what the situation is. First of all, they don't research the problem to the point of finding out anything. If you are going to blame anybody, blame the Congress of the United States that passed the legislation. That's the place to go. Ross was ordered to do a job, and he was going to carry it out, period. I thought he was doing a good job.

RP: The recall action you had in 1990, Manzanar never entered into that?

KB: No, that was before the [historic site] legislation. The recall was all about water.

RP: How do you feel about the Manzanar Advisory Committee at this point? Do you feel it's been effective in getting citizens' and other people's points of view across to the Park Service?

KB: I think so, I think it had a place and a part. We've had the heads of the Park Service and various authorities visit with us and exchange viewpoints. That had some effect on their attitude, or at least they got the feeling of the committee. I think it's

At Manzanar National Historic Site, visitors stand before the names of over 11,000 people interned at Manzanar, 1942–1945. *Author's Collection*

been important that we've had some of the meetings with the Japanese in April [during the pilgrimages]. The number of people who show up, and some of the politicians who've showed up—they get a better idea, maybe, of the attitude of the Japanese.

RP: Keith, what's your overall feeling about the progress on Manzanar—on the historic site?

KB: It's been slow, and again when you get bureaucracy involved there is not a great big hurry to get things done. We can look at a lot of different agencies [the same way], not just the Park Service. If we just keep the flow of money coming, we'll make some movement forward. It *is* moving forward, and we will have a national historic site that we can be proud of.

Afterword

"The West is remote and vast," says historian Patricia Limerick; "its isolation and distance will release us from conflict; this is where we can get away from each other. But the workings of history carried an opposite lesson. The West was not where we escaped each other, but where we all met."[1]

On April 24, 2004, Manzanar was again a meeting place for people and pasts in the Owens Valley, when the Interpretive Center at Manzanar National Historic Site, housed in the restored high school auditorium/gymnasium originally built by Manzanar's internees in 1944, was formally opened with a day of remembrance, celebration, and global news coverage. Of the nearly 2,500 people attending, about half were Japanese Americans. The rest were Owens Valley residents, interested visitors, local, county, and federal officials, and tourists drawn into the festivities by the astonishing sight of a crowded parking lot in this once-empty place. The outdoor program included a performance by the *Owens Valley Spirit*, a Paiute drum group, and the colors were presented by a combined color guard of the Lone Pine Veterans of Foreign Wars and the 100th/442nd Southern California Veteran's Association from the highly decorated World War II Nisei combat group.

Mary Kageyama Nomura returned to sing "When I Can," a ballad of young romance and lack of privacy in camp, composed for her by Louis Frizzell, music teacher at Manzanar High School from 1942 to 1945. Chambers of Commerce from the local towns served lemonade and cookies, Girl Scouts and Boy Scouts passed out programs, and to conclude the day, a Bishop big band played swing tunes of the 1940s.

In the past decade, Owens Valley public agencies, businesses, and civic leaders have joined together to expand the vision of an Eastern Sierra recreation paradise, first promoted seventy years ago by a like-minded group, the Inyo-Mono Associates. Now, important historical and cultural legacies are taking their place alongside the scenic wonders of the region in its growing list of tourist attractions. The Eastern Sierra Scenic Byway is one result of that effort, and the center at Manzanar, where a humble rural town, and later an enclosed barrack city, once stood, is now among the Owens Valley's impressive attractions.

Recreation assets and historic sites notwithstanding, the real history of a place is still to be found in the stories its people have to tell—and in giving oneself over to listening and learning from them. One must "wait its occasions," Mary Austin said of the Owens Valley, and pause for "such news of the land, of its trails, and what is astir in them, as one lover of it can give to another."[2] Memory yields up the stories, that news; stories are history "in conversation with memory."[3] Conversations with fourteen "ordinary" people of the Owens Valley have taken us through the past and pointed to a future that will be defined by how people continue to explain this land all that has taken place there.

Of the millions who visit or pass through the Owens Valley each year, most are in a rush to reach the wilderness playground to the north or enter the solitude of the backcountry; there is little time to stop for stories. Many do stop at real estate offices in Lone Pine and Bishop to inquire about property for sale, perhaps with a thought to moving into the valley. It is an appealing idea: an easy four-hour drive from Los Angeles, a nearly pristine landscape, picturesque towns, breathtaking scenery, and unparalleled recreation. But most would-be residents are surprised to learn that only a fraction of valley lands are privately owned, and available property is scarce. With a countywide population of just under 20,000, the Owens Valley is an anomaly in a state with thirty-five million people. Inyo County's 1.8 people per square mile placed against the 217.2 people per square mile in the rest of the state speaks clearly to the urban/rural dichotomy of the modern West. In 2003, one of every two people living west of the one hundredth meridian—John Wesley Powell's West—was living in California, and among those, fully two-thirds are in the state's urban centers.

Those who yearn to escape to the Owens Valley and places like it, looking for a life, presumably, of greater simplicity and free of the burdens of city living, can be reminded that others, lured by similar ambitions, once "went West." "To be an American is to move on," writes Kathleen Norris— "as if we could outrun change."[4] They will know, too, after hearing the stories of these fourteen people, about the profound sense of place environments like the Owens Valley can engender, and how the burdens of a tumultuous historical legacy are evident in the very landscape itself. In this long land of the West, we have all met, yet someone coming into its astonishing emptiness for the first time might well ask if history of any consequence has taken place there at all.

Appendix I (Narrators, Interviewers, and Transcribers)

Narrators

Keith Bright (b.1915) was born in Taft, California, earned a degree in Petroleum Engineering from the University of Southern California, and built a career in the oil industry. In 1968, Keith and his wife Jane moved with their three children from the Los Angeles area to a cattle ranch in the Owens Valley. Early involvements with state party politics led to an appointment in 1986 to a seat on the Inyo County Board of Supervisors. At the same time, Keith served as a negotiator for the Inyo County–Los Angeles Long Term Water Agreement. In 1993, he was appointed to serve on the Advisory Commission for Manzanar National Historic Site. The Brights live on their historic ranch north of Independence.

Truman Buff (1906–1996), an Owens Valley Paiute, was born at the Fort Independence Reservation and lived there most of his life. Excelling in music and sports as a boy, he studied violin and saxophone at the Sherman Institute, an Indian boarding school in Riverside, California. He later played with dance bands in southern California and in the Owens Valley. Following a tour of the western states with an all-Indian band, he returned to the valley, married, and worked twenty-seven years as a heavy equipment operator for the Los Angeles Department of Water and Power. A talented baseball player, he played for over thirty years with teams in the Owens Valley.

Owen Cooper (b. 1916) retired in 1984 from Chalfant Press in Bishop, capping a fifty-year career as printer and co-publisher of the Owens Valley newspapers. Born in Los Angeles, he moved in 1927 to Independence, where the family operated Jim's Place, a popular restaurant. In 1933, Owens was the lone graduating senior at Owens Valley High School. During World War II, he oversaw printing of the Manzanar War Relocation Center internee-produced newspaper, the *Manzanar Free Press*. A devoted ham radio operator and father of two children, he lives now in San Diego.

Ritsuko Eder (b. 1917) was born in San Diego. At the outbreak of World War II she was living on Terminal Island in Los Angeles with her husband. They lived a year at Manzanar, where their son was born in December 1942, and resettled in Colorado before returning to Los Angeles in 1945.

Nettie Roeper Fausel (1874–1968) was born on her grandparents' homestead in the ranching area near Manzanar. Her grandfather, a German immigrant, went to California in the early

1850s as a prospector. In 1882, the family moved to Independence, where Nettie's father Julius was the butcher, postmaster, and music teacher. Nettie and Max Fausel were married in 1899 and had one daughter. The Fausels lived in a small house on Edwards Street (Highway 395) behind the post office where Nettie was postmistress of Independence from 1903 to 1946. Nettie remained in Independence until her death in 1968.

Dawn Kashitani (b. 1910) was living in Redondo Beach, California, at the outbreak of World War II. She and her husband, a minister, along with their son Paul, lived at Manzanar for over two years before relocating to Pennsylvania. Her daughter Joanne was born at Manzanar in September, 1944. Dawn lives in Santa Monica, California, close to her children and four grandchildren.

W.C. "Stub" Lydston (1870–1957), originally from Maine, brought his wife and three daughters to Manzanar in 1919 from Whittier, a Quaker settlement in southern California. At Manzanar, he owned a small farm and orchard and worked for cattlemen in the area. The Lydstons moved to Independence in 1934, and Stub worked for the City of Los Angeles until his retirement in 1938. At age 68, he began work as a custodian for the Owens Valley Unified Schools. He passed away in Independence at age 87.

Mary Kageyama Nomura (b. 1925) was born in Los Angeles. She lived at Manzanar War Relocation Center, 1942–1945, and graduated from Manzanar High School in 1943 where she was senior class vice-president and a staff member for the annual, *Cardinal and Gold*. A talented vocalist, she is still remembered as the "Songbird of Manzanar." At Manzanar, she met Shiro Nomura, and after leaving in 1945, they married, had five children, and for over thirty years operated a fish and grocery market in Garden Grove, California. With Mary's help, Shi assembled the Nomura Collection of Manzanar photographs and artifacts at the Eastern California Museum in Independence. After Shiro passed away in 2000, Mary moved to Huntington Beach, California; she enjoys her children and grandchildren and in 2004, performed with "The Camp Dance," a musical revue about life in the internment centers.

Emily Roddy (b. 1911) went to the Owens Valley in 1923 from Berkeley, California, and lived at the railroad station at Owenyo, where her family operated the boxcar hotel and restaurant. Emily married and later lived at Manzanar and packed apples. Living in California's Central Valley, she raised two children and worked as a truck driver before returning to Bishop, where she enjoyed church activities and driving her vintage yellow Mustang. She lives now in a Bishop nursing home.

Concha (Connie) Lozano Salas (1915–2003) moved with her family in 1915 to Cartago, in southern Owens Valley, where her father Miguel worked at the Pacific Alkali soda ash operations on Owens Lake. She graduated from Lone Pine High School in 1936, married soon after and raised five children. Connie and her second husband, Silvestre Salas, retired to Lone Pine in the 1960s, and she was active in charities and enjoyed gardening. Connie passed away in Lone Pine in 2003, leaving a family legacy that included her husband, five children, sixteen grandchildren, sixteen great-grandchildren, and one great-great grandson.

Doris Semura (1912–2005) was born in Hawaii, moved to Los Angeles in 1936, and married in 1938. The Semuras and their six-month-old son were sent to Manzanar in 1942; they stayed one year and relocated to Pocatello, Idaho, working on farms until they returned to Hawaii in 1948. Doris served as a house parent for the Diamond Head School for the Deaf and Blind for twenty-six years until her retirement in 1977. She passed away in Honolulu in 2005.

Vic Taylor (1910–1999) moved with his family from Los Angeles to George's Creek, near Manzanar, in 1920. For over forty years, Vic was a surveyor, hydrographer, and civil engineer with the Los Angeles Department of Water and Power in the Owens Valley. An avid outdoorsman, he operated an early ski-tow operation in the Sierras near Independence. He and his wife Eleanor had two children and lived in Independence throughout their entire sixty-four years of marriage.

LaVerne Reynolds Zediker (1919–1996), an Owens Valley native, was the only daughter of long-time Owens Valley cattle ranchers Fred and Hazel Reynolds. The family moved to a ranch near Manzanar in 1928 where they ran cattle and supplied stock for Western moviemakers working near Lone Pine. LaVerne and her husband Jake had two daughters and operated a pack service into the Sierras.

Nancy Connor Zischank (1907–1999) was born in Columbus, Ohio, and grew up in Boston. She married Max Zischank in southern California in 1931 and in 1935 they moved to Mammoth Lakes, where Nan became a championship skier. For over thirty years, they operated the Long Valley Resort at Crowley Lake. Nan lived at Manzanar during World War II and worked as a driver for the War Relocation Authority. She retired in Bishop after Max passed away and remained active in church and civic organizations until her death at ninety-two.

Interviewers

Arthur Hansen (Mary Nomura) is Professor of History, Emeritus, and Director of the Center for Oral and Public History at California State University Fullerton, and is a consultant to the Japanese American National Museum in Los Angeles. He is past president of the Oral History Association.

Bessie Poole and **Jan Hillis** (Nettie Fausel and Stub Lydston) and **Catherine Piercy** (Ritsuko Eder, Doris Semura, Dawn Kashitani) were long-time residents of Independence and Eastern California Museum staff members or volunteers. It is unlikely they had formal training in interviewing. All are now deceased.

Richard Potashin (Vic Taylor, Emily Roddy, Connie Salas, Owen Cooper, LaVerne Zediker, Nan Zischank, Keith Bright) has lived in the Owens Valley for nearly twenty years. A self-taught oral historian with a background in environmental and plant science, he conducted over three hundred interviews while on the staff of the Eastern California Museum in Independence. He is now a Park Ranger, Interpretation, at Manzanar National Historic Site and oversees its oral history program.

Jane Wehrey (Truman Buff) is an Owens Valley native and current resident, a historian and former Research Associate at the Center for Oral and Public History, California State University, Fullerton, and has consulted for the National Park Service on the development of Manzanar National Historic Site.

Transcribers

Diane Gray, former staff member, Eastern California Museum

Leah Kirk, former staff member, Eastern California Museum

Garnette Long, former director, Tapes Into Type, California State University Fullerton Oral History Program, transcribed eight interviews.

Bessie Poole, interviewer and former staff member, Eastern California Museum

Suzanne Walter, transcriber, Tapes Into Type

Jane Wehrey, interviewer and author

Appendix II (Owens Valley Historical Periods)

3500 BC–1834	**American Indian Pre-contact Era**
AD 600	Period of greatest use of Owens Valley by Indian people begins
1769	Padre Junipero Serra establishes first of twenty-one California missions at San Diego, begins Spanish colonization
1781	Los Angeles founded as a Spanish *pueblo* with 44 people
1825–1870	**Early Visions: Exploration, Assessment, Settlement**
1834	Joseph Walker expedition brings first known white presence to the Owens Valley
1845	John C. Fremont party names Owens Valley after expedition member
1848	Gold discovery at John Sutter's Coloma mill on Sierra western slope
1850	California gains statehood as thirty-first state
1855	A.W. Von Schmidt two-year survey and mapping expedition of Owens Valley and Mono Basin
1860	Discovery of Coso silver deposits near Owens Lake; stockmen follow with cattle
1861	U.S. Civil War begins
	Charles Putnam builds first cabin in Owens Valley, a trading post at Little Pine (now Independence)
1862	Homestead Act passed by Congress
	U.S. Army Volunteers establish Camp Independence on Oak Greek July 4
1863	Soldiers remove nearly 1,000 Owens Valley Indians to the San Sebastian Reservation at Fort Tejon
1864	Cattleman John Shepherd homesteads 160 acres at present-day Manzanar
1865	Silver strike at Cerro Gordo produces $17 million in bullion, shapes growth of Los Angeles
1866	Inyo County formed, with Independence as county seat
1870–1900	**Expansion of Pioneer Society and Economy**
1870–1880	Period of mining booms at Aurora, Darwin, Panamint, Bodie
1870	First newspaper, the *Inyo Independent*, published in Independence
1872	Earthquake, estimated Richter magnitude 7.8, levels Lone Pine, alters landscape

1877	Fort Independence closed, soldiers depart.
1878	First irrigation canals dug near Bishop
1883	Carson and Colorado Railroad puts 300-mile narrow-gauge line from Nevada into Owens Valley to serve mining
1885	Inyo Development Company begins soda ash processing on Owens Lake
1890	Sequoia National Park established
1892	First Indian school established in Bishop

1900–1920	**Changing Visions: Agriculture and Water Transfers**
1900	Population, Inyo County: 4,377. Population, Los Angeles: 102,479
1901	Theodore Roosevelt elected president
1902	Congress passes Newlands Reclamation Act
	Bishop Power and Light Company supplies first electricity in valley
1903	Reclamation Service assesses possible water storage project in Owens Valley
	Mary Austin publishes *The Land of Little Rain*
1904	William Mulholland, superintendent of the Los Angeles Water Company, visits the Owens Valley to assess potential water sources.
1905	Former Los Angeles Mayor Fred Eaton takes options on Owens River land for water rights, turns them over to Los Angeles
	The *Los Angeles Times* announces Owens River aqueduct project
	Los Angeles voters approve $1.5 million bond for purchase of Owens Valley land and water rights
	Irrigation developer George Chaffey's interests purchase Shepherd Ranch, other properties and water rights in Owens Valley
1906	Roosevelt backs aqueduct project, passage of Flint Bill granting public land right-of-way for construction
1907	Reclamation Service officially abandons Owens Valley project in favor of Los Angeles municipal plans
1908	Construction begins on Los Angeles Aqueduct
	Los Angeles builds Power Plant 1 on Division Creek, first of eight plants in Owens Valley
1910	Southern Pacific builds standard-gauge line from Mojave to Owens Valley, connects with narrow-gauge at Owenyo
	Chaffey interests form Owens Valley Improvement Company, subdivide Manzanar land
1912	OVI plants 22,000 fruit trees at Manzanar
1913	First Owens River water flows through 233-mile aqueduct to Los Angeles
1914–1918	World War I

1920–1940	**New Visions: Rebellion, Decline, Recovery**
1920	Population, Inyo County: 7,031. Population, Los Angeles: 576,000
	First movie, *The Roundup*, filmed in Owens Valley
1922	Drought conditions increase demand for Owens River water, Los Angeles begins additional land buyouts, consolidation of Owens Valley stream and groundwater rights

1924	Four-day occupation of aqueduct spillway at Alabama Gates protests Los Angeles policies, gains nationwide publicity
1927	Aqueduct dynamited eleven times
	Inyo County Bank closed for shortage of funds, valley residents lose life savings, owners are convicted of embezzlement, resistance to LA collapses
	All property and water rights at Manzanar in LA ownership
	Eastern California Museum opens in Inyo Country Courthouse basement
1928	Failure of the St. Francis Dam, part of aqueduct system, kills over 400 people in southern California, ends William Mulholland's career.
1929	Stock market crash, beginning of the Great Depression
1931	Paved road completed between Mojave and Bishop
	Los Angeles begins purchase of most remaining town and farm property to offset economic losses
	Owens Valley agricultural production down by 84 percent
1933	Los Angeles owns 95 percent of valley agricultural land, 85 percent of town properties
	Death Valley National Monument established
1934	Los Angeles discontinues irrigation to Manzanar orchards
1935	Business and civic leaders form Inyo-Mono Associates to promote tourism, foster economic recovery
1937	"Wedding of the Waters" pageant celebrates completion of final link in Death Valley to Whitney Portal road, receives national publicity
	Owens Valley Land Exchange creates new Indian reservations at Bishop, Big Pine, Lone Pine
1940–1970	**Rebirth, Wartime, Stability**
1940	One million people travel through Owens Valley
	Mono Basin Extension Project adds 105 miles to aqueduct system, taps Mono Lake water
1941	Long Valley Reservoir dedicated to honor late Father John J. Crowley
	Hydrographer and skier Dave McCoy installs first rope tow on Mammoth Mountain, beginning of ski industry
	Japanese attack on Pearl Harbor, U.S. enters World War II
	Colorado River Aqueduct completed, brings water to southern California
1942	President Franklin Roosevelt issues Executive Order 9066
	Manzanar War Relocation Center opens as Owens Valley Reception Center
	Riot at Manzanar leaves two internees dead
1945	World War II ends, Manzanar camp closes
1959	Nearly 200 movies filmed in Owens Valley since 1920s
1960	Last run of the narrow-gauge "Slim Princess" between Keeler and Laws
	California Institute of Technology opens Owens Valley Radio Observatory near Big Pine
1964	Wilderness Act passed, protects nearly 5 percent of U.S. land
1968	Pittsburgh Plate Glass, last of soda ash plants on Owens Lake, closes
1970–2005	**Valuing the Past, Envisioning the Future**
1970	Second Los Angeles Aqueduct opens, increases water export capacity by 50 percent
	Passage of California Environmental Quality Act

1972	Inyo County files lawsuit against Los Angeles, cites non-compliance with CEQA in groundwater pumping
1988	Civil Liberties Act of 1988 authorizes redress payments to surviving internees of World War II relocation centers
1990	First annual Lone Pine Film Festival
1991	Acceptance of a Long Term Water Agreement by Inyo County and the City of Los Angeles
1992	Manzanar National Historic Site established by Act of Congress
1994	California Desert Protection Act passed by Congress
2000	Population, Inyo County: 17,945. Population, Los Angeles: 3,694,820
	Los Angeles begins work on Owens Lake Dust Control Project to meet air quality standards
2001	Terrorist attacks in New York, Washington D.C., Pennsylvania
2004	Interpretive Center opens at Manzanar National Historic Site
2005	Founder Dave McCoy sells controlling interest in $365 million Mammoth Mountain ski resort

Notes

Introduction

1. Sue Irwin, *California's Eastern Sierra: A Visitor's Guide* (Los Olivos, CA: Cachuma Press, Inc., 1991), 9.
2. Ibid., 8.
3. See Ibid, 8–12; Jeff Putnam and Genny Smith, eds. *Deepest Valley: Guide to Owens Valley*, 2nd Ed. (Mammoth Lakes, CA: Genny Smith Books, 1995), 119–148; Warren A. Beck and Ynez D. Haase, *Historical Atlas of California* (Norman, OK: University of Oklahoma Press, 1974), 4.
4. Refers to *The Land of Little Rain*, the 1903 masterpiece about the Owens Valley by Mary Austin.
5. J. B. Lippincott, quoted in Robert Sauder, *The Lost Frontier: Water Diversion in the Growth and Destruction of Owens Valley Agriculture* (Tucson: University of Arizona Press, 1994), 107.
6. See William H. Michael, " 'At the Plow and in the Harvest Field': Indian Conflict and Accommodation in the Owens Valley 1860–1880," MA Thesis, University of Oklahoma, 1993, 8–12.
7. Zenas Leonard, quoted in Harlan Unrau, "The Evacuation and Relocation of Persons of Japanese Ancestry During World War II: A Historical Resource Study of the Manzanar War Relocation Center," 2 Vol. (United States Department of the Interior, National Park Service, 1996), 137; W. A. Chalfant, *The Story of Inyo*, 2nd Ed. (Bishop, CA: Chalfant Press, 1933), 121; Edward Kern, quoted in Unrau, 138; Philip J. Wilke and Henry J. Lawton, eds., *The Expedition of Capt. J. W. Davidson from Ft. Tejon to the Owens Valley in 1859* (Socorro, NM: Ballena Press, 1976), 6–7.
8. Sauder, *The Lost Frontier,* 63–74.
9. Putnam and Smith, *Deepest Valley*, 248.
10. *San Franciso Chronicle*, quoted in "A Truthful Statement," *Inyo Register*, January 1898, 2.
11. Sauder, *The Lost Frontier,* 85.
12. Ibid., 86.
13. Ibid., 108.
14. John Walton, *Western Times and Water Wars: State, Culture, and Rebellion in California* (Berkeley: University of California Press, 1992), 142.
15. Charles Fletcher Lummis, quoted in Walton, *Western Times and Water Wars*, 142.
16. Los Angeles, Aqueduct Investigation Board, "Report" quoted in Sauder, *The Lost Frontier,* 113.

17. See Abraham Hoffman, *Vision or Villainy: Origins of the Owens Valley-Los Angeles Water Controversy* (College Station, TX: Texas A&M University Press, 1981), 208–243, and Gordon R. Miller, "Los Angeles and the Owens River Aqueduct" Ph.D. diss. (Claremont Graduate School, 1977).
18. Hoffman, *Vision or Villainy*, 79–84; *Inyo Register*, August 3, 1905, 3.
19. Walton, *Western Times and Water Wars*, 138.
20. See Jeffery Burton and Jane C. Wehrey, *Three Farewells to Manzanar: The Archaeology of Manzanar National Historic Site*, 3 Vol. Chap. 6: "History Background" Publications in Anthropology 67 (Western Archaeological and Conservation Center, National Park Service, U.S. Department of the Interior, 1996).
21. Unrau, "The Evacuation and Relocation of Persons of Japanese Ancestry During World War II," 164; Walton, *Western Times and Water Wars*, 191–92.
22. Walton, *Western Times and Water Wars*, 212–213.
23. Ibid., 212.
24. Groundwater is pumped to the surface via deep wells and piped to the aqueduct; see also Abraham Hoffman, *Vision or Villainy*, 265–266.
25. U.S. Census, California Quickfacts, Inyo County, California; California Employment Development Department, Industry Trends and Outlook, 2001.
26. T.H. Breen, *Imagining the Past: East Hampton Histories* (Reading, MA: Addison-Wesley in Publishing Company, 1989), xii.
27. Kathleen Norris, *Dakota: A Spiritual Geography* (Boston: Houghton Mifflin Company, 1993), 127.
28. Lopez, "Mapping the Real Geography," 21.
29. Barbara Allen, "Recreating The Past: The Narrator's Perspective in Oral History," *Oral History Review* (1984), 1.
30. See Roy Rosenzweig and David Thelen, *The Presence of the Past: Popular Uses of History in American Life* (New York: Columbia University Press, 1998).
31. See Arthur H. Hansen, Introduction, in *Camp and Community: Manzanar and the Owens Valley*, Jessie A. Garrett and Ronald C. Larson, eds. (Fullerton: California State University Japanese American Oral History Project, 1977; Alessandro Portelli, *The Death of Luigi Trastulli and Other Stories: Form and Meaning in Oral History* (Albany: State University of New York Press, 1991), 50.
32. Kathleen M. Blee, "Evidence, Empathy, and Ethics: Lessons from Oral Histories of the Klan," *Journal of American History* (September, 1993), 597.
33. Portelli, *The Death of Luigi Trastulli and Other Stories*, 57.
34. Ibid., vii–ix.
35. See T. H. Breen, *Imagining the Past: East Hampton Histories.*
36. Linda Shopes, "Popular Consciousness of Local History: The Evidence of Oral History Interviews," Paper given at the International Oral History Conference, New York (October 1994), 4.
37. Wayne Franklin and Michael Steiner, "Taking Place: Toward the Regrounding of American Studies," in *Mapping American Culture* (Iowa City: University of Iowa Press, 1992), 4.
38. Pierce Lewis, "Defining a Sense of Place," *The Southern Quarterly* 17 (Spring-Summer, 1979), 24–29.
39. See Glenda Riley, "Writing, Teaching, and Recreating Western History Through Intersections and Viewpoints," *Pacific Historical Review* (August, 1993), 339–357.

40. Michael Kammen, *Mystic Chords of Memory* (New York: Vintage Books, 1993), 7
41. Donald Worster, "*The Legacy of Conquest*, by Patricia Nelson Limerick: A Panel of Appraisal," in *The Western Historical Quarterly* (August, 1989), 304.
42. See Richard White, "It's Your Misfortune and None of My Own": A New History of the American West (Norman: University of Oklahoma Press, 1991; Patricia Nelson Limerick, *The Legacy of Conquest: The Unbroken Past of the American West* (New York: W. W. Norton and Company, 1987).
43. David Glassberg, "Public History and the Study of Memory," *Public Historian* 18 (Spring 1996), 55.
44. Alessandro Portelli, Lecture, University of California at Los Angeles, April, 1996, notes.
45. G. David Brumberg, "The Historians-in-Residence Program," in *History for the Public*, G. David Brumberg, Margaret M. John, and William Zeisel, eds. (Ithaca: Cornell University Press, 1983), 10.
46. Portelli, *The Death of Luigi Trastulli and Other Stories*, 57.
47. Michael Frisch and Milton Rogovin, *Portraits in Steel* (Ithaca: Cornell University Press, 1993), 19.
48. See Linda Shopes, "Beyond Trivia and Nostalgia: Collaborating in the Construction of a Local History," *International Journal of Oral Histroy* (November, 1984).
49. Arthur H. Hansen, in Garrett and Larson, eds., *Camp and Community*, 2.

One Nettie Roeper Fausel (1874–1968)

1. Mary Austin, *Earth Horizon, An Autobiography* (Albuquerque: University of New Mexico Press, 1932), 234.
2. The Inyo County census for 1870 showed 1,956 residents: 18 percent non-white, 40 percent foreign-born, 15 percent born in English-speaking Europe or British North America, 12 percent from Mexico or indigeneous *californios*, 6 percent from Germany. Others were from China, France, South America, and other western European countries (Walton, *Western Times and Water Wars*, 60–61).
3. Walton, *Western Times and Water Wars*, 63.
4. Ibid., 91–94.
5. Ibid., 94–95.
6. Mary Austin, *The Land of Little Rain* (Boston: Houghton, Mifflin and Company, 1903), xi.
7. Austin, *Earth Horizon*, 286.

Two W.C. "Stub" Lydston (1870–1957)

1. Jane Marie Pedersen, *Between Memory and Reality: Family and Community in Rural Wisconsin, 1870–1970* (Madison: University of Wisconsin, 1992), 4.
2. *Pollyanna* (1920), starring Mary Pickford.

Three Truman Buff (1906–1996)

1. William H. Michael, "At the Plow and in the Harvest Field," 12.
2. Walton, *Western Times and Water Wars*, 50.
3. Ibid., 37.
4. "Institute Tried to Drum 'Civilization' Into Indian Youth," *Los Angeles Times*, February 23, 2003, B4.
5. George Miles, "To Hear an Old Voice: Rediscovering Native Americans in American History" in *Under An Open Sky: Rethinking America's Western Past*, William Cronon, George Miles, and Jay Gitlin, eds. (New York: W.W. Norton, 1992), 54.
6. Limerick, *The Legacy of Conquest*, 214.
7. Julian Steward, "Ethnography of the Owens Valley Paiute" (Berkeley: University of California Publications in American Archaeology and Ethnology 33, 1932–34), 321.
8. U.S. Census 2000, Inyo County Quickfacts.
9. The caves at Fort Independence used by Army soldiers when they arrived in the Owens Valley in 1862 have eroded but are still visible. A state historic landmark marker for the Fort is nearby.
10. When Manzanar was under military administration in the first months, food and supplies were requisitioned from the Army Quartermaster Corps; food not produced at Manzanar was later supplied under a rationing system similar to that of the civilian population at large.

Four Vic Taylor (1910–2001)

1. Hydrography is the "scientific description and analysis of the physical conditions, boundaries, flow, and related characteristics of oceans, lakes, rivers, and other surface waters." (*American Heritage Dictionary*)
2. Wallace Stegner, "Living Dry," in *Where the Bluebird Sings to the Lemonade Springs: Living and Writing in the West* (New York: Random House, 1992), 61.
3. White, *A New History of the American West*, 3.
4. Steve Lopez, "Upside of State's Water Crisis, No More Washing My Car," *Los Angeles Times*, January 3, 2003, B-7.
5. Stegner, "Living Dry," 75.
6. Dave McCoy is founder and former owner of Mammoth Mountain, today one of the premier ski resorts in the West. Born in 1915, he was a champion ski racer at 22 and went to work for the Los Angeles DWP in 1936 on snow surveys. He lives today in Bishop.
7. Second foot: one cubic foot of water per second flowing past a given point.
8. Acre foot: volume of water (43,560 cubic feet) that covers one acre to a depth of one foot.
9. Spreading is the distribution of water over the ground surface to percolate into the soil and replenish groundwater storage. In the Owens Valley, the City of Los Angeles spreads surplus stream water it cannot otherwise store or does not immediately need for the aqueduct. It is later extracted from the ground by well pumping.

Five Emily Roddy (b. 1911)

1. White, *A New History of the American West*, 252.
2. John R. Spears, quoted in Richard C. Datin, Jr., "The Carson and Colorado Railroad," in *Inyo 1866–1966*, Inyo County Board of Supervisors (Bishop, CA: Chalfant Press, 1966), 57.
3. *Complete Report on the Construction of the Los Angeles Aqueduct* (Los Angeles: Department of Public Service of the City of Los Angeles, 1916), 90.
4. White, *A New History of the American West*, 253–255.
5. In 1885, the William Penn Colonial Association, operating out of Whittier, California, acquired 13,000 acres of land near the Owens River and the station at Owenyo. The first irrigation settlement of its kind in the Owens Valley, the Quaker colony used previously dug irrigation canals and built others for a total 42 miles of canals. Alkaline soil conditions and the farmers' inexperience in desert environments left the tract largely undeveloped and unoccupied by 1905, when it was among the first to be sold to Los Angeles.
6. Car whacker: railroad car repairman.
7. Packing and shipping operations were contracted to Consolidated Produce Company, Los Angeles.
8. The City sold fruit from the 300 remaining acres of orchards at Manzanar, usually through a bidding system. Smaller buyers from southern California reportedly sent private trucks to pick up apples left on the ground or not sufficiently colored for regular shipment. Manzanar also supplied fruit to City work camps.
9. The City of Los Angeles prohibits swimming in the aqueduct.

Six Concha Lozano Salas (1915–2003)

1. Observations on early Lone Pine and its multi-ethnic population may be found in Walton, *Western Times and Water Wars*, 67, 124.
2. White, *A New History of the American West*, 320–323.
3. See Sucheng Chan, "A People of Exceptional Character: Ethnic Diversity, Nativism, and Racism in the California Gold Rush," *California History* (Summer 2000), 44–85.
4. White, *A New History of the American West*, 446; "Milestones of Growth and a New Ethnic Order," *Los Angeles Times*, March 30, 2001, CC1.
5. The California Alkali Company plant at Cartago opened in 1917, closed down in 1921, reopened for three and a half months in 1923, and remained closed again until May, 1924. It was then acquired by Inyo Chemical Company and continued in operation until its permanent closure in January, 1932.

Seven Owen Cooper (b. 1916)

1. Robert V. Hine, *Community on the American Frontier: Separate But Not Alone* (Norman, OK: University of Oklahoma Press, 1980), 21.

2. Yi-Fu Tuan, *Space and Place: The Perspective of Experience* (Minneapolis: University of Minnesota Press, 1977), 145.
3. Patricia Nelson Limerick, "Making the Most of Words: Verbal Activity and Western America," in *Under An Open Sky: Rethinking America's Western Past*, William Cronon, George Miles, and Jay Gitlin, eds. (New York: W.W. Norton and Company, 1992), 178.
4. *Inyo Independent*, March 6, 1942, 1.
5. Owen Cooper describes Manzanar on the afternoon of December 6, 1942, just hours before the riot broke out that left two internees dead and nine wounded. A large crowd had gathered in the Administration area as Project Direct Ralph Merritt met with an internee committee negotiating the release of mess hall worker Harry Ueno. Accused of beating another internee the previous day, Ueno was being held in the Inyo County Jail in Independence. As the crowd grew unruly, approximately thirty armed soldiers stood by. The crowd dispersed but returned that evening. It briefly took over the police station, demanding the release of Ueno, by then back at Manzanar. The confrontation turned deadly when soldiers used tear gas, then fired into the crowd.

Eight LaVerne Reynolds Zediker (1919–1996)

1. White, *A New History of the American West*, 615.
2. Ibid., 613.
3. See Teresa Jordan, *Cowgirls: Women of the American West* (Lincoln: University of Nebraska Press, 1992), xxiii–xxxiv, for a comprehensive study of the "cowgirl."
4. April Reese, "The Big Buyout," *High Country News*, Vol. 37, No. 6, April 4, 2005, 10.
5. D. W. Meinig, *The Interpretation of Ordinary Landscapes* (New York: Oxford University Press, 1979), 164.
6. Kenneth Turan, *Sundance to Sarajevo: Film Festivals and the World They Made* (Berkeley: University of California Press, 2002), 144.
7. In the early weeks of the camp, small groups of internees were permitted to shop in Lone Pine under guard. A reported 500 town residents opposed to the practice petitioned the War Relocation Authority, and the trips were halted. Wartime rationing of some goods did not immediately go into effect following America's entry into World War II.

Nine Ritsuko Eder (b. 1917), Doris Semura (1912–2005), Dawn Kashitani (b. 1910)

1. San Francisco *Examiner*, May 8, 1900, quoted in Roger Daniel, *Asian America: Chinese and Japanese in the United States since 1850* (Seattle: University of Washington Press, 1988), 112.
2. Daniel, *Asian America*, 116.
3. *Los Angeles Times*, March 24, 1942, 1. The 1,000 evacuees who departed Los Angeles on March 23, 1942, went to Manzanar in two nearly equal groups, the first by train to Lone Pine Station, and the others in the caravan of private vehicles. See also Burton, *Three Farewells to Manzanar*, 17–25, 45–55; Unrau, "The Evacuation and Relocation of Persons of Japanese Ancestry During World War II," 187–194.

4. Most barracks were initially configured with four apartments, each holding up to eight people.

Ten Nancy Connor Zischank (1907–2000)

1. Yi-Fu Tuan, *Topophilia: A Study of Environmental Perception, Attitudes, and Values* (Englewood Cliffs, NJ: Prentice-Hall, 1974), 109–112.
2. John Cassian quoted In Yi-fu Tuan, *Topophilia*, 110.
3. Remi Nadeau, *The Water Seekers*, 3rd ed. (Santa Barbara: Crest Publishers, 1993), 111.
4. Limerick, *Legacy of Conquest*, 27.
5. Evacuees with advanced cases of cancer and other illnesses, including psychiatric patients, were usually transferred to Los Angeles General Hospital.
6. By 1940–1941, only a very few Issei businessmen were considered moderately wealthy. They were successful in the wholesale produce business, import-export trade, and finance, but figures relating to individual wealth are not available.
7. There were no Japanese American 5-star generals. This may have been Colonel John Aiso, whose parents were interned at Manzanar.
8. Some were infants of unmarried mothers in the relocation centers, others were children of Caucasian mothers who did not go to the camps. Others could not be cared for by their parents for varying reasons.
9. The mass exclusion order for persons of Japanese ancestry living in the west coast military areas was lifted on December 17, 1944, and evacuees were free to return to their homes beginning January 2, 1945. At that time the population at Manzanar was 5,549, down from a high of 10,121 in 1942.
10. Vegetable production at Manzanar, 1942–1944, was 7,747,201 lbs; of that, 847,960 1bs. went to war relocation centers at Tule Lake, California, and Poston, Arizona.
11. MP supervision of internee workers in fields and facilities outside the fenced camp boundary was gradually lifted, and the workers were permitted to wear identification, check out at the gate, and work on their own.

Eleven Mary Kageyama Nomura (b. 1925)

1. Wayne Franklin and Michael Steiner, "Taking Pace," 3.
2. Daniel, *Asian America*, 201.
3. The Willow Motel was built using Manzanar barracks.

Twelve Keith Bright (b. 1915)

1. Thomas "Tip" O'Neill, quoted in Timothy P. Duane, *Shaping the Sierra: Nature, Culture, and Conflict in the Changing West* (Berkeley: University of California Press, 1999), 269; Robert Bellah in Duane, *Shaping the Sierra*, 266, 269.
2. White, *A New History of the American West*, 570.
3. Bellah, quoted in Duane, *Shaping the Sierra*, 266.

4. In 1980, Inyo County voters approved an ordinance giving the county authority to regulate groundwater pumping by Los Angeles. The measure was ruled unconstitutional in 1983.
5. The 1994 California Desert Protection Act placed more than 3 million acres of desert in southeastern California into Wilderness status. Included are areas on the eastern edge of the Owens Valley previously accessible with vehicles. The bill added 1.3 million acres to Death Valley National Monument and designated it a national park.
6. Geothermal energy production at Coso Hot Springs in southern Inyo County is the second largest in the country.
7. Plans for expanded soda ash processing on Owens Lake in the 1990s were stalled. U.S. Borax presently operates a facility there.
8. A California Historic Landmark plaque affixed to a large boulder at the entrance to the former relocation center reads: "In the early part of World War II, 110,000 persons of Japanese ancestry were interned in relocation centers by Executive Order 9066, issued February 19, 1942. Manzanar, the first of ten such concentration camps, was bounded by barbed wire and guard towers, confining 10,000 persons, the majority being American citizens. May the injustices and humiliation suffered here as a result of hysteria, racism, and economic exploitation never emerge again."

Afterword

1. Limerick, *The Legacy of Conquest*, 291.
2. Mary Austin, *The Land of Little Rain*, xi–xi.
3. Richard White, "Tribute to Richard White," Oral History Association Meeting, Los Angeles, 2001, notes.
4. Kathleen Norris, *The Cloister Walk* (New York: Riverhead Books, 1996), 244.

Readings/Sources Consulted

The following sources were valuable in researching and writing this project; others appear in the notes. They do not represent a complete listing of all the works, persons, interviews, or other material consulted, nor do they include all of the possibilities for investigating a broad and complex history.

The Owens Valley, Manzanar, The West

Published Works

Austin, Mary. *The Land of Little Rain*. Boston: Houghton, Mifflin and Company, 1903.

———. *Earth Horizon*. Albuquerque: University of New Mexico Press, 1932.

Bahr, Diana. *Viola Martinez, California Paiute: Living in Two Worlds*. Norman: University of Oklahoma Press, 2003.

Brooks, Joan. *Desert Padre: The Life and Writings of Father John J. Crowley, 1881–1940*. Desert Hot Springs, CA: Mesquite Press, 1997.

Chalfant, W.A. *The Story of Inyo*. Rev. ed. Bishop, CA: Chalfant Press, 1933.

Cragen, Dorothy Clora. *The Boys in the Sky-Blue Pants: The Men and Events at Camp Independence and Forts of Eastern California, Nevada and Utah, 1862–1877*. Fresno, CA: Pioneer Publishing, 1975.

Cronon, William, George Miles, and Jay Gitlin, eds. *Under An Open Sky: Rethinking America's Western Past*. New York: Norton, 1992.

Daniels, Roger. *Asian America: Chinese and Japanese in the United States since 1850*. Seattle, University of Washington Press, 1988.

———, Sandra C. Taylor, and Harry H. L. Kitano, eds. *Japanese Americans: From Relocation to Redress*. Rev. ed. Seattle: University of Washington Press, 1991.

Duane, Timothy P. *Shaping the Sierra: Nature, Culture, and Conflict in the Changing West*. Berkeley: University of California Press, 1999.

Farquhar, Francis P. *History of the Sierra Nevada*. Berkeley: University of California Press, 1965.

Garrett, Jessie A. and Ronald C. Larson, eds. *Camp and Community: Manzanar and the Owens Valley*. Fullerton: California State University Fullerton, Japanese American Oral History Project, 1977.

Hansen, Arthur A., Debra Gold Hansen, Sue Kunitomi Embrey, Jane C. Wehrey, Garnette Long, Kathleen Frazee. *An Annotated Bibliography for Manzanar National Historic Site*. Fullerton: California State University Oral History Program, 1995.

Heizer, Robert F. and Alan F. Almquist. *The Other Californians.* Berkeley: University of California Press, 1971.

Hine, Robert V. *Community on the American Frontier: Separate but Not Alone.* Norman, Oklahoma: University of Oklahoma Press, 1980.

Hoffman, Abraham. *Vision or Villainy: Origins of the Owens Valley Water Controversy.* College Station: Texas A&M University Press, 1981.

Holland, Dave. *On Location in Lone Pine.* Granada Hills, CA: Holland House, 1990.

Hundley, Norris. *The Great Thirst: Californians and Water, 1770's–1990's.* Berkeley: University of California Press, 1992.

Inada, Lawson, ed. *Only What We Could Carry: The Japanese American Internment Experience.* Berkeley/San Francisco: Heyday Books/California Historical Society, 2000.

Inyo County Board of Supervisors. *Inyo 1866–1966.* Bishop, CA: Chalfant Press, 1966.

Inyo Register. Inyo County California Anno Domini, 1912: Beautiful Owens Valley. Bishop, CA: *Inyo Register*, 1912.

Irwin, Sue. *California's Eastern Sierra: A Visitor's Guide.* Los Olivos, CA: Cachuma Press, 1991.

Jordan, Teresa. *Cowgirls: Women of the American West.* Lincoln: University of Nebraska Press, 1992.

Liljeblad, Sven and Catherine S. Fowler. "Owens Valley Paiute." In *Handbook of North American Indians.* Vol. 11: Great Basin. Warren L. D'Azevedo, vol. ed. and William C. Sturtevant, gen. ed. 412–434. Washington, DC: Smithsonian Institution, 1986.

Limerick, Patricia Nelson. *The Legacy of Conquest: The Unbroken Past of the American West.* New York: Norton and Company, 1987.

———, Clyde A. Milner II, and Charles Rankin, eds. *Trails: Toward a New Western History.* University Press of Kansas, 1991.

Manzanar Committee. *Reflections in Three Self-Guided Tours of Manzanar.* Los Angeles: The Manzanar Committee, 1998.

McWilliams, Carey. *Southern California: An Island on the Land.* Salt Lake City: Peregrine Smith Books, 1973.

Mulholland, Catherine. *William Mulholland and the Rise of Los Angeles.* Berkeley: University of California Press, 2000.

Myres, Sandra. *Westering Women and the Frontier Experience 1800–1915.* Albuquerque: University of New Mexico Press, 1982.

Nadeau, Remi. *City Makers: The Story of Southern California's First Boom.* Corona del Mar, CA: Trans-Anglo Books, 1977.

———. *The Silver Seekers.* Santa Barbara: Crest Publishers, 1999.

———. *The Water Seekers.* Garden City, NY: Doubleday, 1950.

Nugent, Walter. *Into the West: The Story of Its People.* New York: Vintage Books, 1999.

O'Brien, David J. and Stephen S. Fugita. *The Japanese American Experience.* Bloomington: Indiana University Press, 1991.

Ostrom, Vincent. *Water and Politics: A Study of Water Policies and Administration in the Development of Los Angeles.* Los Angeles: The Haynes Foundation, 1953.

Putnam, Jeff and Genny Smith. *Deepest Valley: Guide to Owens Valley, Its Roadsides and Mountain Trails.* Rev. ed. Mammoth Lakes, CA: Genny Smith Books, 1995.

Riley, Glenda. *A Place to Grow: Women in the American West.* Arlington Heights, Ill.: Harlan Davidson, Inc., 1992.

Rolle, Andrew. *California: A History.* 5th ed. Arlington Heights, Ill: Harlan Davidson, Inc., 2003.

Rowley, William D. *U.S. Forest Service Grazing and Rangelands: A History*. College Station: Texas A&M University Press, 1985.

Sauder, Robert. *The Lost Frontier: Water Diversion in the Growth and Destruction of Owens Valley Agriculture*. Tucson: University of Arizona Press, 1994.

Smith, Henry Nash. *Virgin Land: The American West as Symbol and Myth*. Cambridge, Mass.: Harvard University Press, 1950.

Smythe, William E. *The Conquest of Arid America*. New York: Harper and Brothers, 1900.

Southern Inyo Association of Retired Persons. *Saga of Inyo County*. Covina: Taylor Publishing Company, 1977.

Stanley, Jerry. *I Am an American*. New York: Crown Publishers, 1994.

Starr, Kevin. *Material Dreams: Southern California Through the 1920s*. New York: Oxford University Press, 1990.

———, and Richard J. Orsi, eds. *Rooted in Barbarous Soil: People, Culture, and Community in Gold Rush California*. Vol. 4, Summer 2000, of the *California History* Sesquicentennial Series. California Historical Society/University of California Press.

Stegner, Wallace. *Where the Bluebird Sings to the Lemonade Springs: Living and Writing in the West*. New York: Random House, 1992.

Steward, Julian. *The Ethnography of the Owens Valley Paiute*. Berkeley: University of California Publications in American Archaeology and Ethnology 33, 1932–1934.

Turan, Kenneth. *Sundance to Sarajevo: Film Festivals and the World They Made*. Berkeley: University of California Press, 2002.

Turner, George. *Slim Rails Through the Sand*. Long Beach, CA: Johnstone and Howe, 1963.

Walton, John. *Western Times and Water Wars: State, Culture, and Rebellion in California*. Berkeley: University of California Press, 1992.

White, Richard. *It's Your Misfortune and None of My Own: A New History of the American West*. Norman: University of Oklahoma Press, 1991.

Government Reports, Theses, Newspapers, Other

Burton, Jeffrey. *Three Farewells to Manzanar: The Archaeology of Manzanar National Historic Site, California*. 3 vol. Tucson: Western Archaeological and Conservation Center, National Park Service, U.S. Department of the Interior. Publications in Anthropology 67, 1996.

Busby, Colin I., John M. Findlay, and James C. Bard. *A Cultural Resource Overview of the Bureau of Land Management, Coleville, Benton, and Owens Valley Planning Units, California*. For U.S. Department of the Interior, Bureau of Land Management, Bakersfield District Office. Oakland, CA: Basin Research Associates, 1980.

City of Los Angeles, Department of Public Service. *Final Report on Construction of the Los Angeles Aqueduct*. City of Los Angeles, 1916.

Cotton, J.S. "Agricultural Conditions of Inyo County, California." 1905. Typescript. Eastern California Museum.

Eastern California Museum: Oral History Collection.

———. Subject Heading and Family History Files.

Inyo Independent

Inyo Register

Los Angeles Times

Manzanar Free Press

Michael, William. "At the Plow and in the Harvest Field: Indian Conflict and Accomodation in the Owens Valley, 1860–1880." Master's thesis, University of Oklahoma, 1993.

Miller, Gordon R. "Los Angeles and the Owens River Aqueduct." Ph.D. diss., Claremont Graduate School, 1977.

Unrau, Harlan. "The Evacuation and Relocation of Persons of Japanese Ancestry During World War II: A Historical Study of the Manzanar War Relocation Center." 2 vol. United States Department of the Interior, National Park Service, 1996.

Van Horn, Lawrence F. *Native American Consultations and Ethnographic Assessment: The Paiutes and Shoshones of Owens Valley, California*. Denver: United States Department of the Interior, National Park Service, 1995.

Wehrey, Jane. A Convergence of Pasts: Remembering Other Manzanars. Paper given at the Oral History Association Annual Meeting. Raleigh-Durham, NC, October, 2000.

———. "Voices from This Long Brown Land: Oral Recollections of Owens Valley Lives and Manzanar Pasts." Master's thesis, California State University Fullerton, 1998.

Oral History, Memory, Sense of Place

Altman, Irwin and Setha M. Low, eds. *Place Attachment*. New York: Plenum Press, 1992.

Amato, Joseph A. *Rethinking Home: A Case for Writing Local History*. Berkeley: University of California Press, 2002.

Bodnar, John. *Remaking America: Public Memory, Commemoration, and Patriotism in the Twentieth Century*. Princeton: Princeton University Press, 1992.

Breen, T.H. *Imagining the Past: East Hampton Histories*. Reading, MA: Addison-Wesley Publishing, 1989.

Dunaway, David K. and Willa Baum. *Oral History: An Interdisciplinary Anthology*. 2nd ed. Walnut Creek: AltaMira Press, 1996.

Franklin, Wayne and Michael Steiner, eds. *Mapping American Culture*. Iowa City: University of Iowa Press, 1992.

Frisch, Michael. *A Shared Authority: Essays on the Craft and Meaning of Oral and Public History*. Albany: State University of New York Press, 1990.

——— and Milton Rogovin. *Portraits in Steel*. Ithaca: Cornell University Press, 1993.

Hareven, Tamara K. and Randolph Langenbach. *Amoskeag: Life and Work in An American Factory City*. New York: Pantheon Books, 1978.

Ives, Edward. *The Tape-Recorded Interview: A Manual for Fieldworkers in Folklore and Oral History*, 2nd ed. Knoxville: University of Tennessee Press, 1995.

Jones-Eddy, Julie. *Homesteading Women: An Oral History of Colorado, 1890–1950*. New York: Twayne Publishers, 1992.

Kammen, Michael. *Mystic Chords of Memory*. New York: Vintage Books, 1993.

Kikemura, Akemi. *Through Harsh Winters: The Life of a Japanese Immigrant Woman*. Novato, CA: Chandler and Sharp, 1981.

Kyvig, David E. and Myron A. Marty. *Nearby History: Exploring the Past Around You*. Nashville: American Association for State and Local History, 1982.

Linenthal, Edward T. and Tom Engelhardt. *History Wars: The Enola Gay and Other Battles for the American Past*. New York: Henry Holt, 1996.

Lopez, Barry. "Mapping the Real Geography." *Harper's Magazine* (November 1989): 19–21.

Meinig, D.W. *The Interpretation of Ordinary Landscapes*. New York, Oxford University Press, 1979.

Norkunas, Martha K. *The Politics of Public Memory: Tourism, History, and Ethnicity in Monterey, California*. Albany: State University of New York Press, 1993.

Norris, Kathleen. *Dakota: A Spiritual Geography*. Boston: Houghton Mifflin Company, 1993.

Pederson, Jane Marie. *Between Memory and Reality: Family and Community in Rural Wisconsin 1870–1970*. Madison: University of Wisconsin, 1992.

Portelli, Alessandro. *The Death of Luigi Trastulli and Other Stories: Form and Meaning in Oral History*. Albany: State University of New York Press, 1990.

Rosenzweig, Roy and David Thelen. *The Presence of the Past: Popular Uses of History in American Life*. New York: Columbia University Press, 1998.

Shopes, Linda. "Beyond Trivia and Nostalgia: Collaborating in the Construction of a Local History." *International Journal of Oral History* 5 (November 1984): 151–158.

Thelen, David. *Memory and American History*. Bloomington: Indiana University Press, 1990.

Thompson, Paul. *The Voice of the Past*, 2nd ed. Oxford: Oxford University Press, 1988.

Tuan, Yi-Fu. *Space and Place: The Perspective of Experience*. Minneapolis: University of Minnesota Press, 1977.

———. *Topophilia: A Study of Environmental Perception, Attitudes, and Values*. Englewood Cliffs, NJ: Prentice-Hall, 1974.

Index